Hannah Roberts

Alice Williams is an author, freelance writer and yoga teacher. At nineteen years old she dropped out of university and lived in a Buddhist monastery in Nepal where she learned that even complete buttheads just want to be happy, so we should probably try and be nice to each other. Who knew? When Alice returned from Nepal, she finished her degree and worked low-level office and hospitality jobs to support her writing. Her first book, *Would it kill you to say please?*, was published in 2007. She celebrated this milestone by having a quarter-life crisis and becoming a yoga teacher. Alice lives in Melbourne with her partner and two young children.

BAD YOGI

Published by Affirm Press in 2019
28 Thistlethwaite Street, South Melbourne, VIC 3205
www.affirmpress.com.au
10 9 8 7 6 5 4 3 2 1

Text and copyright © Alice Williams
All rights reserved. No part of this publication may be reproduced without prior permission of the publisher.

Title: Bad Yogi / Alice Williams, author
ISBN: 9781925712605 (paperback)

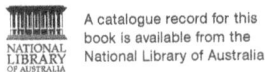

Cover design by Design by Committee
Typeset by J&M Typesetting
Proudly printed in Australia by Griffin Press

The paper this book is printed on is certified against the Forest Stewardship Council® Standards. Griffin Press holds FSC chain of custody certification SGS-COC-005088. FSC promotes environmentally responsible, socially beneficial and economically viable management of the world's forests.

ALICE WILLIAMS

BAD YOGI

To Gil, Charlie and Finn.
In the immortal words of Uncle Monty
My boys, my boys ...

'Memoir is the last place I'd go looking for truth.'
– David Sedaris

Prologue

I'm kneeling on a borrowed yoga mat, as old and worn as the sutras, trying to lift my chest to the fluoro light 'heavens' along with fifteen other women.

The room is quiet, except for the sounds of the city street below, and our own wheezing breaths. Our teacher, Jorge, is dedicating two entire classes to learning how to backbend, beginning with camel, which is my least favourite backbend as it takes every muscle in my twiggy neck not to let my head log back like a partially-beheaded ragdoll. While we kneel here imagining invisible threads lifting our sternums, the rest of the world is enjoying Sunday, like normal people.

We're halfway through the class when Jorge decides we need a break. A tea break? No, no: this is a yoga teaching course – we take breaks to *open our heart spaces*.

'Come, ladies! For this exercise, you'll need to spread yourselves around the room, but first let's just – *Woosh! Woosh!*' Jorge swings his arms to release any bad juju accrued in the morning's lesson, and like rats to their pied piper, the students mirror him.

I gaze longingly through the window at the people clutching aperitifs in the bar across the lane as a busker serenades the late afternoon shoppers on the street below.

'In this exercise, we're really going to "go there" and explore connecting with others *through* our heart chakra, in a way that feels safe.'

A heinous, heinous activity that is met with big smiles from the usual suspects.

'Because this is about *feeling*, learning the language of the heart, we're going to do it in silence. So as you walk around the room —'

We start to shuffle obediently.

'— start to *feel* into your heart spaces. Notice how it *feels* when a particular person comes into your space —'

Other students wander zombie-like into my peripheral vision. Marta is beaming from ear to ear.

'— and should your energy open out to them, feel free to just open your arms like so, and if their energy is open in return, just lean in and embrace.'

What the fuck?

'Remember, ladies, if you feel you need to stay with your *own* energy, then you just cross your arms across your chest like this —' Jorge crosses his arms across his chest like Rick Astley, never giving us up, '— to indicate that you prefer to keep it to me, myself and I.'

Everywhere I look people are slowly raising their arms to hug. I'm not anti-hug. I am, however, anti-*orchestrated hug*. I plaster on a tepid smile while setting a course for the corner.

Too slow. Jo-Jo, the beaming yoga goddess, enters my peripheral vision, aqua lipstick to match her crew cut. She doesn't even wait for the go-ahead before wrapping me in an embrace. What can you do with a person like that? I try to pull away but she just clings on tighter, trilling and *waggling her butt* with glee. Resistance is futile, so I go limp, and after a while I'm horrified to find that I … enjoy it? This is going too far. I pull away politely and shuffle off as fast as my heart chakra allows.

I may be unemployed, broke, depressed and incapable of controlling myself around food – and yes, I may have voluntarily committed myself to this wankiest of courses – but goddamnit, I have my pride! I will not be sucked into this world of eye-gazing and new-age half-wittery. When anyone approaches, I cross my arms and shake my head gently. *I'm sorry. Tonight it's just me, my heart space and I.*

Tiny, sparkly eyed Marta floats into my orbit. There's something warm, unassuming and eager to please about Marta, sort of like a golden retriever hidden inside a five foot three, 45-year-old woman. As she advances, eyes shining and arms floating, I move my arms across my chest. But I'm too late: she's already leaning in and up, eyes closing, an expression of hugging ecstasy on her face.

I step back, my arms crossed, and as she hugs thin air she opens her eyes and smiles, uncomprehending, then takes a further step forward. I shake my head. *I'd love to hug you but, dear me, look at the arms.* She looks at my arms, then back at me, confused. I shake my head again. Her face falls, like a little sparrow, and she drifts off.

Heart opening's a bitch.

1

Denial

Monday 7.50am

The screening starts in ten minutes, and instead of meeting my new colleagues, I'm running by the side of a highway in a godforsaken industrial wasteland. Forget the ten years it took to get this job; the daily commute is like a descent into suburban Mordor. After getting on the tram in the city at 6.30am, I passed several superstores that needed their own postcode before Google Maps alerted me to my stop in the middle of the highway.

When I got off the tram there was no one on the street. There was no *street*, just fields and an anonymous-looking office block surrounded by security cameras. It looked like a corporate version of that orgy mansion that swallowed Tom Cruise in *Eyes Wide Shut*. The only other person who was left on the tram, a twenty-something man wearing a suit and headphones, got off behind me and quickly disappeared into the building.

Google Maps says the studio compound is a block north. All I can see to the north is a field the size of an airport with a pokies joint dumped incongruously in the middle and, far in the distance, a gleaming stand-alone restaurant advertising an all-you-can-eat $15 Chinese buffet. Clearly 'a block' here is different to a block in the city. I surreptitiously check the sky for predatory crop dusters.

The early morning sun is hot as I run. Every twenty paces I have to pause to adjust the floaty floral Alannah Hill shirtdress I bought on sale last week. I *thought* it said 'corporate bohemian who conforms when necessary, but with a touch of *je ne sais quoi*'. But now, as I tug the hem down from my waist to my knees, I'm wondering if it's more 'nineties work-experience prostitute'.

I check my phone: I've got five minutes. Technically I'm only on a trial, but my game plan is 'WEIO': Wow them Early with Insights and Originality. Bursting, red-faced and sweaty into the writers' room as twelve or so people sit silently watching television is not the entry I wanted to make. Finally, I reach the edge of the field, and the only thing between me and my new job is a cluster of McMansions and the wire fence of the studio compound.

At the security checkpoint I give my name and position, and the guard waves me through. My face is dripping and my dress is twisted back-to-front, but I've got two minutes to spare.

One of the producers' assistants flies by with a box of coffees. 'Story trial?' she calls out. 'Follow me.' I jog to keep up with her as we zip through the bright open-plan casting office, occupied by straight-backed ladies with beachy waves and stilettos; past the male-only offices (lawyers and accountants); and on to the furthermost corner of the compound, where they keep the goth-girl trolls and the polo-shirted gay boys – aka, the story department. And in the corner of the corner is the story room – aka, Valhalla.

The story room sounds like a magical place because it is. The walls are lined with *TV Week* covers, the likes of which I used to salivate over as a kid. And the rumours were true: at the centre of the story table is a self-replenishing pile of chocolate. 'Story fuel', they call it. Today it's Cadbury Caramello and mini-Flakes, but the Script Coordinator says it can be anything you want, you just ask and she'll order it for you. (I'm on a cleanse, but chocolate that's free doesn't count. And I brought a box of protein bars, so if I have one on the ninety-minute commute home instead of dinner, it evens out. Winning, as Charlie Sheen would say.)

Everyone completely ignores me and dives on the box of coffees brought in by the Producer's Assistant. There are seven of us storyliners, plus a couple of script editors, one Script Producer (harried) and the Executive Producer (*EP* to those of us who work in show business). The EP is ostentatiously *not* harried. Instead she has a strong post-menopausal 'don't give a fuck' vibe, a tiny faded rose tattoo peeking through a gap in her complicated black-silk cape/dress/jumpsuit ensemble, and a greying faux hawk.

The working week begins with a screening of rough cuts of the five episodes shot the week before. As far as I can tell, screenings are like watching TV with your friends, except here when you yell, 'Why don't you learn to act, dumb-dumb?' someone writes it down as a note and passes it on to the relevant department.

Halfway through the second episode, the EP jumps up, cape flapping, and someone stops the tape. We've just watched a scene where the resident MILF cracks on to the teen heart-throb in her living room. 'I know what you're all thinking!' says the EP.

I think the scene is a delicate testament to the MILF's loneliness and the heart-throb's abandonment issues, but I'm trying to strike a balance between 'hire her!' observations and shutting the hell up so I can read the room.

'It's Austin,' she says. 'How many times have I told them? They've gotta give that boy *better hair!*'

I read the room. Lots of nodding. Sycophants. I didn't come here to blend in.

The next time the EP stops the tape, I raise my hand. Time to enact my WEIO game plan.

'I just noticed that Austin said "youse" a couple of times,' I say. 'Is "youse" a character thing, or …?'

Someone snickers. Why is everyone staring at me as if I'm a monkey who's just learned to yodel? The EP smiles like a wolf in a lace nightie.

'Um, no, it's not a "character thing",' she says, waggling her fingers in air quotes. 'It's a "we shoot five episodes a week nobody has time to give him elocution lessons" thing.'

I cram another mini-Flake into my mouth. Wow them later. Back to shutting the hell up.

•

By the end of the day I have been schooled in audience demographics (kids and elderly conservatives who write in if anything bar hair, make-up or wardrobe is a shade too progressive), and exactly what we can get away with without losing our G-rating.

It may just be a trial, but if I stick to my game plan, I reckon I can score a permanent contract within a month. In the meantime I'm supplementing my income with felt-tipped pens and pads of post-it notes – the large expensive kind – from the stationery cupboard.

Curiously, everyone I know who's written for the show said they ended each day in tears. When I asked why, they just got a faraway look and said, 'You'll see.' Actually, no, I will not 'see'. This morning I got a note in the mail from my publisher to say they were pulping the unsold copies of the book I wrote when I was at uni. Back then I thought writing was easy. You came up with something on a whim, sent it out and someone wanted to publish it! Now I realise it's a kind of masochism. After my book was published, my dad had a liver transplant and nearly died, and I had a quiet breakdown. I couldn't write a decent line to save my life. Since then I've spent five years in the wilderness of call centres and data entry, writing every night and getting nothing but rejection.

Then I got this gig, the first job I've ever had that pays cash money for using my imagination. I've spent too many years banging my head against call-centre toilet walls for this job to be a lemon. Besides, how bad can it be?

It's dark by the time I leave the studio. Around here at night, it really does feel like you're in the country. The stars are brighter, and there are only the lights from the distant highway to guide your way.

As soon as I step onto the darkened street, a car flicks its headlights on, blinding me. I'm just out of view of the studio's security cameras. The car lurches towards me, and through the lights I see that the back seat is crammed with young men. One of the men jumps out of the car and runs up to me. I freeze. He stares at my face then calls over his shoulder, 'Na, s'not her!'

'Fucking slut!' someone yells. The man jumps back into the car and they drive away. I will not be raped today, and neither will the actress they were waiting for. So that's tonight's gratitude journal sorted.

These are the people we write the show for.

Ninety minutes later the lactic acid has finally drained from my body as I walk through my front door.

My boyfriend, Gil, is shooting baddies on the computer and he whips off his headphones when he sees me.

'How was it?' he asks, eyes bright.

'Fine,' I grunt.

'Just fine?' he says, wandering into the kitchen and getting me some leftover pasta. It's 'man pasta', so a huge bowl with no vegetables and lots of bacon. I tuck in. Ninety minutes ago I was sprinting for my life through darkened fields. I need the glucose.

I tell Gil about the rapey fans and his face darkens. 'That's it,' he says. 'We're getting a car.'

I'm too tired to argue that we can't afford it, so I just say, 'Yeah, sure,' knowing that it will be forgotten like so many other plans, then I sink into the couch beside him.

On Friday is the all-important pitch meeting, when each storyliner must pitch two prospective storylines, broken into beats that can be woven in over several episodes. And we get doughnuts!

My trial ends next week, so the window to impress is small. 'The worst thing you can do,' was the advice I had from people who've gone before, 'is try to reinvent the show.' Maybe that was the case for them, but I plan to be *sneaky* about reinventing the show – change things from within.

I have five hours for plotting my pitches, four and a half of which I spend at the shopping centre around the corner looking for cheap undergarments and protein bars. But I am no mindless consumer roaming the food court: I am an imagineer, and ideas need time and retail to percolate.

In the final twenty minutes I come up with two storylines that give a much-needed dose of originality and freshness to the show, and that have enough suspense to keep viewers' watching through adverts for KFC popcorn chicken.

At around five the Script Coordinator summons us all to the story room. The pitch meeting begins with a call for a light and fluffy C-story for the resident sexy dad, Steve, and his young son, Will. The aim is to take the edge off the A-story (fake teen pregnancy) and the B-story (1 hot teacher + 2 cougar mums = PTA love triangle).

The new Script Editor pitches a story about Will taking the class pet snake home for the weekend, and the hijinks that ensue when Steve reveals he has a phobia of snakes. The Script Editor mimes Steve waking up to discover the snake on his pillow, and the squealing and hand-flapping that follows. The story room is in stitches. (Bar me. I have taste.)

Suddenly the Script Producer goes quiet. 'It's a great story,' she says, 'but we can't do it.'

'Why not?' asks the Editor.

The Script Producer sighs. 'The network won't let us de-ball another hunk.'

When it's my turn, my pitches are so profoundly inappropriate ('confusing and needlessly weird' is the feedback) that the Script Producer asks if they can use them in their training manual.

I am undeterred. There is a key to this gig, and I shall find it. I refuse to return to the call-centre wilderness.

After the pitch meeting I head straight to the hospital. Dad rang twice today to complain about hospital food, and I promised to bring him Indian. (One of our tasks as dutiful family members is to get him to eat, even if it means scouring the back streets of Springvale for a particular brand of spring roll he remembers fondly from the eighties.) Five minutes later he rang to cancel the order. 'Would it kill you to bring Vietnamese? But not from that place down the road, get it from Footscray.' I told him I was his daughter, not his flunky. 'Is there any difference?' he said, cackling. Glad to provide opportunity for merriment.

The problem with liver patients is that even though they're gravely ill, they're also incredibly annoying. All the toxins their liver usually processes start to build up in their brain and make merry with their personality in a delightful condition known as 'encephalopathy'. With encephalopathy the patient's toxic brain bears just enough resemblance to their old one that you don't know whether to feel sorry for them or wring their neck because they're being an arsehole. The handbook the liver clinic gave us had just one measly paragraph on the condition: 'If you notice any worrying mental changes in your family member, feel free to discuss it with a member of the transplant team.' *If you notice …* How about 'if the patient shits you to the point you want to kill them, hold off until we can do the transplant first'?

As I watch the leafy outer suburbs speeding past the train window, I eavesdrop on two junkies. The speedy junkie is lecturing the sleepy junkie on the finer points of naturopathy.

'*Milk thistle*, bro!' he yells. 'I'm tellin' ya, it's nature's liver tonic!'

I must inform Dad's doctors. He may be waiting for his second liver transplant in four years, but have they tried milk thistle?

Mum rings as I'm walking from the train station to the hospital. I ask her how he was when she went in today.

'Let's see,' she says. 'I bought him the spanakopita he requested, but when I got there he said it was only lukewarm so I had to find somewhere to heat it up. When I got back to his room he was having a lovely time with his new doctor because, in his words, "he has a PhD, you know, so he really gets me".'

'As opposed to us halfwits who can't even keep his baked goods warm?'

'I left after that and went to my book club,' she says. 'I wasn't going to go but, you know, "they really get me".'

I snort.

'Did you get to talk to his doctor yourself? What did he say?'

'Oh no, I didn't want to bother the doctor,' Mum says vaguely. 'If there's something important they'll ring me.'

Dad's room is on the eighth floor. At this time of night, the liver ward has spectacular views of the sun setting over the north-eastern suburbs, and as I step out of the lift I pause to take it in. I've also learned to pause before going into Dad's room so I can steel myself for whatever mood he's in. Could be distress, could be Attila the Invalid, could be 'Jesus wants a biscuit'.

This time he's sitting up in bed glowering at the sunset and his mood is 'neglected'. Beside him is a fresh bunch of flowers from Mum's garden. 'No one comes to see me!' he wails, and I point to the flowers. *Apart* from her,' he says.

Three other people share Dad's room, all either awaiting transplants or healing from them. Someone wheels in a trolley full of low-sodium dinners. The other patients dutifully take theirs without complaint, but Dad is incensed.

'I wouldn't feed this to a cur!' he declares. I offer him a bit of my protein bar, but he declines with a nasty comment. A nurse comes around to see if Dad's eaten anything. 'I know it's not the nicest, but you really do need to eat something. Otherwise we'll have to get you on a feeding tube.'

'Tell *her*,' Dad says, pointing to me. I may have neglected to pick up his preferred takeaway, so I attempt to distract him with a fun fact about my first week at work: the same production company that makes the show also produced that reality series about organ donation we took part in while he was waiting for his first transplant four years ago. Dad is not remotely interested in the story, but I stubbornly tell it anyway.

With transplants, once you're sick enough to top the waiting list you still have to wait for someone healthy and compatible to die. The producers made the case that if we agreed to have our 'journey' documented, it might tug people's heartstrings enough to sign up as donors.

While networks may not want TV hunks crying on screen, for Heartstring TV, crying is mandatory. Kendall, the director, interviewed my sister Liz and me in our parents' backyard. She positioned us in such a way that the morning sun filtering through the jasmine created a lovely halo around our heads.

'What fun things do you remember doing with your dad when you were kids?' she said to warm us up. 'Hide and seek? Watching Disney?'

Dad preferred Hitchcock to Disney, which meant that we did too. Mum and Dad met at the university cinema society, and they spent the morning of their wedding at a special screening of *Les Parapluies de Cherbourg* at the Astor cinema. Watching Disney in our household was akin to drinking cask in a winery.

Kendall waited expectantly while I tried to dredge up a commercial-TV-appropriate memory. What else did I remember? Him dancing like he was having an epileptic fit anytime *Total Eclipse of the Heart* came on the radio? Him sneaking up on us in the kitchen and taking a karate stance, so we couldn't get to the fridge without going two rounds with a black belt? Or maybe the time I was finally allowed to watch *Psycho*, at eleven years old, after much pestering. Afterwards, when I was in the shower, I heard a strange screeching. Suddenly the door burst open and a black silhouette holding a knife rushed forth. I screamed louder than Janet Leigh and flapped my hands ineffectually. But when the steam parted it was just Dad, holding a tube of toothpaste. 'Oh, darling,' he said, looking thoroughly bewildered, 'I'm sorry. I thought you'd find it funny.'

Fifteen years later I did find that funny, but I had a feeling it wasn't the kind of heart-warming memory Kendall was after.

'Disney movies,' we said. Kendall looked at the sound man and he gave her the thumbs up.

'Okay, this time try and repeat the question in your answer. So if I asked how it feels to know someone's giving an organ to your dad, instead of saying, "amazing", you'd say, "It feels amazing to know that someone's saving my dad." Okay?'

No, it sounded incredibly cheesy. But we were there to do a job, and that job was to make a home viewer cough up a loved one's organ. We nodded. Kendall pressed record on the camera and deepened her voice. 'So, tell me, girls … what would be the hardest thing about losing your father?'

The boom inched closer. She had her head up her own arse if she thought she could get us to cry on camera.

'The hardest thing about losing Dad …' Liz said, choking back a sob. 'The hardest thing about losing Dad would be …' she couldn't get the words out.

'He'd never see grandchildren!' I croaked, and we broke, clutching each other, sobbing. Through my tears I saw the director smile. Tears in the first take! I no longer cared because I had finally said it – the worst thing – and it wasn't so bad. We blew snot bubbles and smiled back.

The sound guy took off his headphones and pointed to the sky. Kendall's smile faded. A plane had ruined the take.

'I'm *so* sorry, could you do that again?' she said. 'But … like it's the first time you've said it?'

When the show finally aired it was like watching a different family. One that had tearful group hugs and strolled arm-in-arm along the beach in a way that didn't look staged at all.

And now here we are again, except Dad's even sicker, has waited longer and there are no camera crews sending our story out to get people to donate a liver.

The windows have gone dark and cold. I lean over to give Dad a kiss before I leave and he holds my arm as I lean in. His own arms, the enormous tree branches that used to throw me over his shoulder, are nothing more than spindly twigs full of IVs and dark-purple bruises. My throat thickens. It's so much easier to be infuriated.

•

On Saturday morning I wake up with a sugar and pizza hangover. I've been eating protein bars for dinner all last week, then ruined it with half-a-dozen doughnuts in the pitch meeting on Friday, so when I walked into the living room last night and saw that Gil had ordered pizza ('none for me, oh look, you've ordered two large by accident') I figured why not just dive in? That's what normal people do on a Friday.

Sugar hangovers feel like you ate a pimply teenage sloth. Your tongue is coated in fuzz, and your energy has crashed so low that all you want to do is drink a litre of orange juice and lie on the couch till about 3pm, when you can top up with a burger.

Usually on a Saturday I would take my pimply sloth to yoga. Today is not one of those Saturdays.

When I started yoga at seventeen it was that quaint time in yogic history known as the 'Pre-Activewear period', when the only people doing yoga were hardcore vegans, ageing hippies and middle-aged mums (yuck!) in comfortable tracksuit bottoms. I'd been suffering from acute anxiety, despite (or possibly because of?) all the bongs my best friend and I smoked in her bedroom. On my way home one night, after a particularly bad panic attack, I furtively checked out the timetable outside my local yoga studio. I went to my first class expecting a nice lie-down, but instead of a soothing hippy crooning gentle instructions, a tiny Mossad agent called Pamela barked out a series of postures designed to torture Palestinian spies. Little did I know it was an Iyengar class, which is yoga taught by perfectionist drill sergeants trained not to show mercy. Looking back, the poses were pretty basic – it was the way she made us tune in to every sensation and thought that was agony.

Pamela rarely smiled in the traditional sense of the word. Occasionally, when I was so far out of my comfort zone that I could see my past life, the corners of her mouth lifted slightly. Then she'd move my slacker teenage body deeper into a posture until a rush of energy swept through me and I felt a high that I'd never quite reached with my friend's Spring Valley bong. So this was yoga! The next day I couldn't walk, and the following week I was back for more.

Every week, yoga brought me face-to-face with my shortcomings, but it was the one place I didn't have to be more than I was. I'd get into a posture and settle in to watch the drama: *This is painful and boring ... Hurry up and call the next pose ... I'm freakin' amazing ... I'm totally crap and can't do this ... Oh my god, I'm doing this ... What happens when I breathe? Oh ... space.*

Though I wouldn't admit it to anyone, there was a little voice in my head that started insisting I wanted to be a yoga teacher. So I started to investigate teacher training. Few places offered it in those days, and I made my then-boyfriend drive me across town at the crack of dawn to check out the one studio that did. The man who taught there seemed austere and intimidating, as if joy was anathema to yoga. I soon realised that even if I could master the poses on the studio walls, I spoke too quickly, laughed too loudly and was not the kind of calm, centred person anyone would take seriously as a teacher. So I gave up.

I still drag myself to a class every week, though I just go to gym yoga instead of a proper studio. It's easier, I can hide and no one pushes me in a way that will bring me face-to-face with my shortcomings. But these days, instead of the sense of peace that used to follow a class, yoga fills me with a curious sense of being a stranger to myself, particularly during the quiet, reflective moments of Savasana. I guess the only reason I go is as a kind of nod to my former self.

·

From the screening room, we get a clear view to the patch of gum trees near the carpark where the actors all gather to smoke. The only one who doesn't is the one who plays Warthog. Warthog joined the show as the fat teen sidekick and somehow survived getting culled before adulthood. When a TV journalist wrote a not-very-flattering article about his appearance he signed a contract with a diet-meal delivery service and now spends his breaks running laps of the carpark. Since he dropped twenty kilos, the writers were told they could start giving him romantic storylines.

This morning he's out there doing burpees and push-ups during the screening. The EP stops the tape so we can all behold his dedication to televisual attractiveness.

'I'd like the hack who wrote that article calling him a "fat kidult" to see him now!' she rages. She's stressed after a meeting with the network, and she stops the tape after every scene to yell at no one in particular.

'What did I tell everyone? Don't give Sasha more than one emotion per scene. You know she can't handle anything complex!' the EP bellows. 'And why doesn't wardrobe have her in something more sexy?'

'Tayla refuses to wear anything tight-fitting,' the Script Producer murmurs.

'Tough shit!' cries the EP. 'We hired her to be the sexy slut; she'll wear the fucking Lycra!' I look around for signs of feminist horror and find none.

Three episodes later I can't take it anymore and lean over to one of the storyliners. He's gay, so surely a progressive ally?

'Why are the women always the ones doing the dishes and cooking dinner?' I whisper. 'And why do they always take their husbands' last names?'

But he just looks confused. 'Do they? I've never really thought about it,' he says. 'It just sort of happens. It doesn't mean anything.'

I will change things from within. But first I need to find the Script Coordinator – we're almost out of mini-Bounties.

The screening finishes with an emotional scene between the teen heart-throb and his dad. After the workaholic father cancels yet another event with his son and leaves to do business with 'the Chinese', the teen heart-throb stands in the doorway and a tear rolls slowly down his cheek. It's a heartfelt scene that I think will resonate, unfortunately, with many kids watching.

The EP throws a Bounty wrapper at the screen. 'No, no, no!' she says. 'The network says we can't show him in tears. We've *got* to get the hunks to stop crying! What's wrong with a wall punch?'

A wall punch? I think of the little boys in the audience, learning the masculine way to show sadness as they wait for their own dads to come home. Then I think of the call centre and the month I spent harassing producers for this trial.

Learn their ways. I write a note to myself: *More lycra, less tears.*

●

I've been skipping yoga the last few Saturdays because we have a new teacher who makes us spend the first ten minutes lying down and 'noticing how we feel', which I find intensely irritating. Then we spend aeons in uncomfortable poses watching our breath, and I'm so grateful I gave up the idea of being a yoga teacher. Imagine willingly volunteering to not only undergo that pain yourself, but to inflict it on others?

But today I pull myself together and go, and just as I start quietly packing up so I can leave before Savasana – corpse pose – the teacher issues a slow, droning yoga decree from the podium.

'Remember, Savasana – "being" with oneself as one truly is – is the most difficult pose of all.' He looks right at me in a way that plainly says 'lie the fuck back down'. I lie the fuck back down. As I watch the ceiling fans, a thought pops into my head. *It may be your dream job but you hate it.*

This is why I hate Savasana.

•

In the afternoon I take the train out to meet Mum at the hospital. Because we live within a few kilometres of the city, I don't need a car, but every now and then I fantasise about a nice, heated vehicle as I shiver at the tram stop. It's bloody freezing, and since dropping two kilos in two weeks I can't seem to get warm, so I've thrown on my largest, thickest wool cardigan, which feels more like a dressing gown.

When I get to the hospital, Mum is waiting in the foyer with a bunch of flowers for Dad. We're going to my aunt's birthday dinner after visiting Dad, and Mum's wearing a beautiful red-and-purple dress she made herself out of rough silk.

I give her a hug; she smells like Issey Miyake *l'Eau d'Issey*. My arms could wrap around her birdlike frame twice, and I hold her gingerly so as not to crush a rib. Which is funny, because there's absolutely nothing frail about her – she can stand on her head and has only recently cut down her daily ten-kilometre runs. She can go all day on a sip of water, a handful of mesclun lettuce and just a sliver of Brunetti's almond torte. If asked to bet on her or Bear Grylls surviving a Gobi desert crossing, I honestly don't know who I'd choose.

'Is that what you're wearing?' she asks, frowning at my cardigan.

'I was cold,' I say, but it sounds like a weak excuse for sloppiness. 'How was Dad yesterday?' I ask by way of distraction as we take a pump of the obligatory hand sanitiser at the lift.

'Oh, you know,' she says, giving me the side-eye. 'His usual charming self.'

Dad is doing leg circles with the physio when we arrive. As soon as we walk in he asks me to run down and get him some 'fizzy lemon'.

Despite numerous attempts, no one has thus far been able to procure the version of 'fizzy lemon' that matches the fizzy lemon in Dad's head. It's not lemonade. It's not lemon squash. It's not mineral water with a dash of lemon. It cannot be found in supermarket or hospital café, beyond hill nor dale. My theory: 'fizzy lemon' is actually code for a game called 'How Much Do You Love Me?' The winner never actually *finds* this mythical drink, they're just the one who goes to the greatest lengths to try. Henry, one of dad's former psychology students, had a crack this afternoon, and though he failed to obtain the right fizzy lemon, he went to Leo's supermarket, Coles *and* the gourmet place down the road, Dad tells me, batting his crazy eyes.

The worst part is, the addled mofo is right. Friends, former colleagues and students come from far and wide to indulge his every whim. My own friends lower their voices to ask, 'How *is* your Dad?' Since it's rude to answer 'fucking infuriating', I murmur, 'Okay – his white blood count's on the up, thanks for asking,' and try to look solemn.

Before we leave I have one more go at the mystery of fizzy lemon. ('Lift? Lemonade? Mineral water with a squeeze of lemon? *Soda* water with a squeeze of lemon?' 'No, no, none of that!') Then it's time for Mum and me to swap the sterile surrounds of the hospital for my aunt's house.

Driving back, I notice that posters and banners advertising the National Gallery of Victoria's retrospective exhibition of my grandfather's work have started appearing on every tram stop and light fixture in the city. (My grandmother drew the line at commemorative tea towels – 'So tacky!' – but I quite liked the idea.)

I'm hit with a wave of exhaustion and I close my eyes for five minutes. When I open them, we're outside my house. I look at my mother. 'Aren't we going to the dinner?'

She smiles. 'I knew you'd want to get changed first.'

My family are already assembled when we get there. In contrast to the bright sterility of the hospital, the lights are soft and discrete, the Beethoven unobtrusive, and the scent more 'slow-roasted Persian lamb' than synthetic-apple hand sanitiser.

Whenever I see my extended family in one room, I'm in awe of how strikingly similar everyone looks. Despite a good decade of silent warfare (moves and countermoves over paintings and wills, before a fragile truce was achieved) somehow everyone still manages to look like they've WhatsApp messaged each other beforehand to coordinate outfits. Clothes cascade over wiry frames as if a single sheath was dropped by a white dove from the highest branch of a silver birch, then fluttered down and draped itself around my aunts and cousins just so. All wear chunky bracelets and necklaces from Dinosaur Designs, as hard and defined as the bones, muscle and sinew they adorn. My cousins could all have strolled out of Gypsy *Vogue*, and I realise that staying in my fugly warm cardigan would have meant letting Mum's team down.

No one asks about Dad. We've just come from the hospital where a member of the family is slowly wasting away, but here it seems everything is fine and lovely and perfect and stylish and I feel like bringing it up would be to enact a kind of verbal violence.

A school friend once told me that the women in my family (myself included) reminded her of skittish exotic birds, presumably pecking our way through life. When I ask if everyone is looking forward to the upcoming exhibition, I suddenly see it. Around the room, pairs of twig-like shoulders lift around ears. Eyes dart and finally Mum says, 'Oh, I don't think anyone's really thinking about it,' before beginning a lively discussion with my aunts about whether you could reasonably substitute mangetout for snow peas in an Ottolenghi summer salad. Then we move on to debating the merits of various nightshades.

'Am I mad?' I ask Gil when I get home. 'The two biggest things going on in the family right now are Dad being sick and the exhibition, and no one is talking about them.'

Gil sighs. 'Your family is that special kind of crazy which is WASP crazy,' he said. 'It's like a river that runs under the house and gnaws at the foundations, but you don't realise it's there until the house is falling down.'

2

Breakdown

After two months at the studio I am officially no longer a trainee but a fully fledged storyliner! I must be doing at least adequately. Plus, this week I get to create a new character!

I've named him after Gil's pot-loving cousin, Cousin Neddy. It's just a one-episode part, but who cares? He's still a living, breathing member of the story world, deserving of a backstory and idiosyncrasies. Viewers will say, 'My god, that character is more real, with more complexity and ongoing dramatic potential than any other – they must make him a regular!'

I go to town. It's the first fun I've had since starting here.

My new desk is so far on the outermost edge of the script department that technically I'm in the art department. I share desk space with a camp set dresser called Albie who has been here forever, is fiercely loyal to the show and is an excellent source of gossip. He explained that actors are split fifty-fifty. Half are NIDA grads and the rest are former child models or hot teens plucked from shopping-centre runways. Albie told me how a new family that moved onto the fictional street banded together and dared to complain about the storylines. 'They forgot they were jobbing and asked for better scripts,' he said, chortling.

'What happened to them?' I asked.

'They turned the dad into a gambling addict, shipped the daughter off to a fat farm and the wife moved to Brisbane.' Brisbane:

TV jail for naughty actors.

A few weeks ago I discovered a tiny room behind the photocopiers where they keep stacks of signed head shots of the actors. Every week Gil gets a saucy postcard from one of the hunks sent to him at work, which has apparently confused/frightened the receptionist.

I have a new game plan: Focus on how Lucky I Am to be Paid to Write Amidst the Undeniable Glamour of Television. (No decent acronym, unfortunately.) Admittedly it's a tawdry kind of glamour. The sets I marvelled over as a kid are so flimsy you could knock them over with a nudge, and even though the actors really do look better than us plebeians, their beauty secrets are not so amazing. Whenever I 'accidentally' touch the actors' hair in the canteen line I'm always disappointed to find that their casually tossed manes are actually helmet-stiff. And that 'luminescent glow' they sport? It's because man, woman, child or stunt-baby, they all get sprayed with light-reflecting particles. I saw one of the make-up women wiping her spray gun before holstering and one more childhood fantasy of over-the-rainbow TV perfection was destroyed.

Everyone is at least ten kilos lighter than they appear on screen. 'We call it "three-month syndrome",' Albie said. 'It takes three months from the time they join the show till their scenes go to air. They see themselves on screen and –' he sucked his cheeks '– they start to constrict.'

As for the writers, we sit around during screenings munching our way through packets of Tim Tams and casting aspersions on the actors. 'So and so's getting an arse,' said one of the male story editors, cackling through a mouthful of chips. 'Let's give her a bulimia storyline!' Normally I'd find this offensive, but this morning two actresses came into the script office and *literally* threw bags of lollies into the story room, then ran away giggling. What do they think writers are, a pack of pimple-faced, cave-dwelling goblins? Or is it their way of bribing us into giving them better storylines?

They've just imported a new Story Editor from a rival soap. She told me what happened when her old show had tried to introduce two lesbian characters as part of the regular cast. 'We got death threats until we got rid of them,' she said. 'It was a steady campaign until the lesbians went to Brisbane.'

Asians and lesbians *are* allowed on the show, they just get moved on quickly. My plan to change things from within is going dismally. During a break in the screening I ask the Script Producer why there aren't any non-white regular characters. 'The only way someone becomes a regular character is if they're related to one of the original families on the show,' says the Script Producer. 'And since there are no Asian families on the street ...' She shrugged – *it's out of our hands*. They do have one Eurasian actress, a former model, but she's white enough that they cast her as a member of an Anglo family.

Ratings are down. Over the weekend the EP read an article about the different sub-cultures of millennials. This afternoon she's called a meeting to brainstorm ways to mutate the current characters to match.

Every time the EP expresses a desire to 'shake things up, be more now', I stuff a mini-sandwich in my mouth. The trick is to package suggestions so that they offer the *appearance* of change, without actually requiring change.

'Emo! We need to make Bella an Emo!' the EP bellows, handing out copies of the article. 'Oh fuck, but we not allowed to do anything with her hair. One of the network execs has a hard-on for schoolgirls with heavy fringes.'

I reach for another fancy sandwich. When you're beginning to suspect you're in the wrong room, wrong job, wrong body, catering helps.

•

I miss Gil. I leave early and come home late. I try not to tell him when I'm down, but surely he can tell. I used to ask him to marry me at least once a week, but I can't remember the last time I did that.

I've been here for four months. For the past two I've been waking every morning with a feeling of dread. I remind myself this is my dream job: I'm contributing to Australia's cultural discussion. Then I look around for something I can eat. The protein-bar dinners have been replaced by huge meals when I get home, then there's usually a box of magnums in the freezer, and if it's been a frustrating day, 7/11 doughnuts after that.

I get my latest storyline back with red scrawls through half of it, plus 'notes' on a guest character I've written. I named her after my sister and gave her a Russian prostitute-like disposition. 'Keep in mind the network execs also read these scripts. Tone it down next time.' Butts!

My first mistake was trying to update a formula that's been going perfectly well for two decades without me.

My second mistake was to assume that any old dolt could write this stuff. Now I'm in awe of the people who can do it well. Someone'll pitch the most mediocre crap you've ever heard ('Sasha finds out about her dad's affair – and disapproves!' 'Bella thinks her boyfriend's cheating – but he's planning a surprise birthday!'), but add a few cliffhangers and a hook (*Is this really the end of Tilly's 'perfect' family? Will Jackson play right into Evie's hands?*) and they're weirdly compelling, just like one more tug on a poker machine. Ratings may not be fab (EP: 'They're *shithouse!*') but they're consistent.

My third mistake, one that I should have seen coming six months ago, is that I don't actually like the show now that I'm an adult. In fact, I hate it.

Some of the people I work with are lovely on an individual level, but as a whole it feels like every person for themselves, and there's a palpable sense of fear running through the department. I have no idea how I even talked my way in here, much less when they're going to work out I don't belong. The trouble is, I don't know where I *do* belong, or even if such a place exists.

I should be grateful to be here. My job looks cool to other people, doesn't it? But what I don't tell them is that the best part of my day is eating stolen chocolate on the tram home and disappearing into my book for an hour and a half. It's lonely.

•

The last few nights I've dreamed I'm standing on a tall building, being chased by blood-sucking zombies who vaguely resemble the script producers. Every night they chase me to the edge of the building and I have to decide. Rather than let them catch me, I jump off the edge and into the abyss, and those brief moments of freefall are such a blissful relief. Then I wake up.

Gil says I'm depressed and I should quit. And do what?

I eat my way through the week and drag myself to the advanced yoga class at the gym for penance. But when we get to the slower postures, whatever irritation I've been keeping at bay all week suddenly grabs its chance to scream in my face.

Is it possible to *think* you've reached some kind of career milestone only to realise you were mistaken?

•

It's late, and Mum gives me a lift home after visiting Dad. When we pull up in front of my house, she asks about work and I'm about to launch into a well-rehearsed anecdote when I suddenly feel like a black hole is opening up in my chest. I know it's not polite to go around foisting your gnawing emptiness on other people, so I try a chirpy 'work's fine' and hope she doesn't notice my flatness. She does.

'What is it, darling?' she says, turning off the engine.

I find myself telling her the truth, despite the warning bells in my head. 'I just feel like I want to do something good, something that gives my life meaning,' I say finally, feeling pathetic.

Mum smiles. I realise I haven't made a fatal error: she understands.

'Darling,' she says. 'Don't you think it's time to realise that a baby will give your life meaning?'

I look at her. What is there to say? I nod and go inside.

I wake in the middle of the night, thinking about my meaning baby. If this was one of the show's storylines, eventually my 'meaning baby' would turn into a sulky teenager. One night we'd be arguing and Meaning Baby would push me that little bit too far and the truth would come out.

'You think your life is so hard?' I'd scream, sweat dripping as I laboured over a hot stove. 'Well you were *supposed* to give my life meaning and *you didn't!*'

Hurrah! *Close on 'Meaning Baby' realising that he has failed his life's purpose and might as well start drinking now (or right after this ad for Tile Mart).*

To keep my sanity, I dig out the short story collection I started writing at the call centre. The first story is based on the time I spent at a Buddhist monastery in Nepal when I was nineteen. The main character is a mafia mother, and when she has to become a police informer to save her son's life, she gives them false information and ends up having to hide in a monastery from the fuzz *and* her son's rivals. To keep her cover, this chain-smoking westie, who thinks meditation is a celebrity perfume, has to act 'spiritual' among a bunch of privileged Westerners trying to find themselves, when all she wants to do is tell them to get their heads out of their arses. (In the second half she'll use her wicked mafia skills to help the monks set up a mini racket *but for good.*)

I think the idea has legs. Lots of legs. But more than that, it sustains me. This could be my way out.

Dad is finally well enough to leave hospital and wait for the transplant at home, and I visit him on his last night in the ward. The hospital chaplain comes around and tells me she is here any time. She is carrying a clipboard with a list of people she needs to tell this to. Frankly, pouring my heart out to someone who has allocated me ten minutes over a cup of tea and a soggy Scotch Finger does not appeal. But it reminds me that I still have a few sessions left on my Medicare referral to see Esther, the psychologist I talked to the first time Dad was sick. I make an appointment.

Oddly enough, what we end up talking about is writing.

'I sit at my desk and feel like I'm literally choking. Like there's something sitting there, blocking my throat, and all I can do is cry.' I am aware of how pathetic that sounds. A clothing factory fire in Bangladesh just killed hundreds of women and children, and I'm boo-hooing over a keyboard.

'So what would your ideal job on your ideal day look like?'

I begin to describe it and then I can't go on, because I'm crying. 'It would be wonderful to create something I felt proud of, that other people connected with,' I say eventually. 'But that seems impossible.'

There's a new trainee storyliner. She's bubbly. I give her the tour I wish someone had given me (chocolate drawer and stationery supply cupboard inclusive) and a few tips on how to make it through the first terrifying pitch meeting.

'Oh my gosh thank you, that is so sweet!' she trills. 'I think I got it!'

At the pitch meeting she delivers three pitches that are so hands-down perfect (the exact combination of blandly inoffensive and G-rated racy) that I can see the Script Producer mentally signing her up on a six-month contract. On my way out I grab a packet of raspberry bullets for the train and try to be happy for her.

On Monday, I'm on my way to a plotting session when the Script

Coordinator asks me to hand a couple of envelopes to the other storyliners. I make a lame joke about state secrets and she says, 'Na, just contract renewals they need to sign.' I shuffle them twice to see if there is one for me.

Is this how they let you know you're fired here? To take my mind off things I offer to restock the chocolate drawer. One packet for the drawer, one for my desk and one for the long tram-ride home. It's three weeks until Christmas.

·

It's my last day. I think. No one has actually said anything, but my contract is up today so I guess this is it? Just in case it is, I've thoughtfully sorted my own goodbye present and spent the last few weeks stocking up on fancy pens, coloured post-its, sticky-tape dispensers and Cadbury soft-centres.

I think technically my boss is the Script Producer. She's been in meetings all week but I finally manage to catch her after much awkward loitering around her office with a stack of next week's scripts for editing.

'Awesome, thanks!' she says. Nothing in her voice says *you're so out of here, never to return*. She begins to rush off to a meeting with the EP and I look at my feet, debating whether to return on Monday and see what happens or humiliate myself now by asking if it's my last day. But at the last moment she puts me out of my misery.

'Oh yeah,' she says, turning slightly. 'And I meant to say, thanks for all your awesome work!' She flashes me a smile and is gone. I guess I'm ... fired?

At the end of the day I email the editors my last storyline. I look around for someone to say goodbye to, but they've all gone into the pitch meeting and closed the door. On Monday I can be sad and afraid for my future. Today I just feel spent.

·

On Monday morning I sit down and make my plan. I have two months' worth of savings. I have a folder of notes for a short story collection that I've been planning to write for two years. I've got 35,000 words of backstories for all the characters. I've got colour-coded storylines broken into beats, written on ~~stolen~~ coloured post-its and stuck to my chest-of-drawers. And I've got three packets of ~~stolen~~ A4 cartridge notebooks, should I get the urge to sketch my short story collection in a visual diary.

It takes less than a week of not getting past the first three pages to remember that *planning* to write a book is wonderful; actually doing it is like turning the lights on after a one-night stand.

'Ahh,' says my writer friend Kate when I ring her for help. 'I see what's happening. You have 35,000 words of backstories and no actual story. Just write the damn thing.'

Easy for her to say. It's like she just sits at her desk when the moon is in Virgo and channels something amazing from the ether. Her book has been translated into 50 million languages (my copy is dog-eared from all the friends who've borrowed it), and the worst thing is that despite all of this she is very gracious.

Three hours later I am still rewriting the second paragraph and intermittently visiting the fridge to see if the contents have miraculously been replenished.

•

I think I have to stop yoga altogether. The quiet parts, when I can hear myself think, are torture. I'm lying in Savasana, perfectly happy fantasising about this New Amazing Book I'm going to write, when that unbidden voice punctuates my high: *Who is going to write this book? You don't even know who you are.* Way to buzzkill by throwing some existential angst on the bloody barbie.

I don't know what's wrong with me. Since I left the show, every morning I turn up to my desk, switch on the computer and cry. I press the keys, shuffle things around, and at the end of the day

I delete what I've written. Then I lie on the couch and eat like I haven't been eating all day. I take half a box of laxatives to push away the guilt, and then I feel better.

⁂

For the past few days I've been gripped by a nameless fear. I feel it locking up my chest and throat so much that it's hard to breathe. I don't want to be alone. Mum dropped off some plants yesterday, and as she was leaving I just wanted to burst into tears and ask her to stay, but I couldn't.

I know if I called Mum or my sister, Liz, they'd come over, but what would I say? I'd have to have a reason. But this fear has no reason, it's just shrouded in a paralysing shame that won't let me pick up the phone.

⁂

Somehow between getting fired and Dad's illness I completely forgot about Christmas. Now it's looming. I hated the show, but working there helped me slide through life without feeling like I had to justify anything. Now it seems like every man and their dog is asking, 'What are you doing now?'

My plan for the evening is 'tune out and get through'. Gil is sticking to his own family gathering this Christmas. I think he's still upset from last year when one of my relatives, on hearing he's a video game designer, said, 'Why don't you go to Syria and see what *real* bombs do?'

Everyone is still on hors d'oeuvres when I arrive. A Bach cello suite plays softly in the background and someone hands me a glass of champagne. They also hand one to Dad, and he accepts. Don't they know he's sick?

He catches me looking. 'Well?' he says.

I don't know what we're allowed to talk about, so I try to join in the fierce debate around Georg Jensen cutlery sets. Which is more satisfying to the palm: the curved simplicity of the Copenhagen set, or the narrow stems of the Arne Jacobsen? My aunt thinks Copenhagen, but Liz insists on the latter.

Is it possible that I was swapped at birth with a child from a bogan family? That somewhere out there are my real relatives, a bunch of degenerates who don't know how to cook, can't tell designer cutlery from normal cutlery, don't all have PhDs and don't think it's rude to mention that one of the people present looks a few weeks from death?

I can see Dad getting bored. I have the perfect emergency anecdote. 'Dad,' I say, 'I was chatting to Kate about a weird fan letter she got the other day and it reminded me of something to do with you.'

Last time Dad was hovering indecisively at death's door, my book was about to come out. Mostly all I wanted to do was sit by the phone and wring my hands, but the one thing I *was* looking forward to was the letters. Kate had an entire shelf dedicated to letters from readers, dutifully filed for reference.

'It's just a side effect of writing,' she said, shrugging. So when my book was published my folders were lined up and ready. Gil was on stand-by, prepped with phrases like, 'Must I share you with the world?'

Then one day I got one. Sure, it didn't justify a folder of its own, but I emptied my tax receipts out of a plastic Hello Kitty sleeve for it anyway.

I saw your profile in the paper about your book, it read. *Jolly well done. The article mentioned your father was a retired psychologist. Is he the same L.W. who worked as a psychologist in the Navy from 1975–1979? If so, I'm keen to renew our acquaintance.*

'And so, Dad, my one fan letter was actually kind of for you,' I conclude, to much good-natured groaning around the table. But not Dad.

'Did you keep the letter?' asks Liz.

'Of course I kept it!' I say. 'It was addressed to me, and the law of attraction means it will breed other letters, which will fill that damn Hello Kitty sleeve and many others. Any day now.'

Everyone laughs, but Dad's face clouds over.

'Well? Did you tell him about my liver?' he asks.

The table falls silent. 'No, Dad. I just wrote to tell him you weren't the person he was looking for.'

Dad drops his fork and stares at me. 'Well, you'll just have to write again and tell him about my liver transplant.'

'But, Dad,' I say carefully. 'You don't know him.'

'It doesn't matter!' he roars. 'People want to know!'

There is a barely perceptible pause before someone brings out the summer pudding my mother made and the table bursts into applause. The exotic birds go back to chattering and the rabid pigeon in our midst is quickly distracted.

For the next twenty minutes I can barely speak. I look around the table. Is this what it feels like to be an actor on stage who's forgotten their lines? Where the other actors keep going until eventually you remember what you were meant to say and can catch up?

I can't believe it's been another year.

When I get home, Gil is out with his cousins, leaving a note and leftovers from his family's Christmas dinner in the fridge. It doesn't take long to get through them.

•

2am: I wake up from a nightmare. I was being followed by a mangy black mutt with matted fur. I'm terrified of dogs, but it would not leave me alone. It kept clumsily nipping at my heels, frightening me, though strangely it didn't seem to want to hurt me. It just wanted my attention, to be near me, but I was afraid and kept running away. Finally I managed to lock it inside a house, but when I did it went crazy. I was pushing the screen door shut, but it hurled itself at the wire, hurting itself terribly in the process.

I wake relieved, but some part of me feels lonely for the dog – like it was just a missing part trying to find its way back to the whole. I didn't want to be near it because it was clumsy, and messy, and painful. And now it is gone.

2.25am: My heart is racing; something's wrong. Is this a heart attack? Something is deeply wrong with me and I just haven't been able to see it. Why didn't anyone tell me? Everyone can see it. I've got to find out what it is before the damage gets worse.

3.02am: There's something very wrong with me. I feel like I'm wearing a mask all the time now, but this mask is killing me. I want to take it off; I want to leave my whole body.

Other people know how to deal with that sick feeling you get when you wake up and realise you're still here and need to smile through another day even though you feel like an alien. Other people know how to live, how to make good decisions and keep a job beyond six months. Other people know what you're meant to talk about. But I feel like a troglodyte who crawled out of their cave by mistake.

I put on my mask, tell the stories, make the jokes, do the voices, act incredulous at the appropriate times, but inside there's a void, like I'm watching myself and wondering how on earth I'm putting on such a performance.

For the past few years I've found myself praying sometimes that I won't wake up, and I have no idea why.

3.15am: Gil is sleeping peacefully beside me. I want to wake him up and say, 'Are you deluded? Why on earth are you still with me?' Does Gil have some kind of secret 'save a troglodyte from loneliness' charity agenda? Everyone must be able to see how incompetent and ridiculous I am – couldn't someone have told me? Maybe they've all been trying and I just haven't listened.

3.35am: I can't lie still; it feels like something is ripping me apart from inside. I mentally rehearse getting out of bed, walking into the kitchen and getting a knife out of the drawer. I start scratching at myself to give myself something immediate, here, now, to get me out of my head.

4am: If anything is out there, either kill me now or tell me what to do. I'm out of ideas. I'm less than out.

4.02am: Jesus Christ. I heard a voice in my head, like my voice but different, and at the same time it felt like someone was punching me in the guts. *If you want something to change, you have to be willing to let go of everything.*

Let go of everything? What does that mean? Become one of those people shouting at rubbish bins?

If I gave up everything – the dream of writing, the dream of being someone – what would be left in its place? What's the point of getting what you want if you don't care about it anymore?

My arms are starting to sting. I turn on the light and see red welts up and down my arms, thighs and stomach, like I'm some deranged ice addict. I can't even write myself off properly. Gil shifts and squints against the light. He asks sleepily if everything's okay. I try to speak but can't, and within seconds I hear him sleep-breathing. What's wrong with me? Someone I love is right next to me and I haven't been able to talk to him about how I'm feeling in months because I don't know what to say. Whatever I'm doing clearly isn't working.

If you want something to change, you have to be willing to let go of everything.

Without knowing who or what I'm speaking to, I say yes.

3

Operation New Calling

Last year's New Year's Resolutions:
1. Sever ties with call centre industry. Get dream job.
2. Lose five kilos (not from face).
3. Write Great Australian ~~Novel~~ Short Story Collection.
4. Get in touch with old friends once achieved first three.
5. Move out of asbestos-riddled, carbon monoxide-trapping hovel then get married in way that totally reinvents institution/shows we are not stuffy.
6. Write 'think about having children' on next year's list.

This Year's Resolutions:
1. Get out of bed before eleven. Shower. Don't become 'person of concern'.
2. Find meaning/purpose so I can get through week. Or just today.
3. Find job where I don't have to talk to anyone.
4. Learn how to talk to people.
5. Start last year's list.

•

Halfway through my session with Esther, I hear myself blurt, 'Sometimes when I get to an intersection on my bike I think, *I could just keep going.*'

Esther makes a 'that's not good' face, which is oddly enlightening.

It's *not* good, is it, letting yourself coast into traffic? I'd hardly call it suicidal, but it's certainly a lackadaisical approach to living.

We start to chat about ways I might firm up my survival instinct.

'The problem is that I don't actually know what's wrong, so I don't know how to fix it,' I say. 'I get out of bed, shower, visit dad, apply for jobs and stare at the computer. But inside I feel like a highly functioning zombie. I don't know what I'm doing here. As in here – on earth.'

'What if you start from there?' she replies. 'Just accept that right now you're in the "I don't know" space. And that that's actually a perfectly legitimate space to be?'

The *I don't know* space. That's the best she can come up with? Sounds like a room in some left-leaning university for arts students to escape law students' oppressive certainty. Serves me right for Googling 'Buddhist counsellors'. But the gift of being ready to scratch yourself to death in bed on Christmas night is that you become open to new ideas very quickly.

'So I'm in the *I don't know* space. Then what?'

'When you're in the *I don't know* space, what you need is *more information*. Look around, investigate, see what you like. But give yourself permission to get it wrong.'

At the end of the session Esther suggests I start seeing her once a week, 'just for a little while'. I think she means 'until you don't have out-of-body experiences when you watch yourself ride in front of a car or take a knife out of a drawer'.

'I don't think I have enough material for once a week,' I say. Esther doesn't seem to think that will be a problem.

·

The first thing is to stay calm. I may be in the middle of the *I don't know* space vortex, but (what did she say?) all I need is *more information*. And, for god's sake, I need to put some pants on that don't have elasticised ankles.

I pack my bag with stolen notebooks and post-its (plus a label maker that somehow made its way from a casting agent's desk and into my bag) and head out to the bakery-cafe around the corner for a business meeting with myself.

Monday 9.45am: I order a coffee and a chocolate-iced jam doughnut (this is serious business, I need reinforcement), grab a window seat, crack open a notebook and ask myself what I want to do with my life. Mmm, good doughnut. What if what I want to do with my life is eat doughnuts and stare out the window? Okay, focus. This is exciting. I am a blank canvas! New year, new me!

But where do I start? (With another doughnut. Thought burns calories, and thinking about your future burns them at twice the speed.) Last time I asked these kinds of questions I was a nineteen-year-old university dropout living in the monastery in Nepal. (I still think a few months in a developing country should be mandatory for wayward youth, like military service. Something about seeing shoeless children with matted hair running up to strange cars and asking for a pen makes you think that if you were lucky enough to be born qualifying for an Australian passport, you should get off your parents' couch, figure out where your talents lie and use them. Unfortunately this sort of trip now comes with labels like 'poverty tourism' and is seen as something young white people do to better themselves. Which it totally is, but young white people are lazy fuckers who need to be better.)

Back then I believed I wanted to be a writer and yoga teacher – *clearly* the wrong path if the last few weeks are anything to go by.

Old goals = gone. Blank canvas. Next?

The Script Coordinator at the TV show took acting classes after work. Well, I do like showing off. And would enjoy being loved by the masses. Isn't that basically what acting's all about? Crapping on and getting claps? And free stuff?

'Take action,' is what Esther said. 'Pick a direction and start walking.'

10am: How do you act? Amber said her classes revolved around a scene study. I scull my coffee, hoover my doughnut crumbs and race home.

10.17am: I download the *Aliens* screenplay and print off the scene where Ripley lets rip on a government flunky. I close the windows just in case the chefs in the laneway over the fence are listening, stride to my mark at the coffee table and prepare to address the couch and my sleeping cat, Ginger.

'These people are dead, Burke!' I squawk. Ginger startles. 'I'm gonna make sure they nail you right to the wall for this! Right to the wall!'

Ginger bolts and I break character by laughing nervously. What if Ginger is an incarnation of a former human, currently trapped in a feline prison and laughing at me?

'No' to acting.

10.37am: I always thought I'd be good at psychology – I love diagnosing my own neuroses, and love diagnosing others' neuroses even more. Economically viable *and* fun.

10.39am: Ring Kate to tell her about my new career. 'Isn't your dad a psychologist? Didn't he tell you once never to do it?' He did. One day I was prattling on about something when out of the blue he said, 'Never be a psychologist. You'd be really bad at it.' What a bastard. I must bring that story to my next session with Esther – it's top-shelf material.

10.45am: What did I enjoy as a child? Dancing. Wildly. And taking my pants off for visitors.

10.46am: Dance break. I see my reflection in the television and frankly, am blown away.

Look up dance careers.

10.48am: Suffice to say if you haven't been in a tutu since age four, your professional dancing options are limited to spirit fingers in second-hand car advertisements, or 'Lap dance for $60, no touching'.

11pm: Little break to Google 'free student massages'. (Technically, I'm suicidal. Don't I deserve small pleasures?)

11.15pm: Hmmm ... The training centre offering student massages clicks me through to a course guide for a diploma in yoga teaching. Enrolments close Friday and the final information session is on Thursday. The course is for classical yoga: no bells and whistles, just units on everything from yoga philosophy, pranayama, something called 'yogic physiology', Western anatomy, meditation etc. It looks thorough, old-school and boring.

11.30pm: I think my brain has an extra voice. My normal thinking voice says, *You can't do that. You can't do wheel pose and you think fisherman's pants are for wankers.* This new voice says things like, *Remember how much you wanted to teach?*

I did. Passionately. And suddenly I can't recall a good reason why I gave it up. Surely I had one. Maybe this is what Esther meant: pick a direction.

Time to step out of the *I don't know* space and get some more information.

11.45am: Back to the cafe. New subject; new notebook. Also, frosted banana cake. When you're on a roll, don't stop the flow. But the woman at the bakery counter remembers me from earlier. 'Wish I had your metabolism,' she says, and I blush. I know she means it as a compliment – if you're a skinny girl with a big appetite, people look at you like you're Jesus. But something about my eating makes me feel ashamed and secretive, though I don't know why. Lately I haven't been able to skip meals like I used to either, and if I get fat, people will know I do this.

11.46am: Which kind of yoga to teach? For the past five years all I've done is 'try to ignore the Pump class next door gym yoga', but apparently there are 600 styles. I narrow it down to four main categories:
1. Iyengar
2. Bikram (plus the many Hot Yoga variations)
3. Ashtanga (including its cousins Power/Vinyasa etc.)
4. Classical (the kind being taught at the training centre)

I should probably try them all before deciding whether to do their teacher training – due diligence. I will need my stretchiest shorts, a yoga companion (when Gil gets home from work I'll let him know he's to be the co-pilot on my voyage of discovery) and … an open mind.

6.15pm: ~~Yoga companion~~

6.30pm: For the first time in five years I set foot in a proper, real-life yoga studio. I tiptoe into the studio, more nervous than my first time because this time I know what I'm in for. Straps hang off walls like chains in a dungeon. No gym bunnies in sight, just a bunch of hard-core fifty-year-olds in tattered shorts strapping themselves into postures I last saw in a book about the Spanish Inquisition.

And there behind a desk, is my old teacher, the pint-sized former Mossad agent. 'Hello, Alice,' Pamela says, the corners of her mouth lifting slightly. 'Long time no see.'

Two hours later I am a bag of pummelled muscle. Somehow I manage to ride my bike home and literally slither from the front door to the couch. Ginger jumps on my lap but I can't even lift my arms to pat him. Gil wants to watch *Cosmos* and I can barely muster the strength to demand *Snog, Marry, Avoid*.

Iyengar yoga was my first kiss, and it has a lovely way of weeding out the yoga try-hards from the serious yoga dogs who've got shit to sort through (like me!). But …

> **I**yengar was
> **Y**oga's fun police. He stood on students' backs and they all looked
> **E**xtremely constipated. I'm
> **N**ot sure I could I instruct people to 'squeeze the outer skin of your
> **G**luteus!' without laughing.
> **A**lthough Iyengar's focus on alignment is awesome, it's also
> **R**eally hardcore and I'm just not that kind of badass.

Also, you have to practise Iyengar exclusively for THREE YEARS before you're allowed to begin the introductory level of teacher training.

1. ~~Iyengar~~ (Though I'll keep going to Pamela's class – it's so good, in a masochistic kind of way.)
2. Bikram
3. Ashtanga
4. Classical

Tuesday 11.30am:

> **Bikram Haiku**
> Bikram yoga room so
> Hot. Roasting hipsters sweat
> Out crap. So holy!

Devotees intense
Teacher barks instructions from
Bikram's script, same-same

Torture heat – don't spew!
Crimson thighs like frankfurters
What fresh hell is this?

Class ends, cool air sweet
What, what's this? Endorphin high –
Holmes this is the shit!

'Hydrate babe!' Teacher
Up-sells me drink. Kombucha
Tastes like lukewarm pee

To teacher train would
Cost twelve grand for just two weeks.
Smart money or scam?

Googling, it's sadly
No. 'Cos Bikram is a
Rapey lunatic

Wednesday 5pm:
1. ~~Iyengar~~
2. ~~Bikram~~
3. Ashtanga
4. Classical

Ashtanga is the ultra-fast, vigorous, jumping-in-and-out-of-postures style of yoga whose streaks-of-sinew devotees (Gwyneth,

Madonna, various Naomis) are what people mean when they talk about 'yoga body'.

I did try a beginner's Ashtanga class many years ago and all I remember is how much I wanted to cry (hurt cry, not epiphany cry) after every session. I opt instead for Ashtanga-Lite: Power Yoga.

A new studio, part of a chain, has opened up near the university and the first thing I notice about the Live Free studio is that it's bright! One wall is covered in graffiti-style peace signs, Hindu goddesses that look like MTV babes and inspiring slogans like *No limits, surrender your fears!* Racks of bright yoga tights line the walls and a potted fern almost glows with vitality. And the whole place smells *clean*, if clean is a smell – unlike Pamela's Iyengar studio above the food co-op, which smells like samosas and tears.

So far so McYoga Glossy, I sniff. A scented candle next to the register subtly masks the smell of non-spiritual commerce, and ambient music pipes through invisible speakers. The trudge through the heat has made me tired, but a gentle breeze through the open window blows droplets of water from the nearby fern onto my skin, cooling me instantly. Well, now that I'm here, I may as well stay for one class.

As I slip my shoes amongst the Birkenstocks in the rack, I notice a tall, tanned glamazon twirling on a chair behind the desk, sun shining through her hair. She looks like one of the models on the cover of *Yoga Journal*. Where do they keep the ugly people? Are they ugly-exclusionary?

'Heeeey girl!' she calls. 'First time at Live Free, honey-bun?'

I swivel to see who is coming up the stairs, but there is no one. The glamazon is talking to me! Her name is Suki and I want to be her friend; I want to be *her*. And if I do the training here, maybe I could be?

The class itself is like yoga summer camp. If the staid precision of Iyengar yoga is like the Catholic nun of the yoga world, power yoga is the hootin', hollerin' revivalist church. Power yoga is more like a traditional workout – you work up a sweat while moving quickly in and out of a sequence of postures, often to music. Is yoga allowed to be that much fun? There is swearing! There is a warrior sequence to Katy Perry! ('Warri-ooors, I wanna hear you roooooaarr!' yells Suki.) There are crazy poses that I can't do, but I don't mind because right when we're straining so hard we think we'll die, Suki comes around and tickles our ribs ('It's playtime *all the time* at Live Free!') and we fall about laughing! Pamela would *never* tickle our ribs!

Even though the class feels like it's on fast-forward and my back goes into spasm when we do a standing twisting balance, I am pumped. Where has this studio been all my life? Pamela is so *slow*, and even though we do hard poses we have to do them *mindfully*. Here you dance in and out of them so fast you don't have to notice anything if you don't want to.

At the peak of the John Lennon 'Imagine' remix, Suki lets out a whoop and says, 'Imagine how good your yoga butt is gonna look on Instagram!' and everyone laughs and for some reason I'm reminded of the TV show's story room, but I feel so good *I don't care*. That was the old, cynical me. Live Free, *I don't know* space me is positive!

Savasana is accompanied by a cover of Steve Winwood's 'Higher Love' that leaves me so inexplicably emotional I have to keep my eyes squeezed shut during our final group 'Om' so no one can see my tears. Endorphins *and* cathartic tears – it's the total yoga package.

After class, as I spritz my mat with organic tea-tree disinfectant, I weigh up the pros and cons. Pro, the whole thing was incredibly aspirational. Or do I mean inspirational? Whatever, I definitely aspire to be as yoga-tastic as my classmates and Suki. Why not? It's a healthy pursuit! And unlike in Pamela's class, the tattoos here are fresh and more 'tribal' than 'prison'.

The only downer was at the start of the class when we had to 'create community and groove with our tribe', which involved introducing ourselves to the person next to us and telling them one fabulous thing about our day. I introduced myself to the woman beside me. She wore a yoga-kini with a white horseshoe symbol on it and looked like she had a really clean liver. Just as I was about to lie about my fabulous day, she flicked me a closed-mouth smile and asked if I could move my mat a few inches away so she had room for her car keys and mobile phone next to her mat. For the rest of the class she did the hardest version of each pose, and it was all I could do to keep up with her.

Curiously, I noticed that without exception all the other students' clothes bore the same white horseshoe logo as my neighbour. Even Suki had it. Perhaps it's the studio logo? Something they give you when you sign up?

Now that the class is over, I ask Suki if it's the studio logo and she laughs so hard she has to put down her mason jar of green juice.

'Nooooo, girl, it's *Lululemon*! They're the most amaaaazing yoga brand from Canada. Everything they do is all ethical-focused and they're one hundred per cent into empowering women to *be awesome*.'

Well, I am sold! I think what I love most about Live Free is that their ethos seems to be 'It's okay to be beautiful and amazing and buy things that reflect that because you're worth it!'

Suki tells me about their teacher-training program and the Six Pillars of a Live Free teacher (I currently embody none, but I think with a change in attitude and shorts I could be on my way). As we're talking, students start filing in for the next class. A shirtless man runs up to Suki and lifts her off the ground.

'Heeeeeey, baby!' she bellows and swats him in the six-pack. 'Come to get your groove on?'

Others file in behind him, all chatting happily and high-fiving Suki. It reminds me of the one time I took ecstasy, but without the three-day comedown. I brush off the feeling of being lobotomised with feel-good clichés. Who cares if it's cheesy when you feel this good? I want to join their tribe!

Google tells me there's a Lululemon factory outlet near the old brothel where Kate used to work. I know I'm unemployed, but if I'm going to join their tribe, I need to look the part.

Inside the outlet the walls are lined with images of thin women with long, flowing hair and round, peachy bottoms in complex yoga postures. Okay, so the beauty myth hasn't spared yoga, but, I remind myself, they're one hundred per cent ethical and have great 'brand values' according to Suki. So I will support their mission to empower women, and hopefully they will give me a round, peachy bottom in return.

A bronzed twig bounces over and offers to 'hook me up'. I think a couple of pairs of tights and some shorts will be plenty if I'm practising every day. Then I see the price. Even with a factory discount a single pair of leggings still cost almost a week's rent. But that's the thing about being a yoga teacher, isn't it? You have to live ethically, which means paying more for clothes that were hand-stitched by unionised Canadians getting a decent wage and free on-site childcare.

On the way home I flick through the Live Free teacher-training program brochure. Hundreds of lithe yoga babes line up in rows in Balinese hacienda, studying units on Stepping into Greatness. Old me would have sneered at such a phrase. New me has tasted of the Power Yoga endorphins and wants more. Yes, I want to step into greatness! Or at least just step into normal functioning. Can I call off the search now?

1. ~~Iyengar~~
2. ~~Bikram~~
3. ~~Ashtanga~~ Power Yoga ✓✓✓✓
4. Classical yoga

Sigh. Esther's *more information* edict means due diligence. I will go to the information night for the classical yoga teacher training course, if only to rule it out.

Thursday 6pm:
The training centre is in a narrow city laneway that specialises in boutiques showcasing the work of cutting-edge fashion graduates who don't believe in armholes. I've dragged Kate along for a second opinion. At the entrance to the building a busker playing Django Reinhardt harasses us with aggressive gypsy music.

We take the lift up to the fourth floor and follow the signs to an enormous double classroom. The building overlooks a laneway packed with restaurants, and the huge windows have a clear view into some upstairs bars across the laneway and tiny apartments in the building opposite. The classroom itself looks directly into someone's kitchen. On the downside, I may miss half the yoga instructions because I'll be too busy watching someone cook spaghetti in their underpants, but on the plus side, if there's a *Rear Window*-style murder, I'll be a great witness.

There are massage tables stacked against one wall and Yoga bolsters against the other. The vibe is more grungy and functional than the 'Fluoro white with a dash of fern' aesthetic of the Live Free studio.

Aside from me, there are two other last-minute prospective teaching sign-ups. The first looks like a Fleetwood Mac groupie, with an aqua crew-cut, floaty dress and some kind of pagan squiggle in the middle of her forehead.

'Hiiiiiiiiii, I'm Jo-Jo,' she croons. 'Are you two gorgeous ladies going to join our sangha?'

One glance at Kate's face tells me she's disappeared to her happy place, so I nod for both of us and pull up some bolsters. On the other side of the circle is Jo-Jo's polar opposite. Mid-thirties, she wears a blazer that I just saw in the boutique downstairs for $750. In contrast to Jo-Jo's aqua crew-cut, her 'sun-faded' balayage die job looks so natural it must have cost a bomb. The only things that I can relate to are the white knuckles gripping her Goldman Sachs water bottle.

An older man of indeterminate age (grey hair, but looks

deceptively sprightly) strolls in and introduces himself as Graeme, the course coordinator. He rah-rahs about the course (it's classified full-time, not because we'll be sitting in class forty hours a week, but because we're expected to put in an ordinate number of practice hours). Since I'm ninety per cent sure the endorphin-pumping 'make me like Suki' course is for me, I tune out somewhere between 'syllabus' and 'core competencies' and focus my attention on mentally pricing the cost of Goldman Sachs' whole outfit ($3,500, if you include the watch and hair).

'It used to be that you found a guru and trained with him – very patriarchal I'm afraid – for life,' says Graeme. 'But we believe each tradition has something to offer, which is why all seven of our teacher trainees come from different lineages.' Indeed, the teaching staff include pretty much all the main lineages, except Goat Yoga.

'What we're really here for tonight,' he continues, 'is to work out if *you're* ready to go on this journey.'

Kate pinches me under the table. If anyone says 'journey' within the first ten minutes I have to buy her a drink.

Graeme takes us on a 'short sprint' through the history of yoga, which begins with the first texts (as in, the first texts ever), the Vedas, which were 'mystical hymns' meant to be sung. Somewhere down the line a bunch of sages thought this might not be the most reliable way to pass on wisdom, and so they nailed down the nuts and bolts of the yoga teachings and compiled them into the Upanishads, which are really focused on getting to know the true self, or the *'Atman'*. 'Yoga has been much diluted over the centuries, which is a shame because the original texts tell us as much as about living well in the 21st-century as in the time, thousands of years ago, when they were written,' says Graeme.

One of the most famous sections of the Upanishads is the Bhagavad Gita, which is all about a great warrior who loses it on the eve of battle. As he looks out over the battlefield to survey the two armies (one of which he's meant to lead) he starts to get cold feet. In steps his charioteer, Krishna, who also happens to be God in disguise (we've all had that wise taxi driver, amiright?) and the whole thing is a dialogue between the two of them, which is really a metaphor for defeating the crap aspects of our inner selves, uniting with our higher self, and basically getting out there and 'living your best life'.

I have to hand it to Graeme: the man is passionate about old-school yoga – the ancient kind, not the high-fiving, Lululemon, 'get your *groove* on, girlfriend!' kind.

'Anyone can qualify to be a yoga teacher these days,' Graeme goes on, 'but only those who submit themselves to the fires of initiation detailed in the first texts are truly yogis.'

Hold up. Is there a way to do this *without* putting yourself through the fires? Could I maybe get recognition of prior suffering and skip the fires? I think of bouncy, happy Suki and can't imagine her ever being broken by 'the fires of initiation'.

Graeme asks us to introduce ourselves and say why we want to be teachers.

Goldman Sachs Bohemian, real name Annabelle, begins: 'I started doing yoga at my gym in London, and now if I go a few days without a class I want to stab my boss in the head.' She gives an icy smile. 'I guess I want to share those benefits with other people.'

I say that I've been doing yoga religiously for ten years (skipping the five I haven't), have always wanted to be a yoga teacher (when I was twenty) and really want to help people. (By 'people', I mean 'myself'.)

Then it's Jo-Jo's turn.

'Where did I get my love of yoga?' she drawls. 'Oh my god, wheeeerre do I staaaaaarrt?' (Desperately hope she doesn't start with her previous incarnation.)

'I'll begin with my weekend, shall I? It was *juuuust magical,*' she coos. 'I scooted along to the Satyananda ashram in Daylesford for their annual women's retreat, and let me tell you, it was *goooooorrgeous.* We rapped about life, and there was so much beautiful goddess energy.' She beams at me, which I take as an affront. Do I *look* like someone who believes in goddess energy?

'The last night of the retreat coincided with the full moon, so *of course* we had a fire ceremony. We got the oils going, a bit of *massaaage* ... It was so organic the way it all came together. '

Graeme tries to interject but Jo-Jo talks over him. 'Because it was just us goddesses we decided to liberate ourselves from our outer layers and just bathe in that beautiful Luna energy.' Jo-Jo smiles at us each individually, and despite myself I eagerly smile back. Stop it! 'And, that's an energy I really want to bring in to my everyday life. You know?'

I know there's no way that Goddess Energy isn't harbouring a serious mental illness. (Not that I can talk, a month ago I was lying in bed trying to scratch myself to death.)

'Well,' Graeme says, smiling in turn at Goddess Energy, Homicidal Corporate Bohemian and me, Miss Ride Into Traffic. 'You all seem like excellent candidates for yoga teachers.'

Afterwards, Kate and I huddle behind a dumpster in the laneway so she can light a cigarette. 'Everyone I know is starting yoga,' she grumbles as I shelter her lighter from the wind. 'I thought you were different.'

'I *am* different, Kate, I'm your cool friend, remember?' Kate has been upset lately because all her other friends have started having babies and moving to the suburbs. ('And Bunnings! They spend entire weekends roaming Bunnings and Ikea. As a destination.')

I agree that it's disgusting and will never happen to us. Kate takes one more puff and stubs out her cigarette. She looks at me through narrowed eyes.

'You're not seriously considering it, are you?'

'Of course not,' I say, peering up at the fourth-floor window.

2am: I just had a middle-of-the-night realisation: since Monday I have ticked off the first two of my New Year's Resolutions without even trying. (1. Get out of bed before eleven. Shower. 2. Find meaning/purpose.)

·

Mum picks me up to visit Dad. He's in hospital again, but just for a few days to get pumped full of steroids. She politely tries to suppress a coughing fit in the living room, which is something I've noticed people do a lot when they visit. Gil and I seem to be immune to the crumbling plaster.

'It's a *student house* and you're not a *student* anymore,' my mother says once we're in the car. But I think we were very clever hanging on to this house. Cheap rent because of hazards you can train yourself not to notice (carbon monoxide heater, rising damp, holes in wall). Prime inner city location, which means we can walk everywhere and don't need a car – and we're behind a mafia-owned restaurant strip, so if we ever decide to start a drug habit, we've only to order a large capricciosa 'no ham', and we're sorted.

On the way to the hospital, we get stuck behind a bus that has an ad on the back for a meal delivery service. I recognise the formerly fat actor Warthog from the show. *Do it for YOU,* is the tagline. *If not now – when?*

At the next set of traffic lights a portly fellow in activewear jogs up to the crossing. 'Oh look,' murmurs my mother. 'He's exercising. If-Not-Now-When?'

I fish into my bag for another protein bar. In order to lose five kilos I have been eating normally five days a week and protein bars the other two. Sometimes I mix it up with high-fat/no carb or carbs only till lunchtime. Lately I've been adding a cheat meal on Friday, but sometimes it's okay if that turns into a cheat meal once a day, as long as I follow it with a protein bar for dinner, plus laxatives and long runs. The only problem is, I've been using this approach for six months and I weigh *exactly the same.*

Sometime during the hospital visit my parents start to tag team with the ever subtle 'What are you doing with your life, going forward?' line of questioning. Something tells me 'yoga teaching!' won't get a good response, so I cram another protein bar into my mouth and say nothing.

•

I get home extremely irritable, and when Gil gives me a hug, I realise it's all his fault and resolve to do something about it.

'When are we getting married?' I grumble romantically. (Getting married for something to do when I'm desperately unhappy seems like the worst idea, but ... what am I doing with my life, going forward?)

Gil pulls away from the hug and gives the sigh of the deeply weary.

'The more you ask –' he begins.

'– the less likely it is to happen,' I snap. 'I know.'

'Isn't yoga supposed to make you ... I dunno, more *accepting*?' he asks.

I ignore him and put on my new Lululemon, cost-a-week's-rent yoga tights. I walk into the kitchen, Gil trailing behind me. I'm just bending down to get the cat food from the bottom of the fridge when Gil says, 'Nice strawberry knickers.' I scurry to the mirror and bend over. Sure enough my fancy tights are so transparent you can see the pips in the strawberries.

I check the label to see if I've washed them wrong; along with care instructions the label says *Made in Bangladesh*. I beg your expensive-cos-they're-ethical pardon? What about the unionised Canadians? The on-site childcare?

I contrast the images I saw in the store – beautiful women meditating on rocky outcrops – with images from the news story on the factory fire that recently killed more than one hundred Bangladeshi garment workers, and the unforgettable image of a young Bangladeshi woman bent over a sewing machine while her baby lies on a thin piece of fabric at her feet.

So much for empowering women.

Further Googling reveals that Lululemon has so far refused to publish the address of their suppliers so they can be externally audited. I also find an interview with Lululemon's CEO who says the tights are *not* transparent – it's just that some women's thighs are too fat to wear them. I think of Suki, the bronzed, taut yoga goddess waxing lyrical about their ethics. Is that one of the conditions of morphing into a yoga demigoddess? That you don't look too closely at anything that might raise inconvenient negative vibes?

I must face facts: I am never going to high-five my yoga-bros or bellow about taut yoga butts mid-class. I will never keep a straight face telling someone to live their best life or saying 'Whassup girlfriend!' to students I barely know. And most of all I will never wear branded yoga clothes in front of students who might get the idea that that's how you become a real yogi. If working on that bloody TV show taught me anything, it's that when I 'try to learn their ways and assimilate' it's not long before I want to scratch my own face off.

No matter how much I'd like to be a yoga glamazon, they are not my tribe. My tribe are povo buskers playing Django Reinhardt. My tribe are aqua crew-cut goddesses who smell like samosas. My tribe are neurotic corporate banshees with white knuckles on Goldman Sachs water bottles. My tribe are seven different lineages that all lead to the same destination.

•

10 things I learned at the Advanced Diploma of Yoga Teaching Introduction Night:
1. One of my teachers is an extra from *Godspell*
I burst into orientation late, red-faced and sweaty, to find twenty-five faces gazing at me serenely. I locked eyes with someone who looked like a centaur mated with a fortune teller, covered in tatts

and piercings. What at first appeared to be half-goat legs were actually furry fisherman's pants (that's fisherman's pants covered in fur; presumably for keeping one's legs warm while poaching seals *in central Melbourne*).

The centaur beamed at my sweaty face – he had a disconcerting way of staring right into your soul without asking first (rude!). *Please, God, let him drop out at orientation.* 'You must be Alice!' he boomed, marking my name on a roll. 'I'm Jorge. Welcome!'

Jesus wept. The centaur is in the faculty!

2. 'Vibes' are an acceptable qualification

Apparently what's most important about a person is their 'energy'. The teachers took turns introducing each other. 'When I think of Jorge ...' the Pranayama teacher clapped as she introduced the centaur, '... the word that comes to mind is *sprite*. Jorge is one who *frolics*. A darling sprite of the cosmos.' Did Jorge have any qualifications? Was he equipped to teach us? Did anyone care? Suddenly Iyengar's military-like yoga training didn't look so bad.

Jorge was the campest sprite I'd ever seen. He had a shaved head with a little patch of hair in a ponytail at the back (lame), six hundred earrings and a dozen Hindu tats on bulging biceps (has he never heard of cultural appropriation?).

Curiously, as the Pranayama teacher spoke I noticed something else. Vibes. Happy vibes? Despite the back-of-the-head soul patch, the starry fisherman's pants, despite all the things that say '*Warning: Byron Bay Mid-Life Crisis*,' Jorge the forest sprite was genuinely buzzing.

3. I am at risk of diabetes

The sweetness and light were out of control as the mutual love between the teachers continued. Dina, the meditation teacher, had long, flowing hair, and her face was a bliss-filled moon. 'What can I say about Susan?' she said, her fingers tracing invisible 'starlight' patterns in the air. 'Susan embodies the divine female energy of Shakti. She's truly a goddess.'

What kind of sorcery is this? Who is this 'Shakti'? And is becoming a goddess something that happens to all ladies who do yoga?

Graeme (married to Shakti Goddess Susan) made us do that thing where you pair off and interview each other, then introduce your partner to the group.

A short plump Greek woman called Marta introduced Annabelle. 'Annabelle is just the most gorgeous woman I've ever met,' she squealed. 'I feel like I've known her all my life!'

Annabelle threw up her hands and blushed. 'What can I say? She had me at *Namaste*.'

They hugged, *people clapped* and I tried not to throw up in my mouth.

Jo-Jo introduced a Grace Kelly-lookalike in a Camilla Franks silk playsuit. 'Grace is *divine*,' she cooed. 'She's *just* quit her job as a legal-aid lawyer to do this training, and her goal is to teach yoga to underprivileged children.' Legal-Aid Grace Kelly smiled and looked into the middle distance. I pointed an imaginary laser gun at her forehead.

(I was paired off with a male nurse called Kevin, who looked as terrified by the love and light in the room as I did. 'I might just go to the toilet,' he said when I asked him about himself. He never returned.)

On the break I saw one of the skinny goddesses grab a curvy goddess's arse: 'Oh my god, your butt is so *juicy*!' In my world, *juicy* means *fat*, but Juicy-Butt just laughed and mimed sitting on Skinny Goddess. I missed the sexist, abusive EP from the TV show. 'The network says no more than two hippies per shot, and tell wardrobe to keep that fat one out of lycra!'

Although it was only orientation, Marta had already ascertained our birthdays from Graeme and not only printed out, but *laminated* individual excel birthday charts for us all so we can coordinate cake-baking and purchase astrologically appropriate gifts.

4. There are sixteen other teacher trainees. THEY ARE ALL GODDESSES (except Kevin)

Along with Goddess Energy Jo-Jo and Corporate Boho Annabelle and Legal-Aid Grace Kelly, there's a social worker, a marketing manager, two vegan superwomen I'd happily slaughter, a grandmother, a scientist and the rest of them all seem to be council workers. Most have the eerie look of children who grew up without television.

I'm beginning to suspect I've made a grave mistake. (Also, there were no other buskers during the entire evening besides Django Reinhardt. He played for three hours.)

5. Yoga teachers have creepy X-ray vision

When yoga teachers smile, it feels like they're also looking three layers into your soul and possibly checking out your karma uninvited.

I could feel their eyes scanning my aura when I introduced myself. *Look away!* I thought, smiling back at them. *Stop staring at my chakras!*

6. We are our own lab rats

'In order to teach, you first have to experience,' said Dina. 'This is why you won't be getting any "teaching" instruction until the second half of the course. In the first half, you'll learn how to use the tools of yoga to strip back your layers and explore your own sheaths before you teach others to explore theirs. You're your own laboratory!'

7. We will do unholy things with salty water

The *shat karmas*, or 'yogic cleansing rituals' are the many and varied ways you can pour salt water into pretty much every orifice and swoosh it back out again, along with stubborn snots, partially digested food, rusted-on faecal matter and other 'toxins'. They include dipping a metre-long length of gauze in salt water, holding one end and *swallowing* the rest. You let it soak up all your tummy juice, and then you *pull* the gauze back up through your throat. (And presumably chuck it in the bin or sell it on e-bay.) Another involves pouring a teapot of salt water up one nostril and letting it pour out the other. (They didn't have Kleenex when the Vedas were written?)

But my favourite one is where you sit naked in a shallow pool of salt water and suck the water up your bum then push it out again, along with any stubborn, tar-like ancient poos. Graeme was quick to point out that although we will be learning the techniques in class, we will have the option of practising and teaching them in our own time.

8. A nervous breakdown is a required course component

'Intense yoga study of the kind you'll be required to do has a habit of turning your life upside down,' said Shakti Goddess Susan. 'You're not just *learning* the philosophy and practices of yoga, you're letting them *transform you*. And I should warn you,' she said, (smiling at *me?*) 'these yoga storms happen to *all* first-years.'

Since my life is pretty much in the toilet already, I figure this won't be a problem. (And frankly, if someone's 'stuff comes up' after a few stretches and an *Om*, they need medication) – wait, is someone sniffling? I looked around the room. Sure enough Annabelle was already sobbing quietly. The teachers beamed at her. What a suck.

9. Goddesses cry, frequently

And when they do, other goddesses pat their backs and say, 'Let it out, honey.'

10. I now report to ... Shakti

We've each been assigned a mentor: someone to serve as a compass in our Yoga Storms, who will help us apply the ancient Sutras to our modern lives and to whom we address our excuses when we need an assignment extension.

Using the sophisticated method of pulling names from a hat, I was matched with Susan, she who embodies the divine feminine energy of Shakti. 'And I got the Iyengar intellectual!' she cried, as if reading my mind. She crossed the room, eyes shining and, brushing aside my outstretched hand, swooped me up into a full-body hug.

I mentally ran through my options. Was it too late to sign up to Live Free? *You've already paid the first year in advance.* Dammit!

I tried not to struggle, but to surrender into the hug. Susan hugged me tighter, and I let myself go limp.

4

A Fishbowl of Dirty Water

I'd pushed it out of my mind, but finally the opening of my grandfather's exhibition arrives. We've been invited to a 'special viewing' of the paintings before the doors open to invited guests. As we descend the steps to the gallery foyer, my heart pounds. Gil gives me the side-eye. 'You're not going to go into one of those dissociative states you get into around your family, are you?'

When I first heard the gallery was going to be doing a retrospective I looked forward to swanning around and letting everyone know I was a direct descendent of the Man Himself, but now I'll consider the night a success if I can get through it without someone asking me what I'm doing. I don't want to watch their smiles freeze as they say, 'Oh... lovely.'

We pass waiters setting up tables in the foyer, turn a corner and all of a sudden we are in the cavernous exhibition space. Devoid of people, it feels like a post-apocalyptic wasteland from one of Gil's video games.

Surrounding us are enormous canvases depicting my maternal grandfather's cold, cerebral and distant take on the world. His four daughters drift around the exhibition like ghosts. On one wall the curator has bundled the pictures my grandfather painted of them as children. Instead of names, he's given them numbers.

I feel ill. I look at my mother and aunts, all beautiful and stylish and far, far away from one another in separate corners of the gallery. Why am I the one who feels sick? Why can't I just pull myself together? Be happy, celebrate, talk about line or form or whatever else you're supposed to talk about while ignoring the nasty underside of this whole experience.

Gil appears beside me. He looks nervous. 'When I'm with your family I feel like I'm in a little boat and you're all in your own little boats,' Gil whispers. 'And every now and then another boat will come up and say, "Oh, hello!" And then it drifts away again.'

I leave Gil to talk with Dad, who is staring at one of the pictures with such rapt attention I suspect he's discreetly tucked in an earpiece so he can listen to the football.

My tall, pedigree-racehorse cousins are scattered around, holding champagne stems and fiddling with necklaces, collarbones and elbows. I make an awkward approach to a small cluster but my throat suddenly closes. It's hard to be effervescent and socialise when you feel hideous inside.

I spy my grandmother by her hair, swept back into a silvery chignon to reveal a long fine neck and a profile I recognise in so many of my grandfather's paintings. I propel myself in her direction to pay my respects, reaching her just as a photographer swoops. I back away.

At 6.30 the curator assembles the family. The guests for the opening are waiting downstairs. 'The time has come,' she says in hushed tones. (Are we about to hold hands and say a prayer, like Madonna and her back-up dancers before a concert?) 'Are you ready to share the pictures?'

The doors open and people pour in. The room is suddenly very loud and the lights seem hotter. I don't understand – these are the pictures I grew up with, but they look different hung like this. I return to the wall of daughters. First daughter, my mother. Second daughter. Third daughter. Fourth daughter. He's painted them as if they're mild curios to be observed, moving subjects rather than flesh and blood. In all the paintings of my mother, her face is turned away.

The crowd behind me shifts and my grandmother, also an artist, sweeps through, leading a tour, and I join in. As we stand before a picture, my grandmother turns to the group. 'What do *you* think it's about?' she asks us. I try to shrink out of view, terrified I'll get it wrong.

An ever-increasing pod of people join the tour. Someone pushes an elbow into my back as the crowd presses in, and each painting becomes more and more cryptic. 'But what about the *phallus*,' says my grandmother in front of a picture. 'How can you not see it? It's right there, staring at you!'

I squint, but it's like a magic eye: the harder you look, the less likely you are to see it. Everyone else is nodding; *they* can see it. Watching a dozen or so heads bobbing enthusiastically makes me feel churlish. I can barely understand the pictures, but that's not what's bugging me. These people love my grandmother and she loves them back, but they're only eavesdropping on the good parts – and I want to jealously guard the good parts. It's hard enough feeling like a part of the family without being squeezed out at the earliest opportunity by people who perform better than I do.

I step back to get some oxygen and six people immediately crowd into the space I leave behind.

Around me people are laughing, chatting, celebrating. Just like at Christmas, I'm overcome with that sense of being out of my own body. There is so little love in my grandfather's paintings of his daughters. Somewhere around here, while art folk celebrate, my mother and aunts are drifting, collateral damage. Suddenly it's like all the pain of their childhood, the sides of their brilliant father that they don't want to talk about, are up there on that wall. And we're standing here drinking champagne, wearing nice clothes and hiding all the mess behind those pictures.

I feel that sickness again, a feeling of heaviness that has been passed down that isn't mine to carry but I don't know how to put it down. I want to make it all right but I don't know how. The noise in the gallery, the heat and the people bear down. It's time for me to leave.

Gil has left early for a family birthday so I seek out my mother to say goodbye. I spot her through the crowd, white knuckles gripping her elbows. She is talking to the patriarch of an Old Money family.

'Oh look!' my mother sees me and somehow manages to reach through half a dozen people to yank me by her side and wedge me between her and Old Money, but he's not to be deterred.

'Your father,' he slurs to my mother, waving drunkenly at the pictures, 'is something else. Your father is good enough to travel. And you know what?' he continues. 'I'm calling it right now. He's good enough for the world stage. He's good enough for New York!'

My mother smiles tightly and I look around for an escape. There are so many people, the smell of champagne sweat combined with the heat in the room is stifling.

I go home, stopping only to pick up a box of mini apple pies from the supermarket, and I nearly kill the microwave defrosting them because I'm in such a hurry that I forget to take the foil bottoms off.

•

I shoot out of bed at 6am on Sunday morning in a panic, pull on my shorts, grab a banana (I haven't eaten processed carbs since the exhibition, but if I don't eat at least six bananas my brain starts to eat itself) and run from our asbestos hovel to teacher training in the city.

As I tear through the near-empty city streets, the rising sun reflects off skyscraper windows. Belching garbage trucks and street sweepers clear the beer bottles and vomit of Saturday night's festivities. The streets are empty, save for a small gang of women in sequined mini-dresses staggering towards taxis, and a couple of guys quietly hurling into the gutter. I suddenly feel extremely well-rested and hydrated. Could this be a taste of yogic smugness? If so, it's *delicious*.

In the training centre alley it's too early even for the Django Reinhardt busker, and as the cafe operators hose off the pavement (is there no end to the vomit in this town?), I bound up the four flights to class.

Across the room, in the corner, the goddesses are crowded around something on the floor. It's Jo-Jo demonstrating reiki on little Marta, while at the head of the room our philosophy teacher, Graeme, sitting pert and cross-legged with a bemused look on his face, patiently waits for attention. Graeme is one of those yoga men whose grey hair puts them past sixty, but whose energy and physique make you wonder if they sleep in a coffin.

'Aaaa-THA! Yoooo-GA! Nu-SHAS-un-um!' he bellows suddenly. No one pays him the least bit of attention.

'Aaaa-THA! Yoooo-GA! Nu-SHAS-un-um!' he bellows again. This time the goddesses snap back to their bolsters like an elastic band.

One of the main texts we'll be working from is the Yoga Sutras of Patanjali, or 'Yoga's original self-help manual', as Graeme calls it. Patanjali, he says, was a 'homely sage' (why are there never any hot sages?) who codified the path to personal, mental, emotional and spiritual liberation into 196 succinct little Sutras, which he jotted down on dried leaves. The Sutras are divided into four chapters, outlining simple step-by-step instructions on how to find liberation. From what? I'm not sure, but it sounds pleasant.

'Traditionally the Sutras are sung, as a call and response. So I call and you respond,' says Graeme, pointing to the whiteboard where he has written *Sutra 1.1: Atha Yoganusasanam* – the first of the Sutras, which means 'And now the practice of yoga begins.' (Which seems quite obvious to me and not worth a Sutra, but I'm no homely sage. *Boom-tish.*)

'Aaaa-THA!' he bellows.

'*Aaa*-tha,' we whisper.

Graeme purses his lips. 'Okay, well ... You've got a year to get it. The thing about the Sutras,' he goes on, 'is that they are incredibly dense. You're not meant to read them like a book, you're meant to study one or two at a time before moving on to the next.'

Several hours of unpacking various Sutras later we're gagging for coffee.

'I could let you out for a break, but how about a hit from nature's pharmacy instead?' says Graeme. 'Let's do pranayama!'

Pranayama? He wants us to breathe our way out of caffeine withdrawal?

'Each pranayama technique works on the body like a pill. You've got your uppers, which focus on the inhale, giving your brain a rush of oxygen, and you've got your downers, focusing on the exhale, which act like a mild sedative. So instead of reaching for coffee, just try a few rounds of "Breath of Fire"' – Graeme flaps his arms, huffs and puffs – 'and it's like a shot of adrenalin straight to the heart!'

And if we keep that up we'll all look like Graeme when we're sixty.

I don't know how anyone can spend ten minutes discussing breathing let alone a six-month class unit, and yet there is apparently a lot to say. (And for our assignment we have to practise three techniques each day and keep a detailed journal about the effects. A whole diary. About *breathing*.) Number one is that I have been breathing wrong for most of my adult life. Apparently your tummy is meant to *expand* when you inhale, not contract, because your lungs are pushing your intestines down. Who knew?

We practise the technique, and although I do feel a nice brain buzz, when he finally releases us there is a very un-yogic stampede of sixteen goddesses down four flights of stairs. We immediately split up into ten different laneway cafes (for faster service), except for Jo-Jo who heads straight to the river, her face tilted towards the sun ('I'm a solar panel for learning!').

I think I love the Sutras. They're wonderful, simple and wise, and by the end of the class I've had many *a-ha* moments and picked out several that will make nice yoga tattoos.

The Sutras go into great detail about the beliefs, habits and attitudes that keep us stuck in illusion, and then systematically give us a recipe for reuniting with the soul – the Atman. Sutra 1:4 – *Vrtti-sarupyam itaratra* loosely translates to 'When we are not abiding in our true inner light, then we are compromised.'

'The path,' explains Graeme, 'is about systematically using the tools of yoga – not just Asana but also Pranayama, meditation, self-reflection – to strip back all the layers of crap that we're covered up with. Strip back all that blocks you from this wonderful inner light.'

As I walk home through the city at five, past the discount stores and sullen teenagers carrying multiple fast-fashion shopping bags, I contemplate this wonderful inner light. Is that really who we are? I think I had it once, a long time ago when I first started yoga. Even though I felt completely lost and was questioning everything, there was something more real about that period in the *I don't know* space than all the years I spent building the mask. I just didn't see it at the time. If I do all this stripping back, will I find this inner light? Do I even have one?

I put the key in the door, wondering how a conversation about 'the inner light' might go down with Gil, but as soon as I step inside I'm overcome with the scent of pineapple icing. There's a box of Krispy Kremes on the table ...

'I'm taking them to Mum's but grab one if you want!' Gil calls before jumping in the shower. It'll ruin the 'no processed carbs' streak. Still, I've never had a Krispy Kreme and everyone raves about them and it's important to remain informed. And then go *back* to no processed carbs.

I try the Krispy Classic. I can't see what all the fuss is about; it's like eating sugary air. So I try the pink one (also average). The chocolate one, however, is great.

A voice in my head pipes up: *you've done it now, you may as well continue.* In for a penny, in for a sweet glazed-doughnut pound.

Ten minutes later Gil comes in and asks where all the doughnuts went. I look at the box. Empty? How can that be?

'Are you kidding?' he says. 'I just put them down ten minutes ago!'

I look at Gil with confusion. I honestly can't remember eating six doughnuts in ten minutes like it was nothing. I'm still thin. It's not weird. I try to look girlishly guilty, like an Instagram model eating pizza. Thank god he laughs.

The voice in my head comes back, but this time it says, *You look okay now, but those calories are converting to fat cells every second. You've got to get rid of it.*

We're meant to be going to his mother's for dinner in ten minutes but I just want to get rid of this food. I don't have time to go for a run. Could I send him out for something at the shops and run up and down the stairs? I could do that all night and it still wouldn't be enough to burn off those doughnuts. But I'm so sick of laxatives. They take a long time to work, and by the time they do, half the calories will probably be laid down as fat anyway. Besides, I use them so much I think my organs are getting lazy.

What if I try vomiting? Not 'bulimically', but just once, to get rid of it. I'm nauseous, aren't I? And when you're sick it's good to get it out of your system, like when you have a hangover. Right?

Five minutes later I'm hovering, awkward and confused, over the toilet. Seriously, am I good for nothing? I can't even master vomiting! I know you're supposed to put your fingers down your throat, but then I don't know what you're supposed to do once they're down there. How embarrassing. Back to good old laxatives – less humiliating.

We get home late from Gil's mother's place and I still can't stop thinking about the doughnuts. Half of me wants to go out and get more. Tonight was the first time in ages I didn't feel sick immediately after overeating. I felt like I could keep going indefinitely.

I have to stop. Every time I binge I make a deal that this will be the last time. Then I do it again the next night, and *that* will be the last time. I thought I would stop when I started working on the TV show. Then I thought I would stop when I left. Then I thought I would stop when I started the yoga course. After the first bite I don't even enjoy it – so why can't I stop?

The other thing that I've noticed is that I can't restrict the way I used to. In the past, whenever I binged I could eat fruit for a day, or no carbs, or protein bars instead of dinner, and that would get rid of it. I remember how good it used to feel, almost like a virtue, to wake up and have a belly that was almost concave. It didn't matter what else was going on, what opportunities I'd fucked up, what low bars I'd set for myself: looking in the mirror and seeing that made me feel good.

Over the years the amount and frequency have been increasing. When it happens now, I don't hear anything else. I don't want to do anything else. Gil might be talking to me, but I don't hear the words. That's wrong, isn't it? When someone you love is talking but it's like there's an ocean in your head drowning them out and all you can think about – *all* you can think about – is how to get rid of food, how to get more food. And the guilt ... it's unbearable. Whatever 'inner light' Patanjali and his homely sage cronies may bask in, either I don't have it or it's buried under the last strawberry-iced Krispy Kreme.

You'd think that having done yoga on and off for ten years I'd have some kind of home practice, but it's so much easier to rock up to a class and be told what to do. I've been mixing up classes at Pamela's hardcore Iyengar studio with the endorphin-pumping classes at Live Free, but part of our training is creating a daily home practice of *Asana* (poses), meditation and pranayama, then journaling about it. I've surprised myself and started looking forward to it.

Every morning I crack open a yoga book and follow the practices. The more I do it, the more I notice the different voices that creep in *(this is boring; you'll never be a real yoga teacher with poses like that)*. They're loudest in the first five minutes, but there's a point where they give up.

If yoga practice is about seeing what's on the lens so we can clear it, I'm definitely stuck in the 'only seeing all the crap' stage. Has this negativity and fear always been there and I just haven't noticed it? Just being able to recognise that, though, is already an improvement, because last week I wouldn't have called it 'negativity': I would have called it 'reality'.

But if I just stay on the mat and keep going, eventually everything starts to feel very clear, and another voice starts to come in. Whatever it is, it seems to know how to do life better than I do, even if it doesn't always make sense. I haven't heard it for a very long time.

How is it possible that a few minutes each day of messing around on a yoga mat and watching your breath can make you start hearing something like that?

•

I need a job. Any job. I've submitted spec scripts to other TV shows, to no avail. By day I'm responding to job ads written in a robotic corporate double-speak that would make George Orwell blush. By night I'm hugging it out in yoga studios and getting in touch with my energy centres.

My sister Liz drops in after work and we sit in the backyard trying to ignore the chefs from the restaurant berating the kitchen hand in the back lane. Liz has inherited the same 'What, this old Comme des Garcons-inspired thing I found at the back of my closet, please I look like trash' style gene my lady relatives have, and she is scarily competent. But what I actually love about Liz is that underneath the efficient exterior, she's a huge dag and lots of fun.

As soon as is politely possible, she asks me what I'm going to do for work.

'What you need to do,' she says, 'is start applying for jobs as an admin assistant. Then in about five years you could work your way up to office manager!'

A wave of sadness comes over me. Suddenly Liz feels very far away again. I nod and say that it's great advice. But an image of one of the goddesses flits through my mind. Every Thursday night we have to fish Goldman Sachs Annabelle out of the toilets before class because that's where she goes after work to cry about a job she hates.

If I play my cards right, in five years' time that could be me!

•

Mum rang to say that Dad's gone back into hospital for a few days. I can hear the relief in her voice. Dad is so frail, there's something comforting about knowing he'll be monitored by machines that go *bing!* if anything goes wrong.

I tell Mum, very carefully, about the yoga course. I'd been putting it off, but she's surprisingly supportive.

'Oh good, darling, you always liked yoga.' I let out a breath I didn't know I was holding. 'Do you need any money?'

Yes, I need money! 'No, no, I'm okay.'

I've managed to eke out my TV money by never, ever going out, and by subtly forgetting my wallet when I'm grocery shopping with Gil, who graciously pretends not to notice. But it's one rent payment from gone. The problem is that if I ask for money:
1) I'll feel like a baby, and …
2) It's an invitation for her to tell me I should have one.

Later I go online to feed my last chunk of savings into my rising damp-ignoring real estate agent's account, and I see that Mum has deposited a large sum of money into my account – enough to pay off the teacher training course and keep me away from the edge of panic until I find work. In the description she's put 'painting money'. My grandmother must have sold one of my grandfather's pictures. The relief is stronger than the shame of dependence.

·

I've finally managed to get an interview as a copywriter for a gas company. The written application involved inventing a personality for a hot water heating system and then posting on social media as your heater. Increasingly, applying for jobs seems to be a test of your ability to sound like a machine, not a human. (Last week I spent two solid days trying to address selection criteria like 'demonstrated ability to perceive strategic environment and laterally conceive solutions'.) Meanwhile 'humanness' has become a commodity, something you inject into products to make people buy them. I psych myself up with a reminder that impersonating a heater is just basic storytelling, character development and a little narrative.

It's my first interview since I began looking for work, and I'm thrilled. But when I arrive there are forty other applicants in reception who have the same interview slot. Oh, joy, a *group interview*. What are they going to make us do, fall and catch each other while men in suits watch behind a two-way mirror?

It's worse. Much worse. The HR rep divides us into two groups and announces the activity: speed dating! But not just any speed dating. We're going to speed date using the personality we created for our hot water heating system on social media. Once we've dated all the other ~~heaters~~ applicants, whoever gets the most dates gets the job.

My heater gets no dates. The feedback is that my heater is up itself; 'not warm'. Afterwards, on the tram, I discretely eye the after-work crowd in their white, navy, grey and black, and I wonder if any of them spend their working hours impersonating consumer goods? Is this what it takes to get ahead?

It's a blessed relief to get to the human morass that is teacher training. When I arrive, half the class are curled around bolsters in the foetal position. Goldman Sachs Annabelle is still in her $750 blazer as she hugs her bolster, quietly weeping while Jo-Jo jabs at acupressure points on her feet. One of the vegans is going around handing out soft orange cow pats ('100 per cent raw cupcakes!') and despite all reason, my shoulders relax, my breath deepens and I feel inexplicably at home.

Tonight we're scheduled to have our first session with the Divine Shakti Goddess, my yoga mentor, Susan (who I am yet to call for the mandated mentor catch-up). This class is on 'embodiment'.

'So many yoga styles are about trying to *impose* a movement pattern on your body,' she says, imitating the admittedly soldier-like uniform poses of Iyengar yoga. 'But before you can practice – before you can *teach* – you need to strip back that conditioning and understand how the primal movement patterns operate in your *own* body.'

I have *no idea* what she means, but the other goddesses nod along, so I do too. Susan explains a few basic early movement patterns (crawling, etc.) and tells us a few gruesome stories about how children trap trauma often in a freeze response in their bodies as they grow and how it affects their 'embodiment' later in life.

'There is no "one right way" to do a posture,' she says. 'When you allow your body to show you how it wants to move instead of imposing a rigid form, it will tell you all you need to know about how to practise.'

Susan tells us to forget what we 'think we know' about moving, and start from scratch. As in, literally, go back to the first movements we made when we were 'pre-vertebrates' and flop around on the floor like fish.

'Give yourself permission to move *intuitively, organically*.'

She puts on some music and has us walk around in the room 'from our bones'. We walk around in stiff, robotic movements. Then she has us do it 'from our muscles'. It's when she asks us to move from our 'organs' that I get stuck. Susan starts to *flow* through the room in an internally directed interpretive dance.

The other goddesses follow her lead and begin floating around the room as if in a Kate Bush video. I flap my arms and try not to look like a tit.

'That's *it*,' says Susan. 'It's an *inquiry*. Now move from your *peri-organ* fluid –' wtf? '– the fluid *between* the organs.'

The goddesses all became shape-shifting amoebas and I lose it. I've spent the day trying to bury all trace of humanity by impersonating a heater, and now I'm supposed to literally embody the sticky mess of humanity? It's a very confusing way to live.

'May I?' Susan says, hovering her hands over my arms. I nod. She places her hands gently on my upper arms. Some kind of voodoo reiki vibration starts in my shoulder muscles and suddenly my whole body softens. 'There,' she says gently. 'Try now.'

My body starts to undulate of its own accord. It feels soft and easy and so horribly vulnerable. I want to cry.

'Uh! You had it, just for a second, then you started thinking about it.'

'Had what?'

'Embodiment,' she says. 'You know, it might be an idea to start calling me soon.'

Instead of fixing everything, yoga is increasingly stirring everything up. I was diligently doing the thrice-daily Pranayama practice but stopped when I suddenly became aware of how much I hold my breath, as if I'm bracing against the world.

This morning I drag my mat into the living room, and within

ten minutes I'm having an anxiety attack in a backbend. It feels like my body is trying to warn me: *hold up, lady, because if you start stirring shit up you don't know where it will lead and what you will see.* I remember how in orientation they told us that yoga could be like stirring up all the dirty water in a fishbowl. Isn't it better just not to stir up the dirty water in the first place?

Another change I've noticed since increasing my yoga practice is that the free-for-all style eating I used to do just once a month is getting to be every few nights, sometimes more. I seem to have forgotten what's a normal way to eat. I don't want to talk to Esther about it, though – that would be humiliating.

Instead I go to a dietitian. Surely a clear plan is all I need, someone to tell me exactly what I should eat and when, so I don't have to think about it. As long as she doesn't tell me I just need to 'love my thighs'.

The dietician gives me some useful information about portion sizes and healthy eating, but sure enough, the 'you need to love your body' angle eventually comes up. 'It's not the weight so much,' I try to explain – I know that's part of it, but I also know there's more to this problem. 'It's the feeling. Food makes everything go away.'

'You don't trust yourself,' she tells me. 'It's important that you're able to trust your body to eat intuitively,' she says. 'Trust that your body will let you know when it's full. If you let yourself eat everything and no foods are off limits, soon your body will start screaming for broccoli where it once screamed for doughnuts. Besides, what's life without chocolate cake?'

Over the next twenty-four hours I intuitively eat my way through five slices of pizza, a box of cakes from the bakery on the corner and a whole lot of chips. I also intuitively skip lunch, then feel an intuitive urge to eat a whole box of laxatives.

I think my intuition is fucked.

Another day at my desk. The sun is shining and I'm inside, working on job applications. It's excruciating.

Giving up is not an option. Suddenly a thought pops into my mind: *food would make this bearable*. The argument begins. *You've stopped doing that.* Yes, I reason, but when I binged last night I didn't feel sick. And unless I *feel* sick, it doesn't count. *So then you have to reach that point today. Then you'll know that's really it. And detox tomorrow.*

I go to the bakery again and buy some cakes. One of the neighbours sees me with the box. 'You'll ruin all that running!' he says cheerily, jumping into his car. I pretend to laugh but I'm mortified.

As I sit at my desk eating, some part of me is watching myself. Has it always been this mechanical? I get pleasure out of it, don't I? My throat tightens but I keep going. You can't stop until it's all gone, or it doesn't count and then you have to do it all again tomorrow.

Finally I'm staring at the empty box. If I wasn't so numb I'd be afraid. I don't understand how I can keep eating without stopping. I have to fix this. Yoga and mindfulness will fix this. Won't it?

I've already booked into Pamela's yoga class tonight. They say you're not supposed to do yoga until two hours after a meal, let along twenty minutes after a binge, but maybe if I force myself to go, tune in to every uncomfortable sensation … maybe that will scare me into being normal?

When I get there, the class is packed to capacity, thank god, so I can hide. I push and pull myself into the hardest versions of the poses I can, but I still can't block it out. When Pamela makes us lie back over chairs, I know we'll be there for a good ten minutes and I fight the urge to run.

'In yoga we create an artificial stress, and it's not long before the craziness starts,' she says in a monotone, as if craziness is normal. 'We can either identify with it, or we can calm the mind and breathe, be the witness to the habitual stories and ask: "Is this who I am? Is this the story I want to keep repeating in my life?"'

On orientation night, Graeme talked about the yoga concept of svadhyaya, which is self-inquiry. I can't connect that to what we do here, on the mat. I can't understand how moving in and out of postures, watching the breath, brings answers. All I know is when I honestly bring a problem to the yoga mat and am willing to be open, something is revealed beyond what I could have conceived myself.

I came here to feel so sick I would never binge again. I came here to get answers as to why I do it. But now that I'm here, all I want is to feel better so I don't have to go home and eat to numb the guilt of eating in the first place.

People settle into the pose and the room grows quiet. As I arch backwards over the chair, I loosen my grip on the legs so I can lessen the intensity, but still, everything inside me is screaming. I try to tune everything else out and focus only on my breath.

Suddenly my mind goes quiet, and out of the silence I hear a voice, clear and simple:

You have no control over this.

Terror. Relief. Somehow, without being conscious of it, I have known this all along. The class moves into the next posture. As I move with them that voice comes back, but this time the voice is mine.

I can't do this on my own. I need help.

I am not someone who loses control. Other people need help. Eating disorders are for fourteen-year-old girls and skinny women whose highest aspirations are marrying a professional footballer.

So what is this that I'm doing? Whether I'm in a binge cycle or a starve cycle, the rest of the world recedes and food and exercise seem like the most important things. Does that even have a name? It's not bulimia. It's not anorexia. Whatever it is, it's getting worse and no deal I strike with myself seems to be able to stop it. And mindfulness, I'm sorry to say, is doing jack shit. I just mindfully feel like crap.

Late that night I hide with my laptop and ask Dr Google. I tick every box on checklist after checklist for something called 'binge-eating disorder'. I look at the website for an eating disorder organisation. It's just stuff on positive body image with no concrete information on how to stop doing it.

I keep Googling. The studies all say it's progressive and that those who recover do therapy as part of a group. One study said people who go to recovery meetings similar to the ones attended by alcoholics (but for people who eat too much, too little, vomit it up and every variety of food fuck-aroundery in between) found relief.

Going to those meetings just seems weird to me. It conjures images of people with odd facial hair and flannel shirts, and coffee and cigarettes in church meeting rooms. Seriously? That could help?

There's a meeting being held nearby two days from now. Which means I may as well eat till then.

•

I get on the tram certain all the passengers know exactly where I'm going. At the last minute I had to change into my 'fat-fat' pants, because my normal fat pants don't fit anymore. Two days of 'last hurrah' eating will do that to a person.

The meeting is in a shopfront on a busy road. Thank god for sunglasses. Inside, the room is pokey and confessional. People sit in chairs lining the walls, which are painted a cheerful canary-yellow that belies the misery everyone here must feel. And yet the dozen or so people sitting around chatting don't appear hideously embarrassed to be there. Some smile at me, and I try to look not-desperate – like I'm here with a friend. An invisible friend.

A couple of people are morbidly obese and one appears severely anorexic, but the vast majority look confusingly ordinary. There's a woman in a business suit who must be here on a lunch break. There's a man in a reflective vest, the kind they wear on building sites. A woman who looks like a model is sewing an elaborate lace dress for a teddy bear.

A list of babyish clichés hang on the wall opposite me: *One day at a time, Keep it simple.* A banner behind the woman chairing the meeting lists twelve steps. 'Admit we have a problem' is the obvious first, and then – GOD ALERT – they start mentioning a higher power. So *that's* what their common oddness is – it's a cult! I'm dimly aware that they use this same meeting structure for anything from drug problems to sex addiction, and yet the whole thing feels very ... informal. One of the others tells me that each meeting is run to certain guidelines, but the people running them are all volunteers and there's no CEO, no marketing department, no advertising. They just seem to ... happen, and people somehow find them if they want to.

I scan the other steps. One mentions listing people you've harmed and 'making amends'. For what? And what the hell does any of that have to do with food? Still, the steps look straight-forward enough: a person of average intelligence could surely knock them off in a day. Skipping the God steps, of course.

The woman sewing the dress for the teddy smiles shyly at me. She reminds me of that British model Katie Price, aka Jordan – professional marrier of football players, pop stars and cage fighters. Her long, manicured nails work furtively on the lace. Her eyelashes are so long I can practically see each individual lash across the room.

Just as I think there's no one there I identify with, a cool-looking girl rushes into the room and plops down in the seat next to me.

'First meeting?' she says, breathless. For someone so thin, her voice is surprisingly strong and confident. She's the kind of person I would ordinarily be intimidated by – expensive haircut and an outfit that takes a *Vogue* stylist to casually throw together. How does someone so pretty and together end up *here*?

I nod and try to hide my shaking hands. 'It gets easier,' she says, laughing. 'I'm Emily.'

The chairperson starts the meeting, reading straight from a run sheet. She could have put more enthusiasm into her voice, but I'm not here to advise on showmanship.

'Are there any newcomers present?' she asks.

Emily nudges me and I raise my hand. Everyone bellows 'Welcome!' and the chair tells me they recommend that people come to at least six meetings. I smile politely, but already know I won't be back. I'm here to figure out what's happening to me, get it sorted and get on with my life as if none of this ever happened. If they want to spend their time stewing in a cesspit of oddness, that's their business.

One by one people take turns speaking. An obese woman sitting on my right speaks about her relationship with her daughters (who sound like bitches), and how instead of telling them not to boss her around, she just endures it and eats. A thin, middle-aged man who reminds me of Norman Bates speaks next. He says his name is Joel, and he was in another program for drugs and alcohol, 'but food is my primary addiction'. As he speaks, his eyes dart nervously around the room and he wrings his fingers in his lap. For some reason his vulnerability frightens me.

As people take turns speaking some talk about overeating, some talk about 'restricting' and then binging, some over-exercise, but many barely talk about food at all. The one thing they all have in common is using food to deal with their problems. No one interrupts anyone, and this seems to clear the usual static so you can really listen. Though the details of their stories are different, without exception each person sounds like they've been following me around for the past two decades.

A folder is passed around the room for us to write and take phone numbers. When it gets to me I pass it straight on.

Soon everyone has spoken except me.

'Would the newcomer like to speak?' asks the chairperson. My stomach flutters. If I open my mouth I can't trust that I won't blurt out the truth, which would be awful. Or cry. But showing vulnerability to these people would be worse – they'll think I'm one of them. And yet … I've come all this way. And I am so, so tired.

Just say the words. Don't cry. Don't cry.

I talk about food, how each day feels more out of control than the day before. And then, have I never said the words before? About the depression? 'It feels like I'm standing on the edge of a precipice and all I see is darkness. I'm terrified I'll fall into an abyss and not find my way out.'

Beside me, Emily nods in a way that makes me think she might know what it's like. If someone has had these feelings, and yet can still look happy and sane … maybe they know something I don't. Maybe I don't have to fall all the way this time.

The woman with the bitchy daughters hands me a box of tissues. It seems like such a movie gesture, but I gratefully take a handful. When I look up, two of the weirdos, Norman Bates and Jordan, are looking at me with such tenderness I want to cry. I don't want to be understood by these people. And yet having them listen and not only not run away, but look as if they actually care … It's a tiny golden thread connecting me back to humanity.

At the end of the meeting someone presses an envelope of pamphlets into my hand and a few people come over and speak encouragingly. But I know I won't return.

I'm about to leave when Emily stops me.

'Hey, do you want my number?' she drawls. Everything she says sounds drenched in irony.

'I never thought I'd end up somewhere like here,' I whisper as she jots down her number.

She laughs and says she thought the same thing. 'Just take it slow,' she says. 'Call if you need to.' I smile to be polite, but that's never going to happen. If anyone even finds out I've been here I'll die.

'Wait,' she says as I get my bag. 'Can I grab your number too?'

'Sure,' I say, 'but I don't really think I'd be much help to anyone.'

'Yeah?' she says in that lazy drawl. 'Well you helped me today.'

It never occurred to me that simply telling the truth could help someone.

5

Black-Hearted Yogi

Tonight we have our first class with Jorge, the 'Forest Sprite' I saw at orientation. Jorge is kneeling in the corner before a portable altar he's whipped up, stacked with spiritual trinkets and images of Hindu gods and goddesses. As Jorge says his yoga prayers in the corner, we set up bolsters in a pagan circle. When he's finished, Jorge joins us, beaming like we're about to go to Disneyland.

Emotional Disneyland. After the horror show of the meeting, I'm desperate to hide behind an anatomy textbook, but there is to be no hiding.

'Backbends,' Jorge says, 'are all about *embracing* your vulnerability. Heart-opening. Being unapologetic about shining brightly and letting yourself be seen.'

Jorge, apparently, has no qualms about being seen. Tonight he is sporting another crime against fashion: a Hindu goddess t-shirt with his usual starry fisherman's pants. And yet he behaves as if the whole world is just waiting to embrace him with open arms. His hands dance joyfully through the air as he elaborates on yogic fairy dust, whereas my own hands are routinely balled into little fists by my side. He claps when he likes something, and laughs like a drunken Hobbit.

It's odd – he's so full-on it seems like an act, and yet there's a sincerity that I find disconcerting. I feel like Dracula having a patch of sunlight thrust upon him.

Worst of all, he is a fan of 'group work'.

'Before we begin,' he says, 'let us close our eyes and join in vibration.'

I reach limply for the hands of my neighbouring goddesses and we close our eyes. Jorge begins a deep, rolling *Om* and we join in.

'Let's trust that each of us has found our way here by divine direction,' Jorge begins. I peep around the circle and see goddess faces scrunched in concentration, plus lunatic Jo-Jo smiling in ecstasy. 'As we send our prayers and intentions into the universe, let us be willing to let go of all that no longer serves, and make way for the universe to reveal to us our unique and precious gifts. Ladies, as it's our first class together, we should connect as a sangha,' he says, beaming around the circle at each of us individually.

'As we connect with one another's energy, let us gaze around the sharing circle, and if our gaze should meet another's, let us hold that space for a moment and, with hearts open to receive, welcome them into the circle.'

Who is this frolicking forest sprite, and why is he so unembarrassed about being so lame? The opposite; he seems to look straight through you in a way that makes you feel utterly transparent, like there's no point trying to hide anything. And yet it doesn't feel mean or judgemental. It feels kind.

A wave of sadness sweeps through me. Yoga is supposed to 'show us who we really are', but since I've been going turbo on my practice, I know less and less who I am. All around me the goddesses are gazing at one another with hearts open to receive, so I plaster on a non-threatening smile. If someone catches my eye I force myself to hold their gaze, but it's excruciating. Forget 'being unapologetic about shining brightly and letting yourself be seen', the longer we go on, the more I'm convinced I have no soul to welcome.

•

The only good thing about being obviously out of control is that you can finally stop pretending everything is fine. But this doesn't *feel* like a good thing; it feels like at any moment a tidal wave – all the things you're trying to keep at bay – could knock you over, and then who knows what will happen? You might stop showering. You might start talking to the empty seat beside you on public transport. You might be one step away from eating cat food and muttering to yourself on a park bench. It's a slippery slope that begins with meetings and ends in consulting crystal healers and not conditioning my hair.

They told me to go to six meetings to see if 'the program' is for me, but at the time I was confident that reading their pamphlets would be enough. It isn't.

So I reluctantly go to another meeting. It's a bit awkward leaving the house because I told Gil I was going to yoga and now he wants to accompany me because 'it's dark outside'.

Finally I tell him he can only come along if he does the class, and that's enough to dissuade him. I tell Gil a hundred white lies a day ('No, I didn't secretly add anything to the stew you've spent four hours making!') but somehow, this time, it feels like shit.

Now that it's my second meeting I'm able to take in a bit more. The woman who looks like Jordan tells her story today, starting with her real name: Malin.

'I spent my twenties off my head on amphetamines, but when I put down the drugs, I picked up food,' she says, not looking up from sewing a lace cuff into the sleeve of a jacket.

'I weighed 45 kilos. I was living at my mother's house and I would stay home and literally binge and purge for hours. After my first meeting someone followed me to the bathroom and said, "Just eat three meals a day. I don't care what they are, but don't get rid of them." So I did, and I guess that's where my recovery began.

'But recovery, for me at least, really sucked at first. I didn't understand why I got so much shittier with everyone the more I stopped using food. What I learned is that the food is just a symptom.

That's when I had to begin the real work of recovery.'

During a break, Malin catches me looking dubiously at her five-inch platform boots. 'I know they're terrible,' she says, 'but I can't stop wearing them.'

'How do you walk?' I ask. Malin totters around like her feet are bound.

'Sweetie, when I first came into program I was walking the streets eight hours a day in them because I'm so vain I didn't want to wear runners!'

I like Malin. From her long, manicured nails to the lace trim on her sleeves and the individually applied false eyelashes, there's a kind of authenticity – an art – in the artifice.

I admit to her that I don't think I really belong here. I'm not overweight, or skeletal.

'It's not about the weight,' she says. 'It's about obsession. You're still using food to cope with non-food issues – whether it's too much, too little, exercise, laxatives, whatever. Trust me, sweetie: you belong.'

At the end of the meeting everyone in the room shares a word or two on how they're feeling. When it gets to Joel – the thin, nervous, Norman Bates-lookalike – he smiles at me and says he's 'feeling happy that the newcomer has returned'.

Don't get too used to me, I think. Isn't it enough of a blow to my ego that I've swapped full-time employment for amoeba-dancing with yoga goddesses talking about 'highways of energy'? Now I have this merry band welcoming me into their fold.

There's something about Joel in particular that irritates me. Every time he shares about his 'ex-girlfriend' I feel like rolling my eyes. 'Just come out of the closet already!' I want to yell at him. 'No one's going to judge you – look where we are!'

Ordinarily I'd feel compassion for someone having discomfort with their sexuality, so why – here and now – does he trigger this aggression? It's like I can smell the blood of someone else's shame and vulnerability in the water, and it's too familiar for comfort. Is this what it's like for bullies? And why can't I tell anyone – my family, friends, Gil – what I'm struggling with?

When I get home, Gil looks up from his dystopian sci-fi video game and asks how the yoga class went. 'What did you get up to tonight? Reading auras with the goddesses?' He chuckles.

How do I say, *'Actually, I'm checking out this other group where we sit in a circle and then talk about how we can't get through life without a sandwich'*?

•

It seems like everyone I know has taken up a new diet and is absolutely loving it. Either they're fasting two days a week or else they've completely cut carbs, or they're only drinking milkshakes from the chemist. They won't eat fruit because it's got sugar in it, but meat for breakfast, lunch and dinner (with a side of bowel cancer) is fine. Even Gil's posse of pot-smoking cousins won't touch a carb unless it's in beer form.

Part of me is jealous. I remember so well that hope and excitement of beginning a diet, and the sense of mastery when the weight starts to come off. I would *love* to go on one more, but I can no longer afford to. One tiny slip, then guilt, then a binge (because I've blown it, and anything less than perfect adherence won't do), then restricting to get back on track, then planning how it will be different this time, and it all starts again. But it gave me something else. Focus. Did I just waste decades of mental bandwidth on the contents of my stomach? We may not be able to control house prices and the ozone layer, but we can control how many grams of protein we chug after a pump class. And yet … think of all the Large Hadron Colliders not invented because people like me we're plotting calorie deficits.

As I walk into a Live Free class, my eyes go straight to Suki's green smoothie. The teachers there are always detoxing and cleansing, and they seem to literally bounce with energy. I'm pretty sure their urine contains more vitamin by-products than a Blackmores lab. Words like 'cleansing impurities' are bandied about as if having a squeaky-clean bowel is akin to enlightenment.

I hear these thoughts as I move through the poses and bristle at my own cynicism. What's wrong with spouting motivational slogans? These women don't seem to lack energy – though admittedly, it's a similar kind of wiry can't-sit-still energy to the anorexic woman who spoke in the meeting.

On the way home, my phone rings. It's Emily, the *Vogue* girl from the meeting. They have my number! Next they'll infiltrate my life and *everyone will know*!

Emily must sense my awkwardness because she starts to laugh. 'This is what we do in program: we call each other when something's going on,' she says. In the meeting they talked about the 'tools' that are supposed to aid your recovery: things like journaling, and picking up the phone instead of picking up food.

I think the idea is that if I'm on my way to Woolworths to buy a pack of chocolate jam doughnuts, first I call and say, 'Hey, Emily, I'm going for an eight-pack, try and stop me.'

'I'm actually calling because I'm on my way to a new job today and I'm really nervous and just wanted to talk to someone,' says Emily.

Thank god. Fixing someone else's problems. That's something I can do. But it seems Emily doesn't want fixing, she just wants to talk about how she's feeling. At the end of the call, she says, 'Thanks, I don't feel so manic now,' and we hang up. The whole thing takes less than five minutes. Is it really that simple?

That night I dig out the pamphlets they gave me at my first meeting and actually read them. I'm glad to see one of the tools listed is anonymity, or as I like to think of it, *The first rule of fight club is you don't talk about fight club.* The last thing I want is for anyone to know I'm a member of this particular fight club.

One of the tools is a 'food plan'. I ring Emily back and ask her about it.

'A food plan isn't a diet where you go on and off, it's basically just working out some kind of structure around food that works for you. Then every day you choose whatever you're going to eat within that structure and don't think about it again until the next day,' she says. Emily is a recovering anorexic, her food plan is about making sure she eats and digests food three times a day.

'It sounds like prison,' I say.

Emily laughs. 'As opposed to the freedom to get yourself stuck in the binge/detox cycle, right? The idea is that committing and letting it go actually creates freedom, because it takes away the obsession. So your food plan can be three doughnuts for lunch if that's what works for you —'

Woo-hoo!

'— as long as doughnuts aren't a binge food.'

Binge foods. That's the other thing. At the meeting they advocated listing any foods that you can't have 'just one' of and then you abstain completely from them, the same way an alcoholic doesn't have wine, even on birthdays. It's the opposite of what the dietician said about moderation.

The thought of stopping altogether is such a relief. Taking away choice means I don't have to wrestle with trying to control it. For me eating anything with sugar is like flicking a switch: if one piece of chocolate is good, then six (or preferably, the whole block) will be better. It's easier to have none.

I tell her about the yoga cleansers. 'I mean that kind of thing must be healthy, right? All those yoga people I see with their green juices and raw food and detoxing and energy make me think that's something I should be aspiring to. Could that be a food plan?'

Emily snorts. 'Mate, the last time I went to rehab literally every second person on the eating disorder table was a nutritionist! It's fuckin' hilarious – plenty of times the whole "eating clean" thing is a way to mask an eating disorder. It's unsustainable, and just another channel for control and perfectionism.'

The last tool listed is sponsorship. Working with someone who 'has what you want', and who can show you how to eat and live sanely. I ask Emily if she'll be my sponsor. She's in a lot of other fight clubs for various addictions and seems to know her way around it all (and she doesn't preach like a born-again, which is a very attractive quality).

'Na. I'm still binging and restricting most days,' she says, like it's nothing. 'Besides, I've only been to three more meetings than you have, and you need someone who's actually done the steps in this program to take you through them.' *The steps, the steps.* I struggle to see what the steps have to do with eating?

'I think if I just cut sugar for a while and get it out of my system, everything will be fine.'

'Yeah,' says Emily. 'It would if the problem was just food.'

Why does everyone keep saying that?

•

I always find it weird when people in meetings call food issues an addiction, but food *is* like a drug; it very effectively blocks everything else out.

'That's why it takes an addict to help another addict,' Malin says at our next meeting. 'Some people just don't get it.'

An *addict*.

The idea that an eating disorder is an *addiction* seems indulgent. Sure, if I'm at a table with certain foods, I can't actually focus on anything else. But how can you be addicted to food when you need it every day? How can you use the same method to deal with food fuck-aroundery that you use to fight alcoholism? And if it *does* have to be an 'addiction', *why does it have to be so fucking uncool?*

Musicians rocking up to meetings in dark glasses and stubble? Cool. A three-page spread on heroin chic and biker boots? Also cool. But 'Peanut M&Ms-and-laxatives chic'? Decidedly uncool. Food issues rank somewhere between a nasty porn habit and chronic hand-washing in terms of social cachet. Maybe even below hand-washing.

As we sit in our circle, Elias, a plumber in his thirties, spells it out perfectly: 'I go to meetings for drug addiction, and if I'm honest there's that little part of me that feels cool, you know? But this shit is humiliating.'

Everyone laughs.

'We make so many judgements about people who have an issue with food,' he goes on. 'Particularly when you're a guy. And for a long time in my recovery it bugged me that I'm one of the only men in the rooms. But after a while I thought, *Fuck it, it's working*. I've run out of belt holes. Which is a quality problem to have, I guess.'

They even use the language of addiction. 'Recovery' – someone points out that it means 'to get something back'. But what are we getting back? Sanity, they say. Whatever that is.

During the break, I go to the back and make a cup of tea. I'm joined by Deb, who's a receptionist in an obesity clinic.

I tell her about my 'intuitive eating' experiment and the dietitian's advice on moderation. She laughs her arse off.

'When we get someone with weight problems, we're meant to explain in detail what they're doing to their health and teach them about healthy eating,' she says. 'But believe me, no one knows more about what you are and aren't supposed to eat than people who struggle with their weight. I work in a clinic and look where I am. A lack of knowledge is not the problem.

'Not every fat person is an addict,' Deb goes on. 'But I see patients at the clinic getting surgery and you know the disease is just going to mutate if they don't deal with the underlying issues. When you work through the steps, you get to the core of what makes you eat. Recovery isn't just about white-knuckling, which is what it sounds like you've been doing – you know, where you don't binge but you still want to. When you work the steps, you actually don't *want* to use food in that way.'

The steps! The steps! Everyone keeps banging on about working the steps. But when I look at them hanging on the wall, only one mentions food, half mention a 'higher power' and the rest are all about working through your shit. How could that possibly help?

I say it sounds great, not believing it for a second. Deb looks at me and laughs. 'Yeah, right. Well, if I could tell you one thing, it's that doing this program half-arsed does bugger all. In my experience you're either all-in or you're wasting your time.'

•

Every time I binge I think it can't get any worse, and then the next one is worse. And yet every time I lose a shred more dignity, I get a shred more willing to try some stupid thing they suggest in fight club. As humiliating as it is, I asked Malin to sponsor me, and I've started calling her most days as soon as Gil's left for work to talk to her about how I'm dealing with food.

She doesn't seem to give a shit what I eat, but she's excellent at spotting when I'm using food to cope with something.

'I actually think the over and under-eating has got worse since I started coming to meetings,' I admit. 'Shouldn't it be getting better?'

'Maybe it just looks that way because it's the first time you've been paying attention,' she says. Malin is a painter, but to pay the bills she makes these ornate porcelain dolls (which explains the little baroque lace-and-silk outfits she's always sewing at meetings). There is a worldwide subculture of collectors who pay a fortune for these things. That's a racket I'd like to get into.

At the end of each phone call a smile creeps into Malin's voice and she asks if I'd like an 'angel reading'. Malin has a deck of cards with a different angel on each one, one for every day of the year. 'Now, sweetie, would you like to pick a number?' she says. I choose a number and 'the Universe' guides me to choose the reading I most need to hear. Sometimes Malin says, 'Nah, that's a shit one. Pick again,' and I choose again until the Universe gets it right. Then her voice deepens and she'll read out something about the Archangel Gabriel telling me to be open to receiving Divine Guidance. Today my reading is: *Now is the time to learn, study and gather information. Enjoy being a student, because in the future you will synthesise your knowledge into action.*

'See?' says Malin. 'And you're studying! That's a sign.'

One of Malin's suggestions was that I write a list of how I've used food in the past. I do. It's like reading about a stranger.

As a kid I wasn't much interested in food unless it contained sugar. One of my earlier memories is sitting on the bathroom floor turning the lid of a bottle of cough syrup around and around, not realising that they make child locks on those things specifically for little sugar addicts like me.

The bingeing, restricting and laxative abuse started on a year-long student exchange to France when I was in high school. If the host father accelerating towards an Arab family in the carpark and pretending he was about to run them over ('That's how we do it in France!') didn't twig me to the fact that I'd landed in the family from hell, the host sister demanding to know how much I weighed on my second day was another clue. The next morning, she and her mother bustled into the bathroom as I was getting out of the shower, and asked me to get onto the scales. The anxiety of the trip meant I'd lost a kilo or two. The daughter looked at the number and ran off crying. I looked at the mother, confused.

'She's upset because you lied,' she said. 'You told her you weighed 60, but you're actually 58.'

Living with that family, I learned that it's possible to piss some people off just by existing. My host sister's favourite activities were getting high, bingeing and purging. (Her favourite expression was, 'Tomorrow we diet. So tonight we eat!' It sounds much more celebratory in French.) I joined her, but not in the purging – once again I couldn't get my fingers far enough down my throat, nor work out what to do once they were there.

I returned to Australia and lost most of the weight with my new friends: exercise, laxatives and Nescafe. Then when I'd lost it, I'd let myself binge for a few days. Since my weight never changed much, I didn't think there was a problem. It got worse at uni. I was so sure the private-school kids who filled my classes would figure out I didn't belong, and I'd stay up all night doing even the simplest essays, eating to stifle the voice that said I would never do it perfectly.

Although I got good marks at the start of uni, the perfectionist voice kept telling me it was a fluke, and I was bound to fail eventually. That's why I dropped out. Managing weight became my focus for the next ten years, while life, work and relationships happened in the background.

I got more efficient, scheduling things so I wouldn't have time to eat. There'd be weeks where I'd have half a sandwich for lunch, the other half for dinner and a run for breakfast, followed by weeks of bigger and bigger meals – anything to squash whatever feelings dared to rise up.

That part of it goes back much further though. In my family, intellect and theory were king, and feelings were something other people had – crazy people who couldn't control themselves. Of course this didn't mean that nobody *had* any feelings, just that we kept them neatly tucked away, or outsourced them to a therapist. Even as a kid I seemed to have the uncanny knack of being able to pick up any unspoken tension that was flying around, though sometimes I didn't understand it. For some reason mealtimes are often stressful, and so eventually I learned to focus all my attention on tuning out those physical sensations and forcing the food down as quickly as possible so I could leave the table.

When I read this all out to Malin, it's like reading about someone else. It's so obvious that it's not normal, healthy behaviour. Why did it take me so long to see it?

One thing I like about program is that you're allowed to feel shitty and not apologise for it. You don't have to look anyone in the eye, much less open your heart space to them.

Joel barely speaks above a whisper, but today he stands in front of thirty people and shares his story. He speaks about feeling like he was born into the wrong body, and even though there are aspects of Joel's story that could not have been repeated in a single other human, there isn't a person in the room who doesn't identify.

At one point in the story he pauses to close his eyes. His head tilts back to the wall and he takes deep breaths. Malin reaches down her French manicured fingers and clasps his hand.

As he nears the end of his story, it feels like we, the listeners, are the ones left raw and exposed, while Joel emanates a kind of dignity. He showed up, this incredibly shy man, not only to tell his story to a room full of people, but to the story itself.

He has one more thing to say.

'I just wanted to say, my sponsor said it would be a good idea if I identified myself within this group as a gay man,' Joel smiles shyly at the group, and if I could channel an angel to beam celestial light on him in celebration, I would. He still seems painfully vulnerable, but now he's shining, as if something had been lifted – something that stood between who he is and the rest of the world.

I tell Esther about the heart-opening thing Jorge made us do and she does her thoughtful silent gaze. For a really long time.

'Everyone is so wholesome at yoga. I can't identify with them,' I say. I tell her about Jorge, how completely open he is in his oddness. Then for some reason I find myself telling her about Joel.

'When I first saw him he seemed so creepy, all I could see was what he was hiding. There was almost something pathetic about him. But it's me who feels pathetic for being so desperate for help that I go along to this secretive group every week. Then when Joel came out of the closet I felt ... proud. In a weird way, I felt kinship.'

Esther waits. 'So what's in your closet?' she says. I stare at an ornamental bowl on the sideboard and will myself not to cry.

That I'm the one hiding.

'What's in your closet?' Esther repeats. I stare at the gap under the door. Fluff under a chair. The picture above the sideboard, fog and seagulls on a beach.

'What's in your closet?'

I hate crying when I'm here. It feels like a gust of wind's blown up your skirt and everyone can see you naked.

'It's just blackness ... A black heart. And if people knew how black it was ...'

They'd run. They wouldn't want to know me. They'd leave.

6

Heart Opening's a Bitch

What's the cure for feeling like you're in the closet with a black heart? Being seen, I guess. Feeling nervous as hell, I go for a walk in the park with Kate, and when we're lying on the grass in the sun I casually mention I'm doing 'group therapy' for an eating disorder. Kate is the most un-judgey person I know – maybe because she used heroin for years and worked in a brothel, she's used to being judged? Or maybe she is just an Old Soul. Either way, I hadn't told her before because I was afraid she'd laugh. Despite the huge variety of people I see in the meeting, in my mind eating disorders are still the domain of teenage girls and rich housewives.

Kate asks why I do it, and I can't really answer.

'I think it's a way of dealing with things.' I say eventually.

Kate looks thoughtful. 'When I was in rehab they made us all watch this documentary by this guy about shame – apparently a lot of addiction is based around shame. We all laughed when they started the tape and this 1970s guy in a fuckin' ugly jumper turns up, but by the end the whole room was in tears. And these were some hard bastards.'

She says she's got the book the documentary is based on and she'll lend it to me. 'Though I warn you,' she says, glancing at me, 'the cover is utterly wanky and self-helpy ...'

Kate obviously doesn't realise I've gone so far past worrying about wanky and self-helpy that I now have a book under my bed called *Breaking Down without Falling Apart*, like secret yoga porn.

'Does it work?'

'It's full-on ... but it definitely works.'

*

After weeks of headaches, irritability ravenous hunger and the insatiable desire to punch people in the head (I guess that comes under 'irritability'), lo, the clouds have parted. Who knew detoxing from copious amounts of sugar and a constant stream of snacks would be so deranging?

In the morning I plan out three basic meals and a snack, based roughly on the portion sizes the dietitian gave me, and then I don't think about food until it's time to eat. At first the whole concept of a food plan sounds anathema to 'not focusing on food', but weirdly enough, it's actually freed up vast amounts of mental real estate. Thoughts! I am having them! Not about food!

I no longer feel the need to see Esther, so I stop going, and I don't have sugar for two whole weeks. The cravings disappear. My head feels clear and I wake up with odd new sensations: clarity, energy, *a conspicuous absence of self-loathing*. It's such a familiar companion that the first few mornings I found myself absently digging around for it – *I know you're* there – but it didn't reply.

I still can't look at the cult-like phrases about God and higher power on the wall at fight club, but so far things seem to be just fine without them.

*

Teacher training at the moment is focused on 'healing'. It's like Dr Phil on steroids. The goddesses are fleeing the room in tears so often ('I'm sorry, my stuff is coming up right now') that Marta has started bringing mini-packs of tissues to whip out at the first sign of sniffling.

As far as I can tell, yoga healing is all about finding your weak spots, then going at them over and over again, like a magpie at a cyclist. When a yogi asks another yogi how they're going, 'I've had a lot of stuff come up lately and I'm just trying to process it all,' is not only an acceptable response, it's expected. If you say 'fine' you're not really sharing.

In addition to being a yoga and meditation teacher, Dina works as a psychologist. Two hours into our first class with her, I realised the whole arm-wavy, hair-flowy, jig was just masking a demon with a penchant for regurgitating entire textbooks and grilling us on them. This morning, she's teaching us about managing emotions, but she's not doing a very good job of it. So far two goddesses have fled the room in tears, and since the course began, one goddess has left her partner and another has quit her job. Healing can be quite deranging to one's personal life.

'Sometimes this process feels like stripping back layers of an onion,' says Annabelle. 'Each time you strip back a layer, you cry and think you've reached some new understanding. But there's always another layer.'

Annabelle is some kind of HR manager. Most nights she comes straight after work in her corporate suits, changes into her corporate yoga Lululemons in the bathroom, and at least once a class she disappears back into the bathroom and someone has to retrieve her, sobbing, from one of the stalls.

'Our society pathologises basic emotions like "sadness", and leads us to believe that if we're not 100 per cent ecstatic all the time there's something wrong with us,' says Dina. '"I'm a yoga teacher, so I shouldn't feel sad, or depressed, or angry" is one I hear *all* the time. But meditation and yoga aren't about feeling a certain way. They're about feeling how you feel.'

Yeah right. As long as you feel like sharing heart spaces, high-fiving strangers and telling them one awesome thing about your day.

'What if how you feel is crappy?' I ask. 'Like, if I had students who ran out of the room crying I'd worry I'd done something wrong.'

'How could giving them space for their stuff to come up be wrong? If your students are able to shed their baggage in your class, believe me, you're doing something right.'

I write it down in my notebook: *Students crying = Good teaching.*

•

They said yoga is about stripping back the crap so you can see the inner light within. They said it would stir up all the dirty water. Program seems to target the same things in different ways. Both are designed to systematically dismantle every defence mechanism you've spent a lifetime building up.

Not only are these 'stripping back' practices stirring up some funky energy, 'putting down the food' also means every feeling, every mood, every aspect of life I haven't wanted to see is right there in my face. Deb said that half-arsed attempts did nothing. All I can see is the food cravings. All I can see is the dirty water. All I can see is my own darkness.

But now I'm too exhausted to care. So I'll do the hugging. I'll go to the meetings and make the phone calls. The breathing, the *Om*ming: bring it on. For Dad, 'healing' involves getting pumped full of steroids to make him stronger. Paradoxically, for us healthy folk, it's about tearing down everything you thought made you strong.

•

I've picked up a bit of freelance work, editing a manuscript for a self-publishing company. It's not much, but enough to get me through the next few weeks. The first manuscript they give me was written by a guy who used to run an insurance company. I think it's meant to be a self-help book about rising to the top (he's really, really fond of that cream metaphor), but so far there's been a lot about why entrenched poverty is just natural selection at work, and we should focus our resources on elevating the cream. My brief from the company is to 'just clean it up', but it's unclear if that extends to writing notes for Mr Insurance in the margins to let him know when he sounds like a Nazi apologist, or if that's meant to be part of the book's 'tell-it-like-it-is' raciness, which is supposedly one of its selling points. Maybe I should just focus on semi-colons and hope it gets better.

'When you give up overeating, the good news is you get your emotions back,' says someone in a meeting. 'The bad news is … you get your emotions back.'

They aren't fucking kidding. Some days they come out of nowhere, like a hurricane. Today, for the first time since the meeting, that voice came back telling me to eat. It's like a tyrant. But I've just had a huge meal and know I can't be hungry. What should I do?

Malin's voice pops into my head. *Feel the feelings.* How do you do that? I sit on the stairs. I'll wait it out. Out of nowhere it feels like my chest is going to explode. *Breathe through it.* But it keeps going; it's like a tornado. *What's the feeling underneath it?* All of a sudden I'm overwhelmed by fear and loneliness. I burst into tears. Two minutes later the sobbing stops abruptly and I sit back, exhausted – and, curiously, no longer hungry.

Has this insanity been there all along? I cannot believe something as insignificant as eating came to play such a large role in how I handle life. The only role. It's still only three months since I lay in bed on Christmas night and wanted to claw my way out of my body, but now, without food to soften the edges, I want to literally crawl out of my skin.

'It's like I've lost a best friend,' I say to Emily on the phone later. 'How sad is that?'

'You have lost a best friend,' she replies. 'That's what's so shit about it. But I guess it's a good place to start.'

•

At yoga today, Dina is teaching us about the nervous system. As soon as the class begins, Annabelle bursts into tears about her job for the eight-millionth time. We goddesses form a heart circle around her. ('Oh my goodness,' says Marta. 'I'm going to have to stop providing free tissues soon!')

'Why don't you just quit?' I say.

She looks at me like I'm mad. 'I have an investment property. And I couldn't live on what they pay in the public sector.' Annabelle cries harder. 'I've spent all my life working to get a job like this.'

'She's there for a reason,' says Jo-Jo. 'The boardroom may not be a vibrational match any longer, but there's still karma for you to burn there, isn't that right, gorgeous?'

For some reason Dina seems unmoved by Annabelle's frequent displays of emotion, and with minimal fuss she gets us back on track. She talks about how the body interprets anxious thoughts as though they're actual dangers.

'Anxiety is an inappropriate activation of the sympathetic nervous system, our fight-or-flight response, in reaction to something that's occurred emotionally, in our limbic system. That fear triggers the SNS to give you the energy you need to overcome the imaginary lion,' says Dina. 'Addiction is a common response when people don't know how to manage their anxiety.'

She shows us how different yoga practices bring the body into the parasympathetic, or resting, state of the nervous system. Number one is Yoga Nidra, a guided relaxation that systematically takes your consciousness through all the layers – physical, energetic, mental – until you're in a kind of hypnotised state.

'In deep relaxation the screen between the conscious and the unconscious is lifted, and our unconscious brings information into the conscious mind that we were hitherto unaware of. It's not unusual to feel great in Yoga Nidra, and then find yourself crying hours later as your mind begins to integrate what your unconscious has brought forth.'

And when these waves of emotion rise up and you don't squash them down (or, ahem, eat over them), then that's healing! And then, supposedly, you feel *great*.

As part of our coursework we have to lead the class in a ten-minute Yoga Nidra. Each week a different goddess does it, and this week it's Marta.

'Oh jeez, I know I'm going to mess this up!' she giggles and I prepare to be indulgent.

We lie down and she guides us into a simple relaxation. Marta is so small, cheerful and unassuming in life, but when she teaches, something changes. Marta has such a warm and guileless presence – her voice is like vocal honey – that she bypasses all my cynicism and defences; I find myself completely giving over to her. And it's only when I hear it in Marta that I realise; teaching is as much in the presence you bring to the room as it is the words you say. In ten short minutes my body feels slow, and all is right with the world.

Is this the reward for all the stripping back? You get to feel this all the time? Why is this not taught in schools? *If you're freaking out, here's how you counteract that so you don't become an addicted stress-head psychopath.* Common sense. Useful. For once.

Dad has gone back into hospital for a few days so they can connect him to a tube that drip-feeds nutrients into his tummy 24 hours a day. That's what I do to myself: drip-feeding my anxiety by continually grazing.

'Sitting with those feelings and breathing into them, letting them go, will actually reduce the anxiety response,' says Dina. 'You stop the "amygdala hijack" that tells your hippocampus to dump a whole lot of cortisol – the stress hormone – into your system.'

This is more or less what I've been hearing in meetings. *Sit with your feelings. Sit with your feelings. Shut the fuck up, put down the gun and sit with your feelings.*

Only problem – I don't actually know what 'feel the feelings' means. Lie around all day feeling sad?

•

Yoga teachers go on and on about the body 'storing' emotions.

'What we resist persists!' bellows Suki in the Live Free power class this morning. 'The more you try to duck and weave from the feelings, the more they follow you around like an ex-boyfriend who just won't quit!'

Et tu, Suki? *Et tu?*

At one point Suki instructs us to 'release the emotions in our hips', but try as I might, I can't connect the stubborn tightness of my gluteal muscles to any deep-buried trauma.

I'm in Pamela's class when it happens. She gets us into a deep backbend called Kapotasana, where you kneel on the floor and lie back over a folding chair, reaching behind you to hold your legs. At first it feels nice to have such a deep opening in your chest, but after a few minutes your shoulders start to scream. Then your triceps, your upper back and even the front of your thighs. And then the mental games begin.

Backbending feels like reverse claustrophobia – you're so open and expanded it's scary. One side of you is screaming 'fight' and so you count, you hold your breath, you clench your muscles to keep them from opening, do anything to avoid the pain.

And the other side of your mind is screaming *Let go let go let go let go*. But if you let go it will hurt more.

I hear the sound that strikes fear into my heart: Pamela's footsteps growing louder behind me. *Fuck off fuck off fuck off, please, god, just fuck off.*

I see her feet first, then I feel her tiny claws take firm hold of my upper arms and start to pull them back. She takes my shoulders and chest back, back, back, opening up until there is a hot angry ball at the centre of my chest, but I know that if I let go for a second that hot, angry ball will break.

'Breathe,' she says, totally impassive.

Energy is shooting out of the top of my skull. On the street below, a young couple hurl insults at each other on their way to score drugs.

And then I remember something Malin said in a meeting: 'No one can teach you to let go.' *Stay with it*, I think. Then something seems to shatter. A visual memory flashes past (a family dinner?), then heat goes through my shoulders like a fireball that bursts at the centre of my chest, flooding my whole upper body. There's a deep sense of release and then tears start pouring out and I am *quietly sobbing*. My shoulders suddenly loosen by about ten metres and Pamela gently pulls my arms back a little further and more sobbing comes out, like I'm a human cry lever. And the next thing I know, my whole body softens around the contours of the chair like it is the most comfortable thing in the world.

'Good,' Pamela says, and wanders off to instruct the next pose.

Good? Decades of feelings have just been unlocked and all you can say is 'good'? Eventually I peel myself ungracefully off the leathery seat and stagger out the door. My limbs are inexplicably heavy. I have no idea how I'm going to ride home.

When I get downstairs, Gil is leaning against the bike rack. 'Oh, hello,' he says looking up from his phone. 'I was just in the area.'

'In Collingwood at nine o'clock at night? Were you looking to score some smack?'

'Something like that.' He grins, then walks my bike the whole way home while I talk about the magical world of yoga.

Why do some postures give us this emotional catharsis? The theory is that whenever we feel stressed, anxious, fearful or sad, we unconsciously contract parts of our body as a kind of defence. When this happens regularly, some of the muscles stay a little bit contracted and never fully let go, trapping some of that emotion – anxiety, sadness, fear – in the body.

Then, supposedly, when you go to a yoga class and do a pose that really gets into those tight areas (and hurts like buggery – good hurt, not short, sharp, bad hurt) it also brings forth the original emotion that triggered the contraction. (This would explain Gil swearing every time I get him to practise yoga with me, and then laughing maniacally fifteen minutes later.) In yoga they call these blocked energies the 'samskaras'.

One of the things I find both wonderful and infuriating in yoga is that nobody *really* knows how it works, but we still come up with all these pseudo-scientific reasons to explain why it makes us feel better, and since few students in any given class actually know enough Hard Science to contradict it, we just go along with it. (I suppose if all those creationist nuff-nuffs can tell themselves comforting stories about how we got here, why can't yoga teachers take a grain of science and spin it into something that motivates people to sit through the harder parts of a practice?)

Ironically, one of the reasons I think Live Free-style classes are so popular is that they move so fast that you can enjoy the endorphins without ever *really* having to feel the feelings. It reminds me of how I used to skip meditation. Who needs the pain?

As Gil and I walk home through the park, he tells me the latest in a long-drawn-out work saga and I notice that as he talks, he's bracing his abdomen so tightly there's no space for the diaphragm to descend. I stop listening to the words and start watching how this makes his breath shallow, and his shoulders and chest tighten in response.

'Try letting your tummy go soft as you breathe in,' I suggest. He's silent for a few moments.

'I feel sick,' he says.

'Like, sick how?' I'm confused. Shouldn't letting go of a tight breath-holding pattern be a relief?

'Relaxing my belly when I walk makes me feel like I'm going to throw up,' he says. Gil was bullied in primary school, and has changed the way he walks as a result – he now walks like a tight ball of 'don't fuck with me' muscle. 'Relaxing makes me feel just intense anxiety,' he says. So I guess his limbic system has told him that 'relaxation' means 'vulnerability to attack'.

Is that why so many macho men walk around looking like Thunderbirds?

They're keeping Dad in hospital a bit longer than planned. I'm glad. He's becoming less and less mentally 'with it' when I visit. He's come off the feeding tube, but tonight when I arrive, his dinner is sitting there untouched. I look around – why aren't the nurses helping him eat? I plonk my aluminium drink bottle on his tray then get busy chopping up his food and feeding it to him, but he's distracted.

My drink bottle has a bit of pink on it and dad zeroes in, pointing at the pink on the bottle and insisting he wants 'some of that strawberry milkshake'. I tell him that if he eats five bites of dinner he can have some strawberry milkshake. Sometimes you hear yourself saying these things and you shake them off because they're so ridiculous they can't be happening. I just focus on getting the next mouthful into him, and fortunately Dad falls asleep before he realises it's all been a cunning ruse and there's no strawberry milkshake to be had. I know I'd be disappointed.

Once the cry lever's been pulled, it's hard to release it. Crying during yoga or while visiting your ailing father in hospital is one thing. Crying when you watch an insurance ad is another. I begin to envy people who go blissfully about their lives, unaware of the cesspit of 'blocked prana' just under the surface.

Without the buffer of food, the world feels like it's been washed clean, and it isn't pretty. I feel raw, like my skin has been peeled off. The sheer effort required to stay on top of being sane and healthy without turning back to food feels like so much *work*, and it's all I can do not to just say 'fuck it' and check out.

During the break in my next teacher training class, tiny Marta asks if we can sing 'Happy Birthday' to Annabelle as it was her birthday earlier in the week.

'I've got a better idea,' says Dina. 'How about we do an *Om Bath*?'

She shows us how to do it. One person lies on the floor, and then everyone else puts their hands on them and chants a rolling 'Om' – over and over until it becomes one continuous sound.

We gather around and I put my hand on Annabelle's ankle.

'*Auuuuuuuumm*,' Dina begins. We pick up the chant. Every time we pause to take a breath everyone else keeps the sound going.

Through Annabelle's ankle I feel the *Om* vibration of everyone else in the room and when she eventually sits up, her eyes are damp. It reminds me of the end of the program meetings when everyone holds hands and says a prayer, and just for a second you feel like part of a whole, rather than an isolated, black-hearted person.

So maybe they are freaks – the goddesses, the people in fight club. But I guess they're my freaks.

•

I'm meant to call 'Divine Shakti Goddess' Susan once a month, but have been putting it off because she seems like all the worst of yoga voodoo compressed into one person. When she invites me up to her place in the Dandenong Ranges, a beautiful forested area just outside of Melbourne, I reluctantly make a list of mentor-appropriate questions about the Sutras and hop on a train.

When I arrive, Susan takes me on a tour of the property. I'm pretty sure the house she shares with Graeme – surrounded by lush rainforest, with little Buddha statues perched on fern-lined walkways

— is on every yoga teacher's vision board. They each have their own yoga room, and even their golden retriever seems infused with yogic calm.

'It's such an idyllic place to live,' I say. 'You guys are so lucky.'

'Uh-huh. See that shack over there?' she says, pointing to a neighbour's shed through the trees. 'That's the local meth lab. And that house across the hill? He's the resident firebug. Lit three grass fires last season, and Graeme's taken to watching him through binoculars on hot days, like something out of *Rear Window*.'

Huh. So much for the Yoga Idyll. I deliver my carefully prepared Sutra questions, which she answers very politely, then after my fifth one, she says, 'Yeah, yeah, yeah, I don't *do* the Sutras. How are *you* doing?' She's caught me off-guard, and as I start to recite a 'well thanks, yoga's so great', I choke up.

'Can I just say?' says Susan, 'I'm *fine* with tears.'

I let it all out: Dad's in hospital, I'm totally incapable of eating like a normal person, I'm unemployable except for helping bigots spread their ideas and I'm never going to master the yoga philosophy.

'You know what?' she says. 'I'm *tired* of philosophy. Fuck the philosophy! If you can sit next to someone who's dying in hospital and not try to change their experience, believe me, that's all the yoga philosophy you need right there.'

Wow! The Divine Shakti Goddess is cool! Later, while Susan takes a phone call, I do what I always do when I go to someone else's house and check out my hosts' book collection. I'm expecting Susan's shelves to be lined with books on ear-candling and kinesiology. Instead it's the mirror image of Gil's bookshelf back home: graphic novels, esoteric science fiction and Ursula Le Guin.

Later on, Graeme joins us for lunch. Other than orientation, I've never actually seen them in the same room together, and it's fun watching serious yoga scholar Graeme and 'fuck the philosophy!' Susan interact. I mention how much the experience of yoga practice seems different from the theory.

'Ahhh,' says Graeme in his yoga-teacher voice. He leans back in his chair and closes his eyes. 'Sutra 1.37: *Vitaragavisayam va cittam.* "When we are confronted with problems, the wise counsel of one who —"'

'Aww, c'mon, Graeme!' groans Susan. 'We're trying to have lunch here!'

I look at Graeme to see if Patanjali's ghost will rise up and smite Susan for her impertinence. But he just laughs, kisses Susan on the cheek and says, 'Right you are.'

When I get off the train that night, Gil meets me at the station and wraps me up in a bear hug. 'The Dandenongs are a dangerous place,' he says, 'full of glass blowers and tree huggers. I thought I might lose you to an incense farm.'

'Never,' I say.

During our next mentoring phone call, Susan tells me I need to start teaching real classes.

'But I'm not qualified yet,' I say. 'What if someone has a stroke?'

'Call 000,' she says. 'You don't learn to teach yoga by looking at a picture of someone with perfect alignment and trying out poses on your yoga-teacher friends. You learn by teaching real people with real bodies.'

I've already started teaching a couple of old uni buddies yoga in my living room once a week for practice, but maybe it's time to teach real people who won't be so forgiving.

'I just think I'm not ... pure enough to teach.'

Susan snorts. 'Yoga teachers are so bloody puritanical! But yoga is whatever *you* need at that time. You don't like chanting? Screw chanting! Yoga means "union", right? So sometimes yoga means *shopping.* It's okay to play in the shallow end. Put *that* in the Sutras.'

Graeme sends an email around his teaching network saying I'm looking for experience. One of his ex-students says I can assist in her lunchtime classes at the workplace gym for staff at the Department of the Environment.

I spend two days preparing for the hour-long class. Once I have the anatomical and spiritual theme (backbends + embracing vulnerability: I'm nothing if not original), I carefully design a sequence and look up the history of each pose so I sound like I know what I'm talking about.

'You do know that half of what we teach in modern yoga classes are just glorified gymnastics that have been given Sanskrit names, right?' says Susan when I email her my 459th question on preparations. 'Yoga teachers talk a lot of crap and everyone laps it up like it's ancient wisdom. It's not!'

That's not very inspiring.

The night before the class I dream that all the students walk out of the room and refuse to come back until a 'real yoga teacher' takes the class. But the next day is gloriously sunny and I ride my bike through the park feeling like the yoga gods are smiling down at me.

At the Department of the Environment, the walls in the gym are lined with motivational posters of a different kind: instead of disabled rock climbers promising that *If you can dream it, you can do it*, staff gaze at images of turtles choking on plastic bags. Inspiring!

As I wait for Farah, the teacher whose class I'm assisting, my heart starts racing and my breath becomes shallow. *Look how stressed you're getting! You call yourself a yoga teacher? You better not pass those terrible vibes on to your students.*

Just breathe. Slow inhale; longer, slower exhale to activate the relaxation response. Seconds later I feel light-headed, but calm.

Farah appears in tie-dye leggings and a Nick Cave singlet. 'Thanks so much for coming!' she says. 'I'll just be up the back observing, then I'll give you feedback afterwards.'

Observing? *Observing?* Boom! Being a yoga junkie means you

can actually *feel* the moment your amygdala hijacks your nervous system and turns you into an incompetent mess. But the group exercise room is already crammed with bodies lying on yoga mats. If I just slip onto a mat beside them maybe no one will notice and Farrah will just quietly start teaching instead?

I slip on my CD, poke at the buttons, then clear my throat.

'Hiiiiii everyonnnne ...' I drawl. What the? Is this my yoga-teacher voice? A few raise their heads from the floor and give me a wave. Keep going. 'I'm going to be teaching you today while the divine Farah chills up the back.' *The divine Farah?* 'Just rooooollll up to kneeling and we'll start with some gentle movements to warm up the spine.'

I sound like a wanker, but the class all sit up and look expectant and no one is walking out asking for the real teacher. *They think you're their teacher. So teach.*

As Susan suggested, as soon as I get them settled into the first pose, I take stock. She was right: you can read about poses, and practise them all you want, but no textbook pose can prepare you for the thirty different bodies with different bone structures performing thirty variations of that same posture.

'Remember,' Susan told me. 'They know much better than you what's good for their own bodies, so guide them to tune in and respond.' I do my best, and the focus in the room seems to become more internal. Halfway through the class, something magical happens. I start to relax and enjoy it. So this is teaching! And yet it's not the perfect class I've spent two days planning. I end up throwing out half the sequence, changing the class moment to moment depending on how the students respond.

It's going so well I figure I can experiment a little and step into my teaching greatness, as Suki might say. I minutely describe every muscle action in every pose and every feeling I think they might be having. 'Where's your *breath* in this pose? Where's your *ego*?' The class are getting restless. *Go back to the theme.* 'Backbends are all about vulnerability – opening yourself up to the unknown,' I prattle. 'As we prepare for the peak pose, think of an area in your life where you're running away – where you're afraid to see what's really there. Bring that into your mind right now. How does it feel in your body? In your cells? In your *peri-organ fluid*?'

Farah watches me with a curious look on her face. Half the class have stopped breathing and appear to be frozen stiff.

'Okay, now it's time to really feel our vulnerability and bust those fears wide-open!'

I guide them into a deep, heart-opening backbend. My motivational yoga teacher voice reaches a crescendo. 'Stay with the vulnerability. Explore it.' People's arms buckle and I quickly get them to lie down so it looks like we were all *meant* to end up on the floor. Okay, what next? Integration. Susan says that lying on your back is bad if you're feeling vulnerable. I ask them to come into child's pose and hold their feet. Child's pose really does look like the foetal position, particularly when your students start sobbing.

I want to give one of the crying students a little pat, then remember what Dina said about how a good yoga teacher creates space for students and doesn't interfere with their process. So I just keep talking over her sobs, while inside I'm high-fiving myself. I really got them in touch with their emotions! I close the class with a guided meditation where they bring their hands to their chest and imagine a tiny hand reaching out from their heart – the hand of the inner child they've locked away and ignored. That's union, I think. Job done!

As I send them back to their desks and their choking turtles, no one seems to want to make eye-contact with me. I take it as a sign that they're still deep in their yogic trance. People pay hundreds of dollars to have that kind of catharsis in therapy, and here I'm giving it to them practically for free! I think I might have a gift.

After class, Farah approaches. 'I'm just wondering, what was your intention with that class?' she says, curiously not enthusing about my natural ability.

'To create a healing experience,' I say, baffled she couldn't see it. 'To open them up and get them in touch with their vulnerability, and then to heal them and make them stronger.' Duh!

'Right ...' she says slowly. 'I admire your ambition ... I just wonder if it is maybe a bit much for a one-hour class where people are practising with their colleagues?' We regard the remaining students as they pack up, red-eyed and sluggish.

'I'm confused. I thought yoga is about stripping back? Peeling off the layers, getting in touch with what's real?'

'It is,' says Farah. 'But think of a snake shedding its skin. You want to allow that to happen organically. You don't want to get in there with a potato peeler.'

Well she didn't have to be gross about it.

＊

When you spend all your time healing, you get very sensitive to potentially negative and triggering energy. Like reading the paper and watching the news. It feels like we can't do anything to help the Syrian children, the starving polar bears, the trafficked women and children. We can't stop the plastic in the ocean or the Yulin dog-meat festival, but by god, we can clear our blocked prana.

'I haven't picked up a newspaper since 2005,' says Annabelle in our next class. 'Too much negativity.' Annabelle gets her news from her chiropractor, who, among other things, believes vaccines cause autism – so now Annabelle does, too. (Any information contradicting that theory is dismissed as the propaganda of 'Big Pharma'.)

Personally, I look to Gandhi. *Be the change you want to see in the world.* And between clearing out my samskaras from the past and protecting myself from the low-vibe energy in the world, I've got enough to keep my attention firmly on my own navel for at least another year.

One Friday night, Gil asks me to go into the city with him. His family has hired a private room in a karaoke bar to celebrate his cousin's birthday.

'I'm sorry,' I say. 'I'm doing some really deep healing right now, and there's a lot of chaotic energy in bars. With where I am in my journey, I just can't afford to pick that stuff up. But have fun!' I don't think Gil's eyes could roll any further back in his head.

The old me would have jumped at the chance to belt out some glam rock. The new me has to get up early for yoga, and frivolity would just be a pointless distraction from working through my issues. Scratching at scabs until they heal, though? The benefits of that last a lifetime.

•

Most people spend the Friday night of a long weekend unwinding with a nice cocktail, but not goddesses. We all signed up for Jorge's workshop on 'Lakshmi's Gifts and Dismantling False Beliefs'. Jorge's studio is above a bar at the grungy end of a wealthy shopping strip. A trail of pink rose petals has been scattered from the street, past the bar and up the stairs to the studio.

I'm coming to appreciate Jorge's storytelling. He has a way of explaining things that doesn't hand you the message, but gives you the context so you can figure it out for yourself, and it's a rude shock to realise I'm not the only one who appreciates this. Jorge has *acolytes*. Dozens of devoted yogis of all ages, from wealthy ladies with blonde bobs and Fendi bags to the vegan hippies with dreads and faded halter tops, sit in front of Jorge, gazing at him with the rapt attention of children being read a fairytale. I bristle territorially.

Jorge begins the workshop, as usual, by having us stare into a stranger's eyes. It's definitely progress that I can now tolerate 'uncomfortable intimacy with strangers' exercises without running screaming from the room.

Jorge then weaves the tale of Lakshmi, a righteous Hindu goddess. A million years ago there was a war between the gods and the demons. Both groups wanted the 'nectar of immortality', but they had to churn an ocean of milk to get it. Out of the ocean rose a number of gifts, which they gladly took, but the final one, nobody wanted, because it was a vial of poison. Unfortunately, though, someone had to take it or they wouldn't get the nectar.

Finally, Vishnu says, 'I'll drink the poison', and takes one for the team. (That's why Vishnu is always painted blue in pictures. Poison isn't great for the complexion.) As soon as Vishnu downed the last drop, out of the ocean rose a goddess: it was Lakshmi, holding Amrita, the nectar of immortality.

'Lakshmi's story is about what is possible when we're willing to face our darkness. But before we can get to the bliss, before we can get 'the nectar', first Vishnu has to drink the poison – do what he doesn't want to do. It's about trusting that if you go through all the crap, but really look at it skilfully, you'll find the sweetness.'

Lots of 'Oh *yeeeaaaahhhs*' ripple through the room, and it feels good; a decent story well told can unite even a 'south of the river' Gucci yogi and a 'north of the river' mung-bean-patchouli yogi.

'Depending on how we treat them, our greatest struggles can either kill us, or become our greatest teachers – our "guru",' Jorge continues. '*Gu* – darkness – and *Ru* – light. A "guru" helps us to become conscious of all the things that are buried deep within us, the poison, so we can use them as blessings to transform darkness to light.

'We're so focused on getting what we want as painlessly as possible,' says Jorge. 'But what if we look at it differently? What if the question is: "What do you have to look at before you can live in the bliss? What poison do you need to drink to get to the nectar?"'

One of the northern Patchouli yogis raises her hand. '"In the cave of your fear is the treasure you seek." Joseph Conrad,' she says.

'Yes!' says Jorge, and repeats it back to the group and we all write it down. I feel brave and inspired until I get out on the street and realise it all just calls for more *stripping back*. More *shedding*.

I stagger home and throw myself on the couch. My phone buzzes and I reach into my pocket, which is stuffed with gypsy trinkets from the workshop – autumn leaves to represent 'shedding of old habits and beliefs', and petals to represent new life. It's Gil texting me to come and meet him and his family at karaoke, but I can't muster the energy to get up, much less peel the bindi, pasted on by my eye-gazing workshop partner, off my forehead. As I empty my pockets, a poem Jorge sprinkled with gold dust flutters onto the table:

Go ahead, light your candles and burn your incense and ring your bells and call out to God, but watch out, because God will come, and He will put you on His Anvil and fire up His Forge and beat you and beat you until He turns brass into Pure Gold.

— Saint Keshavadas

Why is 'feeling shit' a requirement of healing? Jorge says it's about stripping away everything that isn't 'you' until all that's left is indestructible. But the more yoga and meetings I go to, the more destructible I *feel*.

'No more unpacking,' I plead to the ceiling. 'No more unravelling.'

I pick up my phone for distraction. Up pops a motivational quote from a speaker I subscribed to ages ago in a fit of delirium. *Let yourself be completely shattered*, it says.

'Oh, fuck off,' I mutter and pull a blanket over me, shoes and all.

I look at the books on the coffee table. A book on shame, and the memoir of an alcoholic poet. No bloody wonder I'm depressed. I brush off my gold dust and go to bed.

At 2am the phone rings. It's Gil slurring. 'Heybabehomesoon, ohwait, wha?' I hear laughter and glasses clinking.

'Wherreareya? Wish you are hereoh yeh how is … how is … goddess workshop?' He breaks into cackles. 'SORRY! Sooorrrryyy

… I just miss you.' I prepare myself to rip him a new one for waking me when I need eight hours of sleep for my wellbeing … then I hear it. The opening familiar notes.

'Is that "ETERNAL FLAME"?'

'Oh yeah,' Gil slurs. 'The girl cousins get control of the —'

I hang up before he can finish, throw a coat over my pyjamas, and peddle into the city like the Wicked Witch of the East. I chuck my unemployed credit card down on the reception desk, bellow, 'TWO MORE HOURS!' and race into the room where thirty members of Gil's hill-tribe family are drunkenly crooning an Alice Cooper song. I grab the mike off Gil and join in.

Healing never felt so good.

7

Kundalini Rising

Something weird is happening. Who would have thought that all that 'stripping back' and *shat karmas* and 'healing' would actually work?

When I was dipping my toe into yoga, I found it boring and painful, with a post-class high that lasted ten minutes. But since committing to daily practice – even just fifteen minutes with a short meditation at the end of the day – everything has changed.

Number one, I feel *good*. And when people shit me, I silently forgive them and send them love instead of hoping they get molested by a syphilitic donkey.

Sure, I'm still vastly underemployed with no idea how to make a living from this yoga caper, but I think my healing is pretty much done! I haven't binged in weeks; I feel at one with the world. I think this is how we're *meant* to feel. We're *meant* to have energy. We're *meant* to notice when we're tired and then rest for five minutes to get our energy back, rather than chugging down caffeine and sugar only to crash at the end of the day.

It's the carrot and the stick. I started yoga and program because I didn't want the pain of bingeing and feeling like shit all the time. But now I can't imagine *not* going.

I am ready to be a quiet, positive example to all my students. But I won't brag about it, because if you have to tell people you're someone they can learn from it means you're not. They have to figure it out for themselves.

One afternoon after class I feel so great I take a selfie in my yoga wear and post it to social media with an inspirational quote. I just want the world to know that feeling amazing is theirs for the taking! And it gets so many likes!

I crossed the 'yoga wanker' line, and I'm not sorry.

The next day I float home from the gym, endorphins flowing, feeling wonderful – and it's only 8am. 'What's up with you?' says Gil, still in his dressing gown and grasping a cup of coffee like it's the only thing keeping him upright.

I tell him he'd feel much better if he came and did yoga with me, but he just grunts and sits on the stairs with Ginger the cat, glaring sleepily at me as I make breakfast. I've been trying green smoothies. (They're drinkable if you drown whatever greens you have in concentrated fruit juice.)

'Why do you do it to yourself?' Gil asks. 'It looks revolting.'

'I "do it" because it gives me prana – that's "life force" to you, and I am a liker of life.'

Gil sighs. 'I knew this would happen. You're following the herd. Like a brain-dead cultist.'

Ahh. Classic 'one partner threatened by another's growth' scenario. I understand that Gil is a simple man with simple tastes, but sometimes I wonder if it's a problem that he isn't keeping pace with my evolution. He should be threatened by my burgeoning consciousness and lifting his game before I get too far ahead, spiritually speaking. But I simply smile, silently repeat an affirmation at him ('the light in you is all I see') and take my green juice upstairs to do my daily spiritual readings.

I've started subscribing to a spiritual teacher named Gabby Bernstein on the internet, and she says when you're around unenlightened people it's really important to 'be the light'. So, for example, when I start teaching yoga classes, instead of getting down into whatever mood they're in, I should bring them up to my level.

Be the light, and they will be attracted to my classes like moths to a bright and wondrous flame.

I can already feel that happening. Like this morning at the gym, I must have been radiating positivity because this guy came up and started chatting. And because he had a mild facial deformity, I was very polite, to show that deformity does not freak me out. As a result of my light-exuding, he followed me around my entire workout, giving me tips on how I can do everything five per cent better, like we were old friends, even though we are not. If tolerating a little mansplaining for an hour is the price of radiating goodwill and feeling awesome, then it's a small price to pay.

•

'Did you know our bodies are like little drug dispensaries?' I tell Emily on the phone. 'And different yoga poses trigger shots of either an upper or downer, depending on what you want? Maybe you could spread the word in your drug meetings? It's nature's pharmacy!'

'Uh-huh,' says Emily, bored.

'And —' the coup de grâce, '— I haven't binged in *a month*.'

Emily snorts. 'Have you ever heard of the *pink cloud*?' she says. 'It's something that happens early in recovery. It's when you just start working the steps, and you start to feel a base level of good.'

'I feel *fantastic*!'

'I know you do! And that's great. But maybe you partly feel fantastic because you felt like shit for so long.'

'What's wrong with that?'

'Nothing in itself, but it doesn't last. One day the shit hits the fan, because that's what happens in life, and you have to learn how to live life on life's terms. You know there's that saying that when you stop using, whether it's food, drugs, sex or whatever, you're still the mental age you were when you began?'

'Yeah,' I say, snorting. I've heard it, and it sounds like a crock. 'What about it?'

'So, when you're numbing yourself you kind of stop growing. You've been using food since you were fifteen.'

Emily sounds almost cheerful, like she's seen it a million times before. (Maybe she has, but frankly, the pink cloud sounds more like a crack thing.)

'Just stick it out, okay?' she says. 'Putting down the food is just the beginning.'

Why is Emily trying to ruin my vibe? Jealousy, most likely. *Be the light. I am the light.*

·

I think Gym Man might be trying to steal my light, literally. This morning I get on the bike next to the window so I can watch the soccer game outside while catching a ray of winter sun. Suddenly a shadow falls. I look up and Gym Man has wedged himself between my bike and the window.

'You're back!' he says, like the gym is his personal domain and I dropped in specifically to chat to him.

'Oh man, that guy can't play for shit,' he says, pointing to one of the players out on the field. 'See that goal was "offside". What that means is —'

'I know what offside —' I begin, but he's oblivious, and continues explaining the rules of soccer until I go to the bathroom, never to return.

Afterwards I feel bad. Clearly he's just lonely, probably on account of his mild facial deformity? Researchers say loneliness is as bad for you as fifteen cigarettes a day. The least I can do is put myself out for a few minutes to listen to a lonely person.

Be the light. I am the light.

·

Being the light is tiring. Gil came home from work last night in a foul mood. I asked what was wrong ('Nothing!') then he proceeded to huff and puff around the house for several hours, slamming cupboards, and bitching about everything except what was actually bothering him. It was all I could do not to give him the fight he seemed to want.

He finally came to bed at 2am, sighing loudly in my direction. I opened my eyes and he looked at me mournfully.

'Want to talk about it?' I mumbled.

'Ok!' he said brightly, then out poured the work frustrations. I listened attentively, offering suggestions, and twenty minutes later Gil was snoring soundly while I stayed awake for the rest of the night.

•

My friends have been coming late to my living-room classes. Tonight they swan in twenty minutes late ('It's fine to just finish twenty minutes later, isn't it? At least you're at home anyway!') and one of them brings her workmate ('Jade's going through a relationship breakup and I think she'd get a lot out of calming down,' whispers my friend), even though I don't have enough room and it means I'll have to teach squished into the corner under the crumbling plaster wall.

My friend was right, though. Jade totally needs the class, and afterwards she tells me what 'great energy' I have. 'You're going to be an amazing teacher,' she says. Then she kind of slumps and looks at her feet. *Be the light. Share the light.* We somehow get to talking about her relationship and it's midnight by the time she leaves.

The next week she stays back again, wanting to talk about the emotions my yoga class brought up ('you're *such* a good listener'). I'm kind of tired and just want to stop being a teacher for the night, but it's my responsibility to help her process her emotions – after all, I helped stir them up in the first place.

The whole time I sit there, a thought is niggling: is it possible that being the light is making me a super attractor for needy people?

After the next class I subtly angle my body towards the door, saying, 'Well, I'm so glad you got something out of the class!'

Her feet stay rooted to the spot. She looks behind me towards the kitchen.

Without thinking I blurt, 'Er ... do you need a cup of tea?' (Which everyone *knows* is code for 'why are you still here?' 'Would you *like* a cup of tea,' means 'I am happy if you say yes'. 'Do you *need* one' is code for 'don't let the door hit you on the way out'.)

She finally leaves at eleven thirty. I am weirdly too drained to sleep, so because I've been up for more hours than normal, I figure I may as well have second dinner.

•

I send the insurance CEO my first edits on his book on why poor people deserve it and how not to be a loser. So far he's sent me four emails in reply to my suggested edits to *the introduction*. Sample response: *I am happy to incorporate your suggestion of the semi-colon in this instance, however any avoidance of 'sentence flow interruptions' would be preferable by me.*

'Sentence flow interruptions'? Does he mean ... punctuation? In another email he asks if I'd consider ghost-writing his memoir offering 'exposure' in lieu of payment. It takes all my restraint not to point him to the section of his book where he talks about getting people's best work for free – or as he calls it, 'maximising resources'.

•

The early bird avoids the talker. This morning I get to the gym half an hour earlier than usual and Gym Man is already there, yammering at a girl on a treadmill. I am free to work out in peace.

Ten minutes later the girl leaves without bothering to stretch. I quickly put on my headphones and duck my head, but it's no good. Seconds later I sense his beady eyes on me like a laser pointer.

I am an evolved being, and can graciously absorb others' social clumsiness.

It's not my job to point out that he lacks manners. Hell, I wrote a *book* on manners, so it's probably my job to model them for him.

Here he comes.

He's probably just lonely. And really, if I can't spend fifty minutes (he followed me to the free weights and then stretching) cheering up one lonely person, what's the point of Being the Light in the first place?

'Why don't you just tell him to bugger off?' says Gil when I get home. I finish off his ham and eggs because kale smoothies aren't enough when you've used up all your energy smiling and nodding.

'I can't be *rude*. Besides, I did sort of tell him to leave me alone when I moved to the other side of the gym to show him the conversation was over.'

'And what happened?'

'He followed me.'

Gil shakes his head. 'Women are weird. A guy gets into your space, ignores signs that you're not interested, and you're worried you'll upset *him*? He's counting on you not wanting to be rude. That's how he gets away with it.'

Huh! So Gym Man *knows* I find him annoying, he just doesn't care? Rude!

•

I think there's something wrong with my inner yoga light. It used to be like a soft glow, but now it's becoming more like a hot flame that wants to singe people. According to Jorge, that's a standard phase in the spiritual path.

Jorge takes us for a class on the chakras. There are seven chakras (supposedly) from the base of our spine to the crown of our head, that all correlate with different aspects of our mental and emotional wellbeing.

'Are the chakras real things or made up yoga things?' I ask.

'Think of the chakras as metaphors for different psychological states,' Jorge says. 'It's not like you'll find them in an autopsy.'

Sometimes your chakras get blocked (or never open at all) due to 'unresolved issues'. One of the tasks of yoga, then, is to clear out your Nadis and open up the chakras.

The 'Nadis', Jorge explains are 72,000 tiny energy highways that run throughout the body. When the 'highways of the Nadis' merge at different intersections along the central channel of the spine, they create the chakras, or 'swirling vortexes of energy'. Why 72,000? Why not? Nadis are yoga science, which is like normal science, minus the burden of proof. One teacher did admit (under intense questioning) that the Nadis loosely correspond to the nervous system in Western medicine and the meridians in Chinese medicine.

But like much yoga voodoo, eventually, if you practise enough, you start to experience it as real.

Jorge shows us a diagram of the seven chakras. He asks us each to read out one and its description, and, as usual, Marta spends ten minutes giggling ('Ooh, I'm never going to pronounce this right, can't someone else do it so I don't mess it up?') before Jorge gives up and reads it himself.

The first chakra is right in the nether-regions and coloured red like a haemorrhoid. 'The base chakra, Muladhara, is about belonging and identity,' says Jorge. 'It's about feeling stable and grounded in who you are. When it's out of balance, we don't feel like we belong; we don't feel like we have the right to take up space. Unrooted. When it's in balance, we're as comfortable watching football with beer-bellied boofheads as we are in a yoga studio.'

The goddesses chuckle. I think we're all trying to picture Jorge chugging a Crownie with a bogan in front of the rugby.

'When Muladhara chakra is weak, you often get anxiety. Some people turn to food as a literal anchor in an attempt to ground themselves.'

Maybe I have a little work to do on my base chakra.

'The second is the sacral chakra, and it's about creativity, pleasure, sexuality,' says Jorge. 'But people whose sacral chakras are in excess tend to have fuzzy boundaries. They have trouble saying no. And because there are no boundaries, they'll often find other people's energy just pouring into them. In this case you can easily be flooded with energy and not know how to contain it. Addiction, for example, starts in the sacral chakra.'

Check!

'In order to communicate boundaries,' Jorge continues, 'your throat chakra needs to be unblocked. The throat chakra is about *expression* – feeling we have a voice in the world. The throat chakra is also about truth. So work around the throat chakra is often about learning clean, truthful communication.'

At this point I don't care whether the chakras are real or not – I just want to get in there and open them. By force if necessary.

'Yoga and meditation help open up the chakras and bring them back into balance, which frees up all that blocked energy so you start to feel amazing,' says Jorge. 'But it's possible to release more energy than you can deal with. So as a protective measure, the chakras have little corks called the 'gratis', which stop us going too fast too soon. As our attitudes change, we can handle more, and so the corks whittle away. *That's* when you may start to notice a big shift in energy and consciousness, and the serpent begins to awaken!'

The 'serpent' Jorge was referring to is the Holy Grail: lying dormant at the base of the spine like a coiled up snake is a kind of psychic energy called 'Kundalini'. And when you get yourself into alignment and your chakras are spinning at a decent clip, this Kundalini energy travels up the spine, through the chakras, to the crown. This is called 'Kundalini rising', and supposedly it takes you to a higher level of consciousness.

'Now, ladies, be careful with this stuff. When you go too fast, you can get too much Kundalini rising. You might go a little nuts.'

None of us is listening. We're all too busy scribbling down the postures and breathing techniques of the chakra-opening practice.

'And don't be surprised if you walk out of a practice session feeling amazing, then go home and have a fight with your family. That's just the subconscious throwing something up that you're now ready to deal with.'

Is that what Emily was talking about with the 'pink cloud'?

•

This week people are *forty-five minutes* late to class. 'Sorry sorry sorry!' they say, tumbling through the door. I ask very politely if they can try to come on time next week, but they fall about laughing ('Omg, you've got "scary yoga teacher" face!'), and I end up saying it's fine.

But the next night, when Susan is teaching a class on the teacher-student relationship, I bring it up.

'Why the hell aren't you charging them?' she says. 'People don't value it if it's free.'

My fellow goddesses recoil at the mention of money. 'You can't *charge* them – they're friends. It wouldn't be nice,' says Marta.

'Why don't you just do it as an offering to the universe?' says Goddess Jo-Jo. 'That's how it was done traditionally. People can make an offering if they feel called to, like a tithe.'

'Or put a donation box in the corner?' says Marta. 'That's what I do.'

'So tell me, Marta,' says Susan. 'How much do people usually donate?'

'Oh, well ... nothing yet,' she replies. 'But I'm not sure if they know the box is there? I suppose I could have a sign, but I don't want to seem pushy.'

After class, Jo-Jo sees me wincing when I get up. I've been doing yoga like a fiend, but for some reason my lower back's been in agony. Jo-Jo does a few moments of reiki on me. I don't know if it feels slightly better because reiki works, or just because Jo-Jo's warm hands unfreeze my muscles.

She tuts. 'Back spasms. Repressed anger.'

'I don't feel angry,' I say. 'I feel great.'

'Uh-huh,' she says, pointing to my throat chakra.

•

On Saturday there's a family birthday. I've put on a dress, and everyone is on their most charming behaviour.

Mum comes over when I arrive. 'You look lovely, darling,' she says.

'Is everything okay? How's Dad?' I ask.

'He's fine,' she says vaguely. 'You know, the same.' Hmmm. *The same* is not fine.

'What are the doctors saying?'

'Oh, I don't know, just the usual.' *There is no 'usual'*. 'Let's just focus on being in the moment. Isn't that what they say in yoga?' she says.

Silence is called when the cakes come out to allow the fifteen or so people sitting at the table to pause and admire them. 'Now *you*,' the host stands up and points to me, 'simply *must* try some of this one.'

The whole table is silent, watching me. 'Uh, that's okay,' I stammer. 'I think I'm full. But maybe I could take some home?'

'No, no, no! Just one bite. Here, pass it down to her.' I feel everyone's eyes boring into me. To reject the offering would be to reject the host.

I take the plate. After six weeks off sugar, the first bite coats my mouth with a sickly sweetness. The second bite I don't really taste anything, and by the time I'm on my second piece I wonder what the big deal was. Of course, I need to try all the cakes, and by then it doesn't seem worth stopping.

As I crack jokes and pretend everything's fine, I suddenly notice my hand hasn't stopped moving from the plates of food to my mouth for forty minutes. It has always been this way, but this is the first time I've noticed it.

I pause. And in that silence, I finally hear the voice in my head: *Just shut up and be funny.*

I look around the table laden with birthday food, and I can *feel* the unspoken conflicts and resentments humming under the surface. My gut feels like a satellite dish for other people's moods and my superpower is feeling other people's feelings as if they were my own. It's accompanied by a familiar and overwhelming feeling that it's my duty to make them feel better. It seems that somehow I've made it my business to be a human security blanket – not just here, either. And even though it feels like shit, that role has helped me to belong. I've become like an 'emotional prostitute', except instead of money, I'm paid in 'feeling needed'. But now I've started seeing other people as hungry mouths that need feeding with attention, and I am so exhausted by them that I have no idea what my own needs are. So it's become my own hungry mouth that needs feeding. And feeding.

When I get home from the party I sit and eat for hours.

Someone in a meeting said that over and undereating wasn't their problem, it was their solution. For years it's been my solution for everything from run-of-the-mill loneliness to that gnawing sensation of not being enough. Smart enough, successful enough, good-looking enough, popular enough, productive enough – and it's worked incredibly well. Except that it doesn't work anymore and I have no other solutions.

I wait a few hours before calling Malin. I can hear Il Divo in the background, which is her painting music. 'Let me guess, you're already planning on undereating tomorrow and going to the gym tonight?' she says. Yup!

'I just don't get it. I've been doing all the right things and then this happens.'

'Well, how long since your last binge?' She asks.

'I don't know … two months?'

'And before that?'

'Three weeks?'

'And when you came into program?'

'Most days ...'

'And why do you come to program?'

'Because over and undereating is my go-to when shit happens.'

'Mine too. And the moment I think I've beaten it, it's back. But the point is to get out of that cycle.'

'I just wish I could eat like normal people. Everyone must think I'm some self-denying weirdo for not having *just one piece* at birthdays.'

Malin sighs. 'You're still looking for permission. What other people think of you is absolutely none of your business. When I finally got clear on my own boundaries, my whole energy around saying no changed. It was like people could tell that I didn't care what they thought and it stopped being an issue,' she says. 'But ultimately, it's not up to other people to get it. *You* have to get it.'

I found myself telling her about Gym Man. And Jade.

'Wow, that would make me really annoyed. Did you tell them to back off?'

'I don't want to offend them,' I say. 'And, I mean, the gym is a communal space. Technically Gym Man is allowed to talk to me.'

'Uh-huh,' says Malin. 'The thing about overeaters is that we smile and people-please in public, and then we go home later and eat over the resentment.'

'I'm not *resentful*,' I say.

Malin laughs. 'Mmmm-hmmm, who has time to be resentful when they're cramming food into their face?'

Touché.

'The point is,' I say, 'if they just stopped taking advantage of my good manners, there wouldn't be a problem.'

'Of course there wouldn't, sweetie,' says Malin. 'But maybe they're just being them. I remember when I first came to meetings I needed a lot of support. And I could tell who wouldn't be able to say no when I called, so I'd call them and talk about my problems for hours.'

I can't imagine Malin doing that to anyone. But I know what it feels like to be on the receiving end. To me, saying no to someone in need feels like a kind of violence. But I am so tired.

'I think I might actually have this thing called "The Mother Wound",' I say. 'I read about it on the internet. It's the primal pain of being brought up in a patriarchal culture that tells us we must remain small and put everyone else's needs above our own, and it's passed down through the matrilineal line. The ladies in my family are all batshit crazy – maybe that's what's causing me to overeat?'

'A-ha,' Malin says slowly. 'And maybe you just eat because you're a compulsive overeater?'

Malin very gently, in that way that makes me think it was my idea, suggests I try writing an *inventory*. It sounds like something masochists do when they want to hate themselves more. Basically you list all the shitty things you've ever done to people and all the shitty things anyone's ever done to you, including the people you're still mad at, and why. The whole thing is kind of forensic, and everybody in meetings moans about it because it takes ages and is very painful.

I'm not convinced, but Malin is right about one thing: not everyone who's in program has done it, but everyone with long-term recovery has, and they're the ones who seem the sanest and crap on the least about how their overeating is everyone else's fault.

What the hell. I've done enough cockaninny things lately that have worked; what's one more?

⁕

I begin the inventory by listing all the people and institutions I'm resentful of. I didn't think I held grudges, but in ten minutes I've already filled three pages. And I'm just getting started.

⁕

Something has been unleashed, something not good. I think Emily was right about the 'pink cloud'. The more I avoid using food as a coping mechanism, and fill pages of inventory with all the shit I'm pissed off about, the more something else is stepping into its place.

Feelings. Or, more accurately, one feeling:

Rage.

And it feels *amazing.*

Rage has taken up residence in my body like a demon. Every shred of anger I've ever pushed down with chocolate or baked white flour products is now surfacing at 2am. I lie awake in bed all night, on fire with fury, then leap up at the crack of dawn after no sleep, pull on my sneakers and march around the park fuelled by righteous anger, replaying all the times I said yes when I really meant gofuckyourself-NO. All the times I've listened politely to the Jades and Gym Mans, all the times I've done the right thing, sucked it up, made myself less so that someone else could be more.

'Oh, you're such a good listener!'

'Is that what you're wearing?'

'I refuse to talk until the topic is me!'

'Can you edit my book for free? It'll be great exposure!'

'Listen to all my work dramas at 2am because that's when I'm ready to talk!'

'Can you cover my yoga class for free? It'll be great exposure!'

'Nothing to see here. Smile! Get with the program.'

'Wow, you look really grumpy lately, what's happened? You used to be such a NICE GIRL!'

'Don't ask for more money! You don't want them to think you're pushy!'

'Did you tell him about my liver transplant?'

'Take off those headphones so I can tell you the rules of soccer and why you need to mix up your gym routine because I've been watching you creepily for six months and you're not doing it right!'

Jorge says that the more you clear up your shit, energetically speaking, the more that energy starts to rise. Could the rage coursing through my body 24/7 be my Kundalini rising?

I used to have somewhere to take this anger. If I wasn't in the binge cycle I was in the 'run' cycle, where I would literally exercise the anger away. I'd get on a treadmill and spend my run imagining fiery deaths, then leave the gym feeling exalted, calm and *ready to be the light.*

Now I can't even do that. Not long after the birthday party binge, I go to the gym, pick my song, and am just upping the incline on the treadmill when *fingers start snapping* in front of my face. It's Gym Man, motioning for me to take my headphones out.

'Yes?' I hiss in a way that I hope implies, *You better have something important to say like 'fire alarm' or 'Did you know your shorts are falling down?'*

'I've been trying to talk to you for ages!' he whines.

'I didn't hear you,' I say. 'Because I was running. With headphones.'

He looks taken aback, and his hand immediately flies up to touch his face thing (I think skin cancer?) and I immediately regret my coldness. Sweet Jesus. I'm a horrible bitch who can't spare twenty to forty minutes for a man in need of companionship.

I sigh. 'How's it going?' He instantly perks up and spends the rest of my run explaining how the Westminster system of government is different to 'what you might have seen on *The West Wing*'.

When I get home I force myself to meditate the rage away instead of having second breakfast. Gil pops his head in to ask if I want a cup of tea.

'Can't you see I'm meditating?' I bark.

He makes a pinched lemon-sucky face, which I think is supposed to be me. 'Isn't all that meditation and yoga supposed to make you a nicer person?' he says. Whatever the fuck gave him that idea?

・

I can't handle this Kundalini rising. For two weeks I've lain in bed, unable to sleep because every nerve in my body is plugged into an electric socket, lighting me up like a Christmas tree. *Two weeks* since I've been able to sleep more than three hours in a row. This morning I go for a run around the park, my mouth literally moving as I rehearse comebacks to fools I'd like to correct.

At one point I run past an elderly woman walking her dog. The dog whimpers and cowers under her legs. Is it normal to frighten animals and the elderly with one's face of righteous rage?

Every day I literally run myself ragged, but the rage just keeps coming. It's not even about anything specific anymore. I went out for dinner with Kate last night and all I remember is complaining to her about the energy vampires in my life, drawing breath only long enough to scoff a vegan salad before resuming. Jorge told us that clearing the chakra blockages causes energy to flow freely, but I feel like an ancient bottle of champagne whose cork has finally popped. Is there a way of putting it back in?

•

I've been reading Kate's rehab book, *Healing the Shame that Binds You*, and it's given me so many 'a-ha' moments about my childhood, and all the ways I was blocked by an evil, shame-inducing culture, that I'm considering offering myself to Oprah as a six-part documentary. Every time I read it, I weep for the innocent child I was, and the defence mechanisms she was forced to enact. Those bastards!

'Shame-bound' people are perpetually watchful of their own behaviour in case anyone sees that we are inherently flawed. And so we become neurotic perfectionists because we secretly fear we are wild, unruly beasts at heart. At one point the author talks about 'shame-bound family rules', and I list ours:
1. Don't feel
2. Don't talk about what's going on
3. Don't be difficult or a cause of concern
4. And if you do have to be difficult, go away somewhere and do it

in private, then come back when you're ready to perform
5. All of the above applies unless you're a man – in which case, at least try to be brilliant

On the plus side, it's really helping me write my inventory. The more I write, the more I see all the ways other people are responsible for screwing me up. This eating thing is all their fault; they've blocked my throat chakra!

•

Mum comes over unexpectedly one night. Once we're settled on the couch, she says, 'Well!' about sixty times.

'I just thought I'd mention something. It really isn't that important.' *Uh-huh*. She pulls an auctioneer's art catalogue from her bag and flips it open to one of the pictures up for auction. It's the picture my grandfather painted of her as a child.

'Is it weird to see it up for auction?' I ask.

'Not really,' she says, holding opposite elbows across her chest and smiling. 'It doesn't mean anything much.' The seller is listed as *Private Collection* and I ask who she thinks might buy it. Mum shrugs. 'Probably some merchant banker,' she says, pursing her lips.

I look at the painting. Like all my grandfather's pictures of Mum, her face is turned away. 'How do you feel about it?' Mum looks away. 'You know ... Like it's somebody else.'

'Don't you feel angry?'

'Oh ... not really.'

Well I am enraged on her behalf. Why can't she just say *it sucks*?

•

Being a nice girl has turned me into a seething, isolated, disconnected, raging lunatic. The question is, what am I going to do about it?

The answer comes in Dina's class on 'interpersonal skills for yoga teachers', which turns out to be assertiveness training for wet blankets.

'Feelings and emotions are just information,' Dina says. 'We get into trouble when we label them "good" or "bad", which we all do. And yoga teachers can *especially* fall into the trap of thinking we're so spiritual that certain emotions should no longer apply to us. An angry yoga teacher? No, thank you.'

Now I'm listening. Emotions, according to Dina, are just 'energy in motion', and we need to get that shit moving.

'Anger is one of the most misunderstood emotions. We know anger is *bad* without acknowledging that it's also *useful*. It gives us the courage to deal with injustice. Think about it – how do you feel when you're angry? You feel strong. You can stand up to bullies. But we can get addicted to it. We look for injustices to get angry about. We all know that 'angry' person. Sure, they've always got a reason to be angry, and if they don't, they find one.'

I think of the thousands of times I've shut that feeling up with food.

'So if anger is just "energy in motion", when you suppress that energy and don't let it move through you, anger gets stuck in your body and mutates, coming back as resentment, or passive aggression.'

Check!

'The key word when you're dealing with emotions is "appropriate". Sometimes anger *is* the most appropriate response. We deal with anger inappropriately when we store it and unleash it. We might feel unsafe expressing it at the time, or we don't want the other person to think we're 'not nice'. So we often store it up and direct it at someone else. Or ourselves.'

I smile, thinking of the nice people I'd like to unleash on.

Dina writes three columns on the whiteboard.

1. Passive   2. Assertive   3. Aggressive

'Most of us have a tendency towards one end of the scale. Not standing up for yourself is passive, but standing up for yourself *too much* can be aggressive. Can anyone give an example?'

I raise my hand. 'Bashing someone in the head?' Dina puts that in column three.

'Now what about passive? Let's say someone habitually tells you what to do. What would be a passive way of handling it?'

'Doing what they say then bitching behind their back!' says Annabelle.

'Errr, kind of ...' Dina creates a fourth column: *Passive-Aggressive*. 'Ideally you want your behaviour to sit in the 'assertive' column. What would be an *assertive* way of handling that situation?'

'Telling them to go eff themselves,' declares Goddess Jo-Jo, who has two teenage daughters.

Dina sighs. 'Assertiveness is more about bringing it back to yourself with an 'I' statement. Something like "When you ____, I FEEL ____ and I would prefer ____" is a good general script to use.'

The goddesses and I exchange glances. As if real people talk that way!

•

I've almost finished my inventory, but there's one column that remains consistently blank.

'I just can't see my part in a lot of this,' I complain to Malin over coffee. 'I am genuinely confused.'

Malin asks a few leading questions to see if I'll figure it out myself, but I do not.

'Maybe your part is people-pleasing and not enforcing your boundaries,' she says finally. Malin tells me some of the things her alcoholic/borderline-personality-disordered mother has said to her over the years, and I can't help but laugh – they're so pathologically cruel. Yet Malin doesn't seem bitter, nor is she denying that the relationship is painful.

'My mother's just doing what she's always done. If I expect her to change and hope that this time she won't say something horrible, then I'm the idiot,' she says, stirring her latte. 'The key is to create some boundaries for yourself and stick to them. For me, I can handle four hours with her at Christmas and a ten-minute phone call every Monday. If she starts to get horrible before the ten minutes are up, I just say I have to go and then I call her the next Monday.'

'Wouldn't it be better to talk to her about how you feel?'

'Why? She's not going to change, and anyway, who am I to tell her how to be? I just have to work out how to still have a relationship with her in a way that's not damaging to me. You can't expect people to guess what you need and then get resentful because they act in ways that give you the shits. All you can do is state your boundary, and if people still give you the shits … walk away and call them the next Monday. So to speak.'

'It just sounds a bit harsh,' I say. 'Like you're cutting someone out of your heart.'

'Think of it more like shaking someone off who's holding your ankle while you're trying to swim.'

Stone cold! I'm too embarrassed to admit to Malin that I still think it's my responsibility to be pulled down if it will make someone else feel better.

We pay for our coffees and hug goodbye on the street.

'Just one more thing,' she says, buttoning up her coat. 'People are used to you behaving in a certain way. When you have a boundary, be prepared for them to push back. But they don't have to like it, and before you know it they'll move on to someone else.' Malin smiles grimly. 'When I stopped reacting to my mother, she just started calling my sister six times a day instead.'

'Didn't you feel guilty?'

'Nope,' she says. 'I felt free.'

Tonight, after teaching my living-room yoga class, I'm determined to usher Jade out with everyone else. 'WELL GOODBYE, EVERYONE!' I say as people leave.

Jade hangs back and looked expectant. 'GOODBYE, JADE!' I say. She looks confused and sits down on the stairs. 'I just have to do up my laces,' she says, untying and retying her laces. I wait by the open front door. I feel like a bitch. Inhale – *Be the light.* Exhale – *from afar.*

Finally she wanders to the front door ... then turns around and starts talking about this new guy she's been seeing.

'I just don't know if he likes me. What do you think? Let me show you this text message he sent.'

She digs around in her bag.

'Actually, Jade, maybe don't,' I say. She frowns for a split second, then resumes digging for her phone.

'No really, Jade, I'm actually quite tired.'

'Ah, here it is, just take a look and tell me what you think.' She holds the phone in front of my face and I finally understand; there are some people who see your boundary, they just don't care for it. Time to lay down some 'when you ... I FEEL ... and I would prefer...' I take a deep breath.

'Jade, when you tell me about your personal life after class, I feel very tired, and I would prefer it if you spoke to a friend.'

She looks at me like I'm a dolphin that's just risen out of the sea and offered her tax advice.

'Wow,' she says, putting a hand on her chest. 'Well that actually makes me feel really hurt.' I'm about to go into paroxysms of apology, but she cuts me off. 'I've only been coming to your classes as a favour to give you teaching experience.' She snatches up her bag and leaves before I can respond – fortunately, because all of a sudden I find my throat chakra has cleared and I'm ready to fire.

I ring Emily, even though it's late. 'What a bitch!' I say. Then, 'Was I too mean?'

'Hell no! Her feelings about the boundary are not your responsibility. If you've got a yard and you plant a sign saying, *Keep off the grass*, if people don't like it they should get off the fucking grass.'

•

I'm on the cross trainer, listening to my music. I see Gym Man and resolve not to avoid him. He waves; I wave back, but don't take my headphones out. He motions for me to remove them.

'What time do you call this?' he says. 'You've been sleeping in! Getting lazy?'

I think they call it banter. I hate banter. 'See these headphones?' I say. 'When I'm wearing them, it kind of means I just want to be in my own space. Like, I don't feel like talking.'

He looks at me and blinks. Then laughs. 'Woooo, someone got out of bed a little cranky,' he says, holding up his hands and backing away. So easy!

But then he comes back!

'You know, gyms are a communal space,' he begins.

'Exactly!' I say. 'And when you keep talking to me after I've indicated that I'd prefer to be alone, I feel disrespected and I'd prefer you backed off.'

Gym Man gapes at me. 'Suit yourself,' he says. As he walks away I hear him mutter, 'Bitch.'

It hurts surprisingly less than I thought it would.

•

Dad has lost so much weight and muscle he now needs a wheelchair to get around. I stay over on the weekend so Mum can take a break.

How can someone who looks half-dead be so annoying? Dad issues minute-by-minute directives from his armchair. Apparently I have not been pouring his drink correctly.

Cirrhosis of the liver causes 'ascites', where fluid builds up in the abdomen and needs to be periodically drained via a tube. Because of the build-up of fluid in his belly, Dad is on limited fluids, and so beverages have become an obsession. Add encephalopathy – brain toxicity – to the mix and he becomes a dictator, supervising anyone foolhardy enough to offer him a drink. 'Now get the glass,' he instructs. 'Not that one, the medium one. Then get the soda water – yes, that's right, open the fridge. Now cut the lemon, just a small squeeze, then pour – no – STOP! What did I say? Just three-quarters full …'

I don't know whether to hand him the drink or tip it over his head.

I have accepted that I am no longer the bloody light; I now just want to survive the weekend.

To go to the toilet, he needs me to help him into the wheelchair, but he forgets that he can't do it himself. At night he wakes up every hour needing to pee and wanting a drink. I'm sleeping in forty-minute bursts and am down to my last patient nerve.

Sometime around 3.30am I wake to a sharp cry. Dad has tried to get into the wheelchair on his own and has fallen to the floor. Half-asleep, I clumsily lift him up and feel a sharp stabbing pain in my back as I do. It's the last straw. All the rage and frustration I've been feeling for the past several weeks shoots through me and I direct it all towards my ailing father, confined to a wheelchair, who has just fallen because he didn't want to bother me.

'You tried to do it yourself!' I scold when I'm finally wheeling him down the corridor. 'And where did that get you?'

I think I just found out how mad it is possible to be with someone you love who is near death. And how mean.

•

'I'm so angry all the time,' I tell Kate. We're having a drink in a city bar, and for the past twenty minutes I've been recounting my 'a-ha's' from the book she loaned me on shame and addiction.

'I'm learning so much about why I am the way I am. It's a revelation!'

Kate raises her eyebrows and says nothing. I suddenly stop and see myself as if for the first time. 'I've been ranting for weeks, haven't I?' I say.

Kate smiles kindly, as only a long-suffering friend about to tell you the truth can. 'About two months.'

'It's that shame book,' I say, slumping back into the couch. 'You said they gave it to everyone in rehab. Did you all feel like this after you read it? Really mad at everyone?'

'Oh *god*, yes!' Kate laughs. 'After they gave it to us everyone was so messed up about it, blaming their families, the rehab people had to arrange for us all to have individual counselling. But even that wasn't enough.'

'Everyone was still mad?'

'It got to the point where the counsellor had to call a group meeting and explain that our families weren't bad people, they were just raised in the same way we were – or worse – and were all just doing the best they could.'

'What, so they give you a book that tells you all the ways you've been messed up, and then say you're not allowed to be mad about it? How is that fair?'

'It's not that they said "you can't be mad" – obviously you can't pretend everything's fine if it's not. It's just that you can't live there.'

I sink back into the leather couch and stare at my empty glass, not feeling like a picture of an independent woman who has her shit together.

•

Malin has been at me for weeks to go to a special fight club she goes to, south of the river. She tells me it's for people who want to deal with family issues, and it's helped her to manage her relationship with her mum. The meeting is in the posh part of town. As the boutiques close up for the evening, women with plump, still faces totter into restaurants on stilettos, while buff men cruise the block, trying to find a space for their convertibles and luxury SUVs.

The meeting is held in a church around the corner from shops selling $5000 handbags. I guess dysfunctional people can live anywhere.

We're early, but there are already about forty people here. Some wave to Malin, and she greets them like old friends.

It's an eclectic group. Some look like they've had hard lives, others look like they have six boats and a corporation. One man looks like a comedian from a TV show, but scruffier.

'Is that ...?' I whisper to Malin. She raises one perfectly arched eyebrow at me and tilts her head. *Yes, but shut up because we're not supposed to show that we know.*

Malin steers me to two free chairs in the enormous circle. It feels too exposed. I shouldn't even be here, I only came to get Malin off my back. 'Don't be nervous, sweetie. If you get asked to speak, just reach inside and say whatever is true for you right now.'

It is surprisingly brutal. Nobody actually speaks about the dysfunctional people around them – they speak instead about how *they're* handling (or not handling) things. No one blames anyone else.

As I listen to them speak, I feel that sick sense of recognition. Defining your worth in relation to others. Constant anxiety about doing enough, being enough. Carefully judging the mood of everyone around you so you can give them what they want and not set anyone off. Feeling that you have to earn your keep on the planet as a human being. And always, always focusing on someone else's problems over your own.

Then it's my time to talk, and it's a completely new experience. I talk about growing up feeling like the only crazy person in the room, and everyone nods like they felt that way too. Is it possible none of us was crazy?

I feel like I've inherited things I don't understand. I keep thinking back to my grandfather's exhibition, and the image of his daughters wandering the gallery like ghosts. He spent his life painting humanity, but he was inhumane to those closest to him, and the consequences of that are woven all through my family. It strikes me suddenly that we've all been trying, in a way, to save ourselves from that pain, but we've only managed to make an art of covering up.

When I finish, Malin squeezes my arm and whispers. 'Great share, sweetie. Really solid.'

After the meeting I step out into the cold night air, everything looks different.

•

That night I have a gruesome dream. I'm in a cabin in the bowels of a cruise ship. We hit something in the water and the ship capsizes. I walk out of my cabin into the corridor to a scene of carnage. Disembowelled passengers line the floor, moaning in agony. Their intestines hang outside their bodies getting tangled up with other people's, connecting them by the guts.

I stagger through the carnage, not knowing how to rescue everyone, how to untangle their intestines and put them back. And then someone hands me a safety card with step-by-step illustrations: *If you find yourself disembowelled, and your intestines have enmeshed with someone else's,* the card says, *this is how to separate.* You do it by rocking together in unison until what's yours is taken back and what's theirs is taken back.

I wake up in horror and recount the dream to Gil. He gives me a hug. 'It sounds horrible,' he says.

'I just wish I knew what it was about.'

Gil looks at me as if it's obvious. 'You're kidding, right?'

'If you know, help me out.'

'Didn't you say you went to some group thing last night? For people who have weird families?'

'Yeah.'

'The guts intertwining. The safety card. It's saying "this is how you tell what's your shit and what's someone else's".'

And these are the steps to do it.

•

Dad was readmitted to hospital after the night he fell out of his wheelchair, and he's going to stay there until there's a transplant available.

He's asleep when I visit this time, but I think he knows when we're there.

'The doctor was here a minute ago but you *just* missed her,' says the nurse. I ask if she can call her back.

No one is very clear about what's happening with him. The doctors regularly update Mum, but she still brushes Liz and me off when we ask what's happening, as if we're making a big deal out of nothing. I have to try to piece together what's going on from Mum's vague recollections and what we see with our own eyes. What I see is someone thirty kilos lighter than my dad, someone yellow who looks like they'd be lucky to metabolise a Panadol, much less survive major transplant surgery. Which is concerning, because if they don't think he's fit enough, they won't risk wasting an organ on him.

I wonder if there's a way we can make him *look* healthier? Maybe some blush? One that blends nicely with the jaundice …

I hold Dad's thin hand and look out the window. He's in the best bed this time. The room has three other beds, but he's right next to the eighth-floor window. The thick glass drowns out all noise, and so everything looks peaceful: softly glowing streetlights illuminating leafy suburbs, the traffic just a silent glowing line of ants.

Eventually the doctor arrives, and I ask her how long Dad has until he's too sick to get a transplant. She starts talking about 'viral levels' and 'counts'. This time I just don't have it in me to nod along politely, pretending to know what she's talking about.

'Uh-huh. How long till he's too sick?'

She pauses. 'Just focus on this week,' she says eventually. 'This week he's good.'

'Okay, Dad,' I say once she's gone. 'Now she just has to say the same thing next week.'

•

Jorge has been saving the crown chakra until the end of the unit.

'The crown chakra is our connection to something greater than ourselves. It's about connecting to our spirit and, by extension, to each other, and to the greater, universal consciousness. Letting go of that sense of separation – that isolated "I". It's about recognising that when we harm others, we harm ourselves.'

He guides us into closing meditation where we imagine a single golden thread moving through the chakras, then up and out of the crown of our head, extending to everyone else in the room. Eventually all the threads meet up and connect to others around the world.

A lump forms in my throat chakra, and when I look down, Marta is pressing a tissue into my hand.

8

Surrender

Dad wakes up less often when I visit. When he is awake, he wants fluid more than anything else in the world.

Lately I can't seem to get more than two weeks abstinence from 'food fuck-aroundery'. Sometimes I despair of ever getting better. I haven't binged in a while, but the old food behaviours – restricting, exercising, obsessing and controlling – have crept back in.

'You may not be binging, but if you're still trying to control it, you haven't fully surrendered,' says Malin on the phone. Malin is all about 'Surrender':

'Malin, I binged again.'

'Blah, blah, surrender.*'*

'Malin, I didn't binge, but I actually think it's okay for me to not eat for the rest of the day because —'

'Blah blah blah, you're not surrendering. *You're not* letting go.*'*

Letting go? What is this 'Letting Go' they speak of? My motto is, 'If at first you don't succeed, squeeze the mother-loving life out of it until you do.'

'I don't get why saying I'm powerless over something isn't just admitting defeat?' I say.

Malin sighs. 'When you acknowledge powerlessness over something, it actually *gives* you power. But if you're trying to control it by finding the perfect food plan, or having rules around cheat days or whatever, it's like an elastic band. You control, control, control, and then you snap. Surrendering isn't about rolling over. It's about freedom. But if you're still getting something out of doing things your way, nothing else can get in.'

I think Malin has been trying to introduce the idea that there might be someone 'upstairs' who can help, but the whole concept is just so alien.

I ask Susan about the yogic view of God ('Is it Sutra 1.24: "An incorruptible form of pure awareness"?').

'Just go for your centre. Forget all that other stuff,' she says.

So, no help whatsoever.

•

I've started paying closer attention to the people in fight club who seem to be doing well. Better than well – I look at people like Emily, who no longer seem to struggle with food, and wonder why the hell they still come to meetings.

Emily shares her story today.

'I was a chubby teenager, but the bingeing and purging didn't really start until uni. And to be honest, it's what got me through,' she says. 'I did exactly what I was supposed to, studied hard and got a degree with straight high distinctions. I always thought the next milestone would be the thing that made me happy. Once I got a great job, I'd stop bingeing. Then, straight out of uni I did land my dream job.

'Of course, I didn't actually acknowledge that my dream job made me miserable, because that would mean I'd have to do something about it. Besides, I was too busy bingeing and purging. And the more I did that, the more compliments I got, so I kept on doing it and ignored signs that someone who worked for me was doing it too.

'Eventually, though, I could no longer hide the fact that I was miserable. So clearly what I needed was a great-looking husband, right? The next milestone, then I'd be set. And I'm a nice, charming girl —' everyone laughs, '— and so I found a nice, Sydney trust-fund boy, just like my hippy parents would hate, and we got married.

'While I was waiting to walk down the aisle, I clearly heard this voice telling me it was a bad idea. I knew it was a bad idea, but I did it anyway. Just stuff it down, get the pictures, get on with it. And on the outside we lived this amazing life. We were earning great money, travelled a lot and everything was great. And when it wasn't great, we found the perfect beachfront apartment. And when that wasn't enough, we started talking about buying a boat. That was the point where I could no longer kid myself that "the next thing" would fix how I felt.'

I look at her. She had all that? Why didn't she just get a divorce, sell the house and live it up? If I'd had her life there's no *way* I'd be sitting here.

'So I went back to my first solution which was controlling food. I worked out what was enough food to keep me alive and that became my focus. If I had a gram over that, that was it. I'd binge for three days. I'd go to functions where they'd have all this free food, and I would literally not hear what anyone was saying because I had a mental GPS on all the waiters so I could get the most food possible. If there was leftover catering from a meeting, I'd offer to get rid of it. Which I did in the car on my way home. One hand on the wheel, one shovelling hours-old pastrami sliders into my mouth, changing lanes on the freeway.' Now everyone is laughing.

'By this stage I'd done so much damage to my teeth that my dentist, who could obviously tell what was going on, told me if I didn't stop I'd lose them all. So I stopped purging, but I kept bingeing. Needless to say, I put on weight. I worked in fashion; in my world, you could be a serial killer and keep your job so long as you didn't get fat. My marriage started to go downhill – or rather, I no longer cared enough to pretend that it was what I wanted. I felt like I was going through the motions of someone else's life, but inside I was desperate to just stop being me, basically.

'One day I was about to cross the road when I saw a bus coming, and the thought came into my head that it would be just so easy to step in front of it. No one needed to know it wasn't an accident. At the last minute I stepped back, and as the bus went past I saw it had a huge advertisement on the side that said, *Are you depressed?*'

Everyone laughs.

'The ad was for a rehab centre. I checked myself in the next day for depression, but it soon became apparent that I had an eating disorder. I went to my first meeting in rehab, and even though I got abstinent pretty quickly, I knew that if I didn't keep coming to meetings once I got out I'd relapse. So here I am. And thanks to my higher power, I've been abstinent one day at a time since then.'

There it is again. God talk. Oh, Emily. Not you too?

•

While Malin says a higher power is about connecting to something larger than yourself, in yoga we're learning about marketing, and how to make everyone want us to be their yoga higher power.

Elena, one of the course coordinators, begins our 'Business Skills' workshop by pouring a bunch of brochures for yoga studios onto the floor. It's Sunday, so Django, as ever, is serenading us from the street below while we goddesses, with our unruly bodies and mismatched activewear, sprawl over the floor and pore over the brochures. Judging by the imagery, there are three ways to market yourself as a yoga teacher:

1. Aspirational
Typical picture: Skinny white lady (mixed-race acceptable) in hip yoga outfit perches somewhere improbable (boulder in flowing stream/boulder on beach at sunrise) doing complicated backbend/balance pose not achievable ever by majority of students. Let alone on a boulder.

2. Urban Zen
Vibe: *Me time.*
Typical picture: Close-up of water trickling over rocks/statues of Hindu gods or Buddha. Conspicuous absence of sticky-fingered toddlers, dust, annoying co-workers, and people saying, 'When are you having children?'

3. Divinely nonsensical
No images, just long passages of hard-to-read text in rainbow colours. The class and teacher descriptions have very little practical information, but liberal use of words like 'divine', 'mystical', 'flowing' and 'healing'. Words like 'price' or 'cost' are banished in favour of 'offering' or 'investment'.

As far as I can tell, none of this imagery represents my (or I dare say my fellow goddesses') experience of yoga.

'I am *so* not ready to promote myself,' says little Marta, gazing at a picture of a woman lying on her back in full splits, one calf tucked under her head, muscles rippling below her Lululemon crop top.

'Good!' Elena says. 'The point of this exercise is to notice how different images make you feel. Think about what kind of yoga teacher *you* want to be and how the imagery you choose to promote yourself can reflect that.'

I have absolutely no idea what kind of yoga teacher I want to be. Actually, I do: one who can balance her feet on her head while standing on her hands. In the surf. But humble.

'Then think about what kind of students you want to attract, and how your marketing will reflect that,' says Elena. 'What's *your* particular appeal as a yoga teacher? How can you communicate that?'

I think about my most recent yoga student, Gil's cousin Neddy, who came over to watch the soccer last night. He was stressed out because he's giving up pot, so I set him up on a bolster and sat next to him for ten minutes telling him to relax his tummy and breathe slowly. When he sat up and said, 'Oh man, that's almost as good as a joint!' he did actually look a bit stoned. Should that be my teaching tagline? *Almost as good as a joint.*

I'll get the chance to shoot my photos for the assignment this weekend. Gil and I are borrowing his aunt's holiday house for a few days. While we're away I need to squeeze in some teaching practice, so I ask Gil to be my guinea pig.

I feel incredibly guilty about having a holiday when technically I'm still unemployed. My latest interview, another 'watch how the monkeys perform in a group' experience, was for a job as a Christmas casual at a department store. I was the only white person in my group, and the only one to get a callback. So props to me.

We hire a car and drive along the winding Great Ocean Road to Apollo Bay. At work, Gil is designing a car racing game, but he hasn't yet gotten around to getting a drivers' licence. For the last stretch of the trip, where the road gets super windy and narrow along the cliff edge, I ask him to take over the wheel.

'For driving experience,' I say, but really, it's my way of getting him back for all the nights he's made me test his car racing game and give it a 'fun rating'.

'What are you laughing at?' he asks, white knuckles clutching the wheel as he peers at the road like a near-sighted octogenarian, a line of twenty cars crawling behind us.

'Nothing,' I say. 'It's just that from now on whenever I hear someone say that video games cause violence, bad driving and shooting people, I'm going to remember what you look like behind the actual wheel of an actual car.'

I still haven't been able to bring myself to tell Gil that I go to weekly meetings for odd people who can't manage one of life's basic functions. He already thinks I'm losing it after walking in on me pouring salt water up my nose. I'm afraid if I tell him about fight club he'll think I'm crazy, or make some horrible joke about it that

I won't be able to bear. It's too painful. And yet *not* telling him, and sneaking off to meetings I call yoga, feels like a secret that's getting bigger and bigger.

•

The first thing I do is ask Gil to set an affirmation at the start of the class ('Life is suffering and pain!' he declares) and it's downhill from there. Apparently literally everything we do 'hurts', and instead of exhaling deeply into the poses, he sighs and says 'mother-fucker-mother-fucker-mother-fucker' until he has no breath left. I crack it after the fifth 'mother-fucker'.

'You're not in *pain*,' I croon. 'You're *reaching your edge*.'

'I'm begging you, stop doing the voice,' he says.

'What voice?'

'The "I'm a calm yoga teacher" voice. It sounds so fake. Why don't you use your real voice?'

'As you well know, my real voice is a high-pitched lisp and I am *trying* to inspire confidence in my abilities!'

'But I love your lithp!'

'Please just shutthefuckup and do it!'

Somehow the whole thing devolves into a screaming match. As far as teaching experience goes, Gil is teaching me a lot about patience. And hopefully it's the last time I tell a student to go screw themselves for not following my yoga-structions.

•

Fish and chips on the beach at sunset. Lovely. Sometimes all you need is an appreciation of the people you're with and the present moment. Like the golden sun illuminating the water and the gentle breeze in your hair.

'Do you have your phone on you?' I say, jumping up. 'This would be a perfect shot for my yoga bio.' Sure, it's a cliché, but at least I'm not in a bikini.

'Yoga yoga yoga,' Gil grumbles, getting out his phone.

I attempt Natarajasana, a standing backbend where you balance on one leg. It will look good, but yoga on the beach is surprisingly awkward, and the wind keeps blowing my hair into my face un-serenely. The pain in my lower back has been increasing, and I wince as it starts to spasm.

'Are you okay?' Gil calls above the wind. 'You look really uncomfortable!'

'Just hurry up and take the photo before I fall!' Sure, grimacing in pain doesn't look like yoga, but he has no idea what Photoshop can do.

•

On our last day we go for a long walk along the clifftops. One of the things I love about bushwalking with someone is that there's a kind of silence you can fall into that feels more intimate than any conversation.

At one point we round a bend and the path dips into a lush green valley, giving us a beautiful and unexpected view of the sun setting over the hills. It's stunning.

We sit on a warm boulder and bask in the late afternoon sun. The light bounces off the ocean to our left and glistens off the wet fields to our right. As the sun dips down over the hills I hold Gil's warm hand and close my eyes. It's one of those rare and perfect moments.

Gil clears his throat and starts to fidget.

'This is one of those beautiful moments, isn't it?' he says.

'Uh-huh,' I say, opening one eye. Gil is not usually one to wax lyrical. Or get nervous.

Oh, Jesus.

'So ...,' he says, picking up a rock and trying to skim it off another rock, then breaks into weird, high-pitched laughter, like a hyena. 'It's one of those perfect moments, you know, HAHA ...'

Since the night we moved into our health hazard shack together, I've spent ten years proposing and he's spent ten years refusing, so that now it's almost become a weird kind of schtick for me to ask once a month: he refuses and we get on with our lives. At least, we did ...

Be cool.

'One of those perfect moments, that if someone was going to propose this would be the moment.'

Annnd ... silence.

I look at Gil. He's gazing across the valley in contentment, as if the conversation has reached its natural end. This better be some comedic, 'tell our children one day' warm-up.

The sun starts to disappear over the hill, dimming the valley, my hopes, and any chance Gil has of 'just forgetting this whole thing', which is what he'll ask me to do in a few moments.

'Yeah, so anyway.' Gil says brightly. 'I guess we should head back?'

'*What was that?*' I ask.

'What?' he says.

'You were going to propose just then.'

'No I wasn't! Oh, well, maybe, but whatever, the moment's gone. Pub?'

We take the shortcut back to the car. I use the twenty minutes to make Gil, in his words, 'ashamed, chastened, embarrassed and very sorry he ever thought about proposing in the first place'. Job done.

●

On our last morning I bend down to get milk out of the fridge and a searing pain shoots through my lower back. This time it doesn't fade. It hurts to walk. Gil asks what's wrong and though we've been learning about back issues in yoga anatomy, the only technical back term that comes to mind is 'stuffed'.

On our return, Susan books me an appointment with her

chiropractor. My only knowledge of chiropractors is that one gave my friend a neck adjustment which caused him to have a stroke, and Annabelle's chiro is telling patients that vaccines cause autism. Pain, however, makes you open to new things very quickly. Susan's chiropractor sends me for X-rays, then sticks them to a lightbox and points to an area of my lower spine. Instead of being straight up and down, it curves laterally.

'Maybe the radiologist got the angle wrong?' I say.

'Right!' The chiropractor laughs as if I made a joke. 'See how those vertebrae curve off to the side, like a snake? They're meant to be straight. And right in that crunchy bit there, your nerves are getting pinched. You have scoliosis.'

I blink at him. 'I can't have scoliosis. I'm a yoga teacher.'

'No kidding!' He gets out a pen and writes down all the poses I should never do again. So in answer to Elena's question of what kind of yoga teacher I'll be? The kind who instructs from a banana lounge.

•

'Is there a reason you're lining up your hips that way?' asks Susan. She's doing a three-day workshop called 'One class, many bodies'. It's all about how utterly inappropriate the poses we teach will be for half our students. It really inspires confidence.

Halfway through, she halts the class so they can gather around me in Trikonasana, a pose I've done hundreds of times before. 'Let me guess: you were taught to line your hips like they were between two planes of glass?'

'Yes. That's the pose,' I say.

'Okay, so you tell me,' she says turning to the group. 'What do you see?'

'She's collapsing into her joints then propping herself up by locking them!' 'There's no integrity to the pose!' 'There's no internal strength!'

Susan smiles at me.

'How does your lower back feel in the pose when you do it the "right" way, the way they do it in all the yoga books?' she says.

'It aches a little bit, I guess. But I'm probably just not flexible enough yet.'

'Right. So even though it's straining your back, you're forcing yourself into it because "there must be something wrong with you" that makes it hurt. Where did we get this idea that "real yoga" means pushing our bodies so they look like the photos on a studio wall? Here's a radical idea – your yoga practice is meant to serve *you*, not the other way around.'

Susan gives me the tiniest nudge and I fall over. 'Your deep, "feel the burn" practice is opening you up, but you're already open. When there's flexibility but no internal strength, you're actually vulnerable. There's no stability. Try it again, this time with the back leg out wider so there's more space for your hips,' she says.

It isn't the sleek, precise Iyengar I've been taught. 'This is not real yoga,' I grumble, though I do what she asks.

'How does your back feel now?' I have to admit it feels strong, and I'm able to breathe more deeply. Susan pushes me again, harder. This time I remain stable.

'Excellent. You've just found *your* Trikonasana pose, which will be different to the person next to you,' says Susan as I sit down with the others, suitably humbled.

'People come to your classes, you instruct a pose, and they do their best to contort their body into the shape you asked them because 'that's the right way'. What are they feeling? They don't even know. They probably don't even think it's important. When their entire practice is about trying to copy what you're doing, or the ex-gymnast slash dancer next to them is doing, they're not doing yoga, they're playing Simon Says.'

To illustrate how inappropriate certain poses are for different body types, Susan grabs a skeleton and shows us how women's femurs are set wider in the pelvis, and we have much more flexibility in the ligaments – all for childbirth. But when yoga postures force this area open, they actually create too much movement, which creates lower-back pain.

As Susan systematically goes through different postures using her male and female skeletons to show us how they fuck up women's backs, the yoga I know is dismantled, and I realise the mind-numbing, anxiety-blocking masochistic yoga pain I prided myself on enduring has been all for nothing.

'If it's bad for you, why do they make the pose that way?' I ask.

Susan rolls her eyes. 'Because the majority of yoga styles are created by men, for men, using male bodies as their models.'

Oh my god! Yoga is *sexist*.

On the second day of the workshop, Susan puts up a variety of X-rays from people with different kinds of joints. Looking at the huge variation in anatomy, it's so obvious there can never be a 'one size fits all' yoga, and no amount of stretching will allow some of us to do certain poses if our arm bones literally aren't long enough, or our vertebra haven't been worn down as child gymnasts.

Just for fun, Susan sticks up some of her own X-rays from her twenties, when a car accident broke her neck. Seeing the mess she was in at the time – and realising how patiently she must have worked to rebuild a broken body – gives me a newfound respect for her as a teacher. Then she puts up my X-rays.

'Ooh, look!' says Annabelle. 'No cervical curve!'

'And with that curve in your lower back, you can kiss goodbye to deep backbends. They'll just force the vertebra to go more deeply into that sideways curve,' Susan adds, grabbing her model spine, twisting it sideways and forcing it into a backbend.

'How is anyone going to take me seriously as a teacher if I can't do a decent backbend?'

Susan snorts. 'Be *grateful* for your idiosyncrasies – they'll force you to learn what it's like for your students.'

The session finishes with an exercise designed to get us to tap into our 'prevertebrate' movement patterns, which involves lying on the floor, flopping around like a fish. Sometimes I wonder if our teachers are secretly taking the piss.

•

I can't believe that just as I had to relearn how to eat, now I have to relearn how to move. I sneak off during the lunch break to pillage Target for cheap underwear with Kate.

'What are they doing to you? I mean, what's the point?' she asks when I tell her about the fish exercise.

'I think we're unblocking our psyches by unlocking our prehistoric body memory,' I say, wondering if there is such a thing as a bra that is both suitable for yoga and non-sex-repellent.

Kate has just returned from a whirlwind tour of Europe. Her partner is on lots of important sounding boards, which means Kate got to stay for free in the best hotels in Cannes and Monaco while he had meetings. I quiz Kate on the glamour: are the rich wives of board members (no husbands of board members) all snobs? Did she stay in the *To Catch a Thief* hotel? Did she meet a royal?

The answers are, 1: No they just complained about their spoiled kids 2: Yes, and it was not as fabulous as the Bendigo Motor Inn where we stayed on our last road trip. 3: Just Prince Albert.

That's when I notice we're in the maternity bra section. I look at Kate. She blushes. I burst into tears.

'That's so amazing,' I gasp, but she waves her hand.

'I always want to punch my friends in the face when they tell me they're pregnant, so I do know how you feel,' she says as I sniffle behind a rack of coral-coloured maternity knickers.

I can't believe my IKEA-disdaining cool friend is gestating a human! Next stop a move to the suburbs, Tupperware containers of lukewarm omelette and … real life with real concerns. I will instantly lose my companion in long dreamy afternoons that turn into cheap Chinatown dinners where nobody has to rush home to burp a dependant (giving my cat arthritis medication doesn't count).

I am happy for her, deep down, and looking forward to witnessing the Kate–Mother transformation. But I can't help feeling everyone is moving ahead with their lives while I'm still flopping around on the floor like a fish, waiting to evolve.

•

After months of 'guest teaching' I've finally been offered my first paid teaching job at the government department where I've been assisting Farah. I am a REAL YOGA TEACHER!

Unfortunately Susan's workshop is completely undoing everything I thought I knew about yoga. I turn up to the Department of Environment class I've been teaching on and off for months, but instead of seeing 'one class' I see thirty different, complex bodies, all with their own unique bone structures and conditions, and am thrown by how totally unsuitable many basic poses are likely to be for a large percentage of students. I end up racing around the class suggesting modifications, wondering why more people don't stagger out of the forty-to-a-class Live Free classes in agony (maybe because the majority of the students are six years old). My own practice has shifted dramatically. Instead of being the first to put my hand up for any demonstrations, and trying to keep up with the demi-gods who arc gracefully into advanced backbends and handstands, I'm up the back doing the easiest version and loving it. Instead of obsessing over how my body looks, for the first time I'm noticing what it *does*. And ironically, doing the easiest version of every pose, but being more mindful of how my body feels when I'm doing it, means I leave every class feeling strong and powerful. Not broken.

•

Dad has become increasingly distressed. He's started having seizures and the doctors have no idea why. I visit with Mum and we find

Dad sitting in bed beaming, his eyes unnervingly clear. The eyes of a savant.

'I'm the head of a new country.'

An idiot savant.

This happened last time too. Dad was so overloaded with drugs that he began to hallucinate – the nurses called it 'Mad Day'. 'When you see Mad Day, just smile, tell them you'll come back the next day and walk out,' I remember them saying.

I grin. 'What's your country called, Dad?'

'We haven't decided yet,' he replies.

'And what do you do in this role?'

'We have to make all the decisions.' He points to his phone. 'This is redirected from my desk.'

'How long d'you think you will be head of this new country?' my mother asks.

'Till they hold an election, I guess.'

He might be mad, but at least he isn't a dictator.

·

Dad's Mad Day continues. When he hallucinates, it just seems kinder to play along. Dad's often frightened. He has waking nightmares that go on for hours, but for every nightmare there is a celestial reprieve. He describes how in the midst of one of his nightmares, he sometimes senses the presence of a young man comforting him.

Sometimes there are breaks in Dad's craziness. One night I bring hair clippers to the hospital. Dad closes his eyes and submits, but I struggle to clip his beard around all the tubes.

'You're being very patient, Dad,' I murmur.

He opens his crazy eyes. 'And you're being very kind,' he replies.

·

The next time Mum and I visit he shows no emotion. 'I'm dead,' he whispers.

'He's been saying that all morning,' says the nurse.

'Well if you're dead, how come we can see you?' my mother asks.

'You're dead too,' he replies.

The nurse tells us to visit another day, but the next day it's the same again. I go in alone and he stares at me blankly.

'I'm dead,' he whispers. Outside it's the kind of beautiful wintry day where people who aren't conversing with the dead are frolicking in city parks, lying in the sunshine. I ask Dad to look out of the window and tell me what he sees.

'Nothing,' he replies. 'I'm dead.' Outside, a hobby plane drifts languidly through the sky, like it has not a care in the world and nowhere to be.

'What about clouds. Can you see clouds?' I ask.

He frowns with concentration. 'Yes. I can see clouds.'

'And trees?' I ask. 'Are there trees outside you can see?'

'I think ... yes. I can see trees,' he says.

He turns his blank eyes to me. I look for something else to point out, to ask him about. Anything to distract from where we are and the questions I have resorted to asking my brilliant father.

'You're dead too,' he says. 'So why are you crying?'

•

Overnight they moved Dad into the Intensive Care Unit. His seizures are getting worse and no one knows why. Mum, Liz and I make a rare joint visit. If there's one thing I've learned, it's that serious illness blows open the cracks in a family like nothing else.

We're only allowed to see him in pairs, so we end up spending a lot of time in the ICU waiting room. It can be a surprisingly buoyant environment, with mini family reunions and people sharing snacks. We take turns going in to see Dad and getting coffee to break up the intensity. And it is intense. At some points Dad is so agitated he tries to pull out his lines, and they have to shackle his wrists to the bed. You see it happening – the straps and buckles – and your mind goes completely blank. Susan was right – you can read all the yoga philosophy in the world, but nothing can teach you 'presence' like being with someone you love in intense suffering and not trying to change their experience.

Since Dad first got re-admitted, my mother has been upbeat and 'it's all a bit of a drag, isn't it?' about the whole thing.

Then one day it all turns to shit.

After almost continuous seizures they kick us out of the ICU while they do god-knows-what. It's the weekend, so the waiting room is unusually crowded with families chatting and catching up. Eventually the doctor comes out to see Mum, Liz and me in the waiting room. Usually my efficient sister takes charge and plants herself in front of anyone medical, but this time the doctor ignores us, kneels in front of my mother and looks right into her face.

'At this stage we don't know exactly what's wrong,' she says. My mother stares back. The doctor takes my mother's hand and looks her in the eye, speaking slowly, as if trying to force comprehension.

'I'm sorry. It's hour by hour,' she says, then disappears back into the ICU.

Mum closes her eyes and starts to cry, her whole body rocking. Liz and I lift her to her feet. As we lead her out, the waiting room falls completely silent. The families filling the rows of seats all stare at their hands as if a funeral procession is passing, when it's just the dam of denial finally breaking.

•

At the meeting tonight, a guy named Eric, who started the same time as I did, shares. I like Eric. We've chatted a few times and both agreed that program is fine and well but the God stuff is not for us. He always wears the same big black cape and fedora, and reminds me of André Leon Talley – if Andre Leon Talley were a nurse in a psychiatric ward and not the fashion editor at *Vogue*.

Eric is very big, and perhaps even here he's self-conscious about it. Because of that, he rarely talks about food. On the few occasions he has shared in a meeting, it's just been to recount the latest funny-horrific work incident: being projectile-vomited on, saving someone from their latest suicide attempt and then getting verbally abused because of it. He tells these stories with garrulous pleasure, as if our shocked laughter is his stress relief.

Today he tells this horrendous tale from his night shift at the hospital, but this time none of us laugh. He's quiet for a moment. 'One of the things I really struggle with in this program is that I don't believe in God or a higher power. But when I got home I was so fucked … I actually wondered what would happen if I asked God for help.' He looked at his hands and sucked in a breath. 'But when I thought about asking, all I could think of was God refusing my request.' He closed his eyes and began to shake. 'And before I knew it I was surrounded by packets of food.'

I know what he means, to be afraid that any God worth believing in wouldn't be interested in helping me.

•

Dad finally stabilises and is let out of the ICU and back into the ward. After the meeting I go and visit him. He's asleep for most of the visit, and when he's awake he asks for fluids, then goes back to sleep.

I've been 'stripping back' and 'healing' for months, but nothing feels like it's getting better – the opposite, it all feels like more work than ever. Yoga is work. Fight club is work. And staying present to what's happening with Dad, without running back to food or rage or blame, is the hardest work of all – and there's nothing to buffer it.

On the train home I plan my binge and buy what I need on the way back from the station. Gil's away for the weekend visiting relatives in the country, so I have the house to myself.

Afterwards I lie on the couch feeling nothing. It's such a familiar numbness.

The numbness was the destination, but right now it doesn't feel so good. It feels like a kind of death. What's wrong?

I stare up at the ceiling, and some kind of fight leaves me. In my head I hear the words *Aren't you ready to give up yet?* as if something outside is speaking the words straight into my brain. Something inside me breaks, and I realise there has to be something bigger than me out there, because I can't do this alone, and program and Malin aren't enough.

•

The next morning I drag myself to the Sunday meeting, sweating with anxiety and self-loathing. I don't belong with all these recovered people.

Emily is chairing. She raises her head when I walk in, takes one look at my face and nods me a silent welcome, and I know I'm exactly where I need to be.

When it's my turn, I open my mouth thinking *keep it together*, but I can barely speak through the tears. And these are no dainty goddess tears, but fat, salty, snotty tears that don't stop. There are times when just that simple act of speaking the truth, as messy as it is, and having people listen is more healing, more detoxing than any yoga I know.

•

The backyards grow bigger and leafier as the train travels deeper into the outer suburbs. The days are getting colder and shorter, and night is falling by the time I get to the hospital.

Dad's room is quiet when I arrive: his roommates are either asleep or in other parts of the hospital. He wakes briefly when I arrive, points to my pink drink bottle, then goes back to sleep. There is no dinner to be chopped up and fed, no vomit to catch, no fizzy lemon to find. Nothing to do but sit beside him and wait.

I think of a woman whom I heard speak at an event for organ

donors and recipients. She was about to host her son's eighteenth birthday when he took his new motorcycle out for a ride. Hours later, this woman gave her son's heart, kidneys and lungs to people she would never meet.

When you imagine being left behind after someone dies, you think that having time to tell them how much you loved them is the most important thing. But maybe it isn't. Maybe it's more important to know that on average you spent more time awkwardly clipping their hair in a hospital bed than berating them in the dead of night when they fell on the floor. If you can't say that's the case, what you need is time to redress the balance.

It is only possible to successfully harvest and transplant organs in one per cent of all deaths. Potential donors must, of course, be the same blood type as the recipients, and they can only be brain dead, not dead-dead, because in order to use their organs, it's vital for them to get fresh, oxygenated blood right up until they are harvested. That means doctors must ask families to consent to donation while the person they love is still alive. It is not an easy conversation to initiate, and there is little time to decide. If a person has indicated to their family their preference to donate, it can make that final decision – and its repercussions – that much easier. We agreed to do the TV show documenting Dad's transplant the first time around in order, as the producers said, to get people to 'initiate the conversation'. But ultimately it's up to their family.

Perhaps no one knows this better than my father. Mum told me that the producers asked Dad to dig out a photo of his brother Mark for the show, but in the end, the scenes relating to Mark were cut. Dad only spoke to me about his brother once. It was when he told me he needed a second transplant.

Mark was a year younger than Dad and had followed him to Melbourne from their home in country Victoria. He enrolled in the same course at the same university. When Mark was a passenger in a car crash, Dad got to the hospital first. The corridor was lined with Mark's friends but, Dad said, he couldn't bring himself to look at them. The rest of the family were hours away, so at twenty-three years old it was Dad who was asked to give consent for doctors to remove Mark's organs. Which he did. For years afterwards he had nightmares that in signing away Mark's organs while he was still alive, he had effectively killed his younger brother.

When Dad was at his sickest, having nightmares and hallucinations, he said he felt a presence: a young man curled around him in bed, cradling him in his arms.

Dad's hand is dry and cool. I think he has a week, two at the most before he'll be too sick for them to risk an operation, or a donor organ.

The view from the eighth floor takes in most of Heidelberg. The lights of peak hour move slowly, and out there in the suburbs televisions are switched on to the show I used to work on, and dinners are being cooked. It will happen to them too.

'They have three more days,' I tell my sleeping father. 'Then I'm stalking the back streets with a baseball bat and a blood-testing kit.'

Lights come on in the houses below while Dad sleeps beside me, and the ward is softly humming. Then something in my chest breaks wide open and the room is still with peace.

At quarter past six the next morning, Mum rings to say there's a liver for Dad. A real one. A healthy one. We get to see Dad before he goes in. The prep and surgery itself will take hours, and we won't know till tonight how it goes. But even if Dad doesn't make it through, the wait is finally over.

I ring Gil, who is still in the country visiting relatives, and he gets on the first train back to Melbourne. He gets home in the late afternoon and we go walking together in the park. As we approach my favourite avenue of oak trees near the fountain, my heart beats faster and my throat starts to tighten in that terrible choking feeling when there's something you want to say but can't. I'm so sick of being evasive and telling half-truths.

'What is it?' says Gil. I burst into tears. Gil holds my hand and we sit on the grass. I finally tell him about the binging and going to meetings. It's excruciating. It must sound so alien and freakish and stupid to someone who doesn't experience it. I brace myself for questions, but they don't come. Gil just puts his arms around me and tells me how much he loves me.

At nine o'clock, Gil's mum comes over and they watch *X-Men* on the couch while I pace behind them. It's the kind of movie that you can follow with only forty per cent of your attention and not miss anything. Junk food for the mind – just like the TV show I worked on what seems like a lifetime ago. Maybe I underestimated it. Maybe there are times when mental junk food is enough.

Five minutes before the end of the movie, Mum rings to say Dad made it through the surgery. She sounds exhausted. Gil and his mother whoop for joy. I sink into the couch, feeling a hundred years old.

•

If you want 'your stuff to come up', try to plan an end of semester gathering for yoga teachers. It's like herding cats: everyone is all 'someone else decide, I'm happy with anything, oh, except everything you've just suggested.'

One of the vegans is sulking because her suggestion of a vegan cupcake bake-off for her daughter's school fete was met with embarrassed coughs. And Jo-Jo ('Wherever we go is perfect cos we bring the prana, baby!') is just happy to be inhaling and exhaling.

Plus, we're all so in tune with our own needs now, and have the assertiveness to express them, that everyone requires a different venue. Legal Aid Grace Kelly is on a Vedic cleanse and needs to be somewhere overlooking the water to anchor her Vata energy, Annabelle can't eat anywhere the staff are 'too in your face' (make eye-contact) because it's like they're projecting their mood onto you and that's not cool. (I, of course, don't do brunch because if I skip breakfast I will die, and if I have lunch too early I will need a whole other meal in the afternoon, which will trigger overeating guilt and a need to call Malin to explain it all, the price of which will be an angel reading and listening to the latest on her cat, Monet's, stress-related UTI.)

The most recent plan is 'chant and chai' night at a local studio, where we can all sing our praise of Hindu gods none of us worship – in Sanskrit – sip lukewarm tea and, if it's anything like every other yoga event I've ever attended, smile at one another with gratitude.

'How about we go out, eat some food and get hammered?' I ask.

Fourteen goddesses look at me like I've just said I was having Bikram's love child. Then Annabelle roars 'YES!' and Goddess Jo-Jo says 'I am loving your decisive energy!' and it's decided.

•

The problem is our systems are too pure. We're in a karaoke bar and they're not behaving like goddesses. There have been scuffles over the microphone, someone is crying in the corner and it's the second time in a row Annabelle has made us sing 'Gangsta's Paradise', and since no one else can figure out how to work the song request buttons, we're stuck with her choices until either she gets tired or Marta wakes up and shows us how.

In the darkness, Legal Aid Grace Kelly does a solo, dirty dancing to Prince's 'Cream' before disappearing into the night. (To hook a tradie, I like to think.) One of the vegans ordered so much sake I'm going to hurl, but it was so she can use the cups for the vegan schnapps she's snuck in.

We eventually get booted out when the security guard can't get Jo-Jo down from one of the tables ('I'm not loving your energy right now!') and the vegan is busted with her BYO schnapps. Now I'm walking home but have stopped for a little rest. There's a weird noise when I walk. I don't like it.

2.10am: There is familiar person. Did I ring him? He is walking towards me.

2.15am: 'What's that rattling sound?' says Gil. He is so smart. He shakes my coat, which makes the sound worse. He reaches into pockets and counts fifteen sake cups. Who put them there? What is that in my hand? A sake jug.

'Try not to stick this one up your nose,' says Gil.

Cleansing sake. Healing sake.

9

My Holy Goat

There's a difference between what makes a good story and the reality. What makes a good story is someone coming to a meeting and telling everyone how screwed up they were, then the story ends with the day they got on their knees, said, 'God, if you're real, help me!' and God entered their hearts in a whoosh of energy ('I just *felt* it, you know?'), struck them abstinent, and the only reason they still bother turning up to meetings is to give the rest of us hope.

The reality, for me, is that there are a few small barriers to getting on the God train:

1. I am genetically incapable of belief
I come from a long line of atheists who believe that anyone who needs a spiritual blankey has simply made a lifelong commitment to deluding themselves.

One of my earliest memories is my grandmother on my father's side driving by a church and pointing out all the 'CRAZY MICKS' outside. It took me many years to figure out that Crazy Micks was not some kind of discount electronics store. I'm not sure if it was the same church my grandfather was booted out of for the egregious sin of questioning the priest too closely, but either way, true love blossomed.

On my mother's side, Jesus was a quaint little trinket clutched by the lower classes. At my grandmother's eightieth birthday, she told us all about the day my mother rushed home to tell her some Good News about a man they'd learned about at school.

'He really is the most incredible man! He does miracles, and he turns water into wine!'

'That's wonderful, darling,' said my grandmother.

'But people were so mean to him and drove *nails into his hands*!' My mother wept.

'Oh, dear. What was his name?'

'Jesus!' sniffed my mother. 'No one *you'd* know.'

For his part, my father is the biggest atheist of them all, if you don't include the three weeks around the time of his first liver transplant when he wasn't. One day he told Liz and me about his new BFF who was having great chats with him – in the desert. That friend's name? Jesus.

'Which Jesus?' asked Liz. 'Old Testament or New?'

'Oh, definitely old,' he replied. 'You should have seen his angry face!'

My own religious education was fairly simple and came courtesy of Julie, my best friend in primary school, who became a born-again Christian with her mother when her stepfather left them for his secretary. That's when she told me the Awesome News not only about Jesus, but also his father, God, and the Holy Goat.

'The Holy Goat is everywhere and in everything, even me!' she said.

That sounded cool! But, Julie informed me sadly, as a non-Christian, the Holy Goat wasn't available to the likes of me, and I was forever locked out of God's love. What a bitch!

As soon as I got home I asked my mother, who was making spaghetti sauce, 'Do we believe in God?'

She studiously kept stirring the sauce. 'I don't,' she said casually. 'But you can if you want. And we did christen you as a baby just in case.'

But the next day at school Julie said my parents holding my sister and me over the kitchen sink while our new godmother (a lesbian!) doused us in champagne didn't count.

2. Among my acquaintances, admitting you believe in God is akin to farting at the dinner table

Clearly, any kind of investigation into a higher power will have to be done covertly.

I get an opportunity when Kate, who is on one of those magical PR lists where they send you free things, rings to say she has free tickets to the opening night of a comedy show by a celebrity atheist. The name of the show? 'God is a crock!' I surgically remove my yoga pants for the occasion.

The comedian, who grew up with a seriously screwy religious education, is a gifted performer, but anger rolls off her in waves and it's hard to relax enough to laugh. The show devolves into a two-hour rant.

How is it possible that atheists are the new rabid fundamentalists? It's exhausting. As soon as it's over, Kate whispers, 'Drink?' and we skedaddle.

It's true what they say about pregnant ladies: even with her black hair, black nails, black jacket and black shirt (only slightly bulging), Kate seems to exude a sunny wholesomeness.

In the crowded bar I ask Kate something I'd meant to ask for a long time.

'When you were using ... did you ever go to NA?' (I actually know a couple of people who go to Narcotics Anonymous, and they say there are cool groups there, just like high school. Needless to say, we do not have a cool group in our merry band of foodies.)

'*God* no,' Kate shudders. 'I mean I did go to one meeting. But that was only to score in the yard outside. Why do you ask?'

I gurgle something about the show and change the subject.

3. Assholes exist and innocent people suffer. Where is God in Syria?

I don't have a single clue. Not one. I don't think Palestinian children get shot by soldiers so that we can all learn a lesson in gratitude. I don't think Syrian children get chemicals thrown on them because God wants the rest of us to learn a jolly good lesson about free will and using it wisely.

What I *have* noticed is that it's often the people who've been through the worst hell imaginable who claim that it's their faith that got them through. And who is anyone else to say 'Sure, but if you look at the situation logically, you'll see very clearly that God Does Not Exist.' Maybe God is in the survival?

Equally, remaining closed to the idea of a higher power as a form of solidarity with people suffering seems like riding someone else's misfortune. Are we really honouring the people suffering in the world by renouncing faith from the comfort of our lounge room, or patronising them?

4. The scientific improbability of a magic man controlling everything from the sky

And if God can control *some* things ('It's a miracle I survived – that was God's doing') then why not *all* things?

I've watched enough 'quantum physics for duffers' documentaries to know that there are all sorts of whacky God-like phenomena that point to some kind of universal consciousness.

Personally I like the idea of God being something akin to the Buddhist idea of 'Buddha nature', which is a capacity for great love and wisdom that's present in everyone, we just have to wake up to it.

Ultimately I can't prove a higher power *doesn't* exist. In program, many people seem to skirt this whole issue by making their higher power mean 'common sense'. Or as one woman put it, 'My idea of God is Good Orderly Direction. It's the voice in my head that says "take a nap" when I'm tired, and "leave the room" when someone's a prick.'

5. Higher powers don't like cynics
I'm not the kind of person any kind of higher power would choose to help. I have mean thoughts. About rich people. And lucky people. And people who thank God at awards shows for choosing them and not the other nominees. And people who put soft drink in their baby's bottle, give them surnames for a first name and walk around on hot days in sunnies and a hat while their baby lies in the pram squinting into the sun. I also have spiteful thoughts about SUV drivers, people who enjoy watching animals forced to race for entertainment, people who say, 'I know, right?' and people who say 'disorientated' instead of 'disoriented'.

The truth is, there are some people in the world, like Oprah, (horrible childhood and decades of hard work notwithstanding), who are the preternaturally lucky chosen ones, and some, like me, who miss out on celestial help because of our giant festering seeds of doubt.

Take Jorge, who is forever banging on about 'divine consciousness'. Who cares if it sounds delusional? It seems to make him not only ecstatically happy, but also preternaturally *lucky*. He's always coming to class BEAMING (he speaks in capitals) because of some wacky coincidence (a KITTEN he just saw under a RAINBOW), that was surely a sign of the DIVINE IN ACTION. This morning he burst into class clutching an AMAZING FREE COFFEE from the new cafe manager downstairs who had somehow neglected to see me when I was there five minutes earlier. And despite the six hundred earrings, Hindu tatts and bald-head + mini-ponytail combo, even conservative-looking people go out of their way to help him. Even when things go wrong, he beams and looks for the divine lessons within. Jorge truly is one of those lucky few who seems to win the celestial lottery on a daily basis.

Since he's taking us for philosophy this morning, I've decided to figure out what his and yoga's version of a Holy Goat is, and believe in it. Two hours later I think I've got it.

The first thing to know is that yoga philosophy is actually very, very simple if you just remember they have six names for the same thing. So yoga *does* have something that equates to what Christians would call God, they just call it Ishvara. And sometimes Brahman. Occasionally Purusha. Pick one and go with it! A rose by any other name.

The second point yoga has to make is that we each have a seed of God, or Brahman, or Universal Consciousness, within us – like the Buddhists have Buddha nature. This seed is called our Atman, otherwise known as our soul, or 'Divine Nature'. Yoga, then, is the union between our Atman – our individual consciousness – and Brahman – divine consciousness. (You know those fleeting moments after a yoga class when everything feels like it's flowing? I think that's when your Atman is flowing nicely with Brahman. Maybe.)

Yogic philosophy says that we *all* have an Atman, or universal intelligence, within us, we just have to get rid of what blocks it and connect to it.

Troublesome thought #1: If *all things* have a divine nature, by that logic *I also* have a divine nature, even if I find that hard to believe. Is that even possible? Jorge told us a bit about Tantric philosophy ('What do you know about Tantra? Sex!' He yelled. 'Actually, there's a bit more to it than that'), and how at its heart, 'Tantra is the ability to see divinity in all things.' Even our dark, cynical selves.

Troublesome thought #2: If yoga is about getting rid of all the crap that blocks 'union' with this divine nature, then all we have to do is kidnap Rupert Murdoch, and ISIS, and put them in a room and make them do headstands? But how does that explain Gwyneth Paltrow? She's been doing yoga since she chucked Brad Pitt, and she's only slightly less annoying than a mosquito.

To illustrate, Jorge tells a story about getting sick in India and how he came home flat and unshiny because he was so disconnected. Somehow I doubt this very much. On Jorge's flattest day I would still need six coffees and a red bull to match him.

'So where *do* you get your energy from?' I ask. Whatever yogic elixir of goji berries and yak fat he's drinking, I must have it.

'Let me flip that around. Where do you get *your* energy from?' he says.

'I don't know ... vitamins? In food?' He wags his head: *try again.*

Annabelle raises her hand. 'From the *inside*? Like ... your Prana?' Prana is another word for 'life force'. And breath. Actually I'm not 100 per cent sure what it is.

'Close,' says Jorge. 'But what is the *source* of Prana?'

Clue! 'The Source!' I yell. 'Universal Consciousness! Like a little bit? ... In all of us?' ... Even cynical me?

'Not just a little bit.' Jorge smiles. 'What if inside you was the whole of the universe? And what if you considered the idea that you are not bound by the limits of your mind or what you perceive as the physical body, but rather that there is a universal energy, a life force that you can draw on whenever you needed it?'

Oh. 'Well ... that would be pretty cool,' I reply.

'So,' says Jorge, turning back to the class. 'If we all draw from the same source, then the next question you want to be asking is: How is that divine nature expressed through me? And what's the *next* step in bringing me closer to my source?'

While Jorge bangs on about a retreat he's leading to India to see Amma, the holy Indian hugging saint, I'm turning this over in my mind.

I have a divine consciousness that is connected to universal consciousness.

Even me. If lucky Jorge has it, and 'everything she touches turns into free cars' Oprah has it, then I do too.

And it expresses itself in me differently to the way it expresses itself in others.

And that's OKAY. That's a GOOD thing. Not a freaky thing.

How am I going to teach all this in my yoga classes? Between downward dog and cobra pose?

•

I come home on a spiritual high and find Gil absorbed in the highly pedestrian, earthbound task of stuffing rosemary and garlic into a leg of lamb. I plant myself in front of him and start explaining the yogic idea of Universal Consciousness.

'Oh god, no,' he groans as he tries to get past me to perform some mundane domestic duty. 'You come home every Sunday preaching that holy roller shit. Can't we just relax and watch a movie?'

Typical. I've come to see movies as bits of mindless entertainment that don't bring me any closer to my source. I suggest a documentary instead, and he unenthusiastically accepts. Honestly, I know Gil has an Atman too, but I'm seriously doubting that he even has a *desire* to connect with the Brahman, much less the ability. So at the moment Gil, too, equals 'not bringing me any closer to Universal Consciousness'.

Later, we're watching a documentary on the director David Lynch. Someone asks how he stays sane while directing, and he says, 'I meditate and get into the Atman.'

'See? Proof!' I say to Gil. 'I hadn't even heard of Atman before today, so it's a sign!'

'It's a *coincidence*.'

'*Coincidence*,' I inform him, 'is Latin for "God saying hi".'

Gil gives me a look that can only be interpreted as 'long sufferance' – or as I choose to view it, 'You're right, I just don't want to admit it.'

But in the morning I wake up and my spiritual high has vanished. I flip through my notes from Jorge's class the day before and all I see are two excited scrawls: '*Unite your* Atman *with your*

Brahman!' and *'Draw on life force!'*

What the fuck? And how does all this relate to food and keeping me abstinent? If I connect my Atman to my Brahman will I not want to binge?

I ring Malin and we arrange to meet at a spot on the bike path by the Yarra River. I wear runners, tracksuit pants and a hoodie. Malin arrives in platform heels, eyelash extensions and a denim jacket with a Matisse picture on the back. As in, a picture of her cat, Matisse.

I gabble breathlessly for ten whole minutes about the seed of Universal Consciousness, God and seeing the divine in all, until finally I start confusing myself.

'Are you finished?' Malin says, laughing. It's a weird feeling, being laughed at by someone wearing a photo of their cat. 'It sounds like you're all caught up in your head. Your higher power is personal, no one else can define it for you. Sure, you can choose a traditional religious God or yoga philosophy, but it's really about the relationship you have rather than nailing the perfect definition.'

'That's just it. I don't have a relationship. I don't even know what I'm praying to, and I'm certainly not hearing anything back. I'm just barely hanging on to abstinence – the cravings come back every time life gets difficult, and even though I've been praying for a job more than anything, I'm teaching two yoga classes a week for free and mooching off my boyfriend. I think my higher power is screwing with me. Or just doesn't exist.'

'You know, they have a saying that you can't be too dumb to get program, but you can be too smart?' I haven't, but I like that she puts me in the 'too smart' category. I think. 'Stop analysing it. You've said yourself that you've been insane where food is concerned, right?'

I grunt in reply.

'Right. So clearly you don't have the answers, but maybe there's a greater wisdom you could hand all your crap over to instead. It's not religious, it's spiritual. You have to work out whatever that power is for yourself.'

That's just too much choice. I just don't think I can be like, 'Alright then, I believe!' Either you believe, or you don't, right?

I point to a tree hanging over the river. 'So what if my higher power is a weeping willow?'

Malin shrugs. 'In my experience, faith isn't something I just have,' she says. 'I have to work at it. First of all, I had to at least have the willingness to *try* it. I obviously was not getting anywhere on my own, and I could see it made life easier for people like me. And from a purely scientific point of view, there are plenty of studies showing that people who have faith in something larger than themselves are less anxious and stressed than people who think it's all just them and that's it.'

I guess that's where I'm at now.

'Recovery is basically very simple,' Malin goes on. 'You can find ways to intellectualise and complicate it, but it works best when you just take the next step and forget about getting it "right".'

'But how exactly do you do it? Put a higher power that you don't believe exists in charge of your life?'

We get to a bench by the river and sit down. Malin turns to face me. 'I started acting as if I believed in something greater than me – praying, saying thank you when good things happened in my life – and over time my faith grew. More importantly, my life got better. I felt less stressed, less out of control, and good things started happening. I sold more paintings, my relationships improved and I'm generally happier. Maybe start with making a list of all the things you need your higher power to be, and act as if that's already in your life.'

'It sounds like self-delusion.'

'Why not just give it a try before you decide if it's for you or not,' she says. '"Act as if" for a few weeks and see if it works.'

'What if I "turn my life over" and my higher power wants me

to be fat?' Even Emily agrees that's a deal-breaker. 'Or sentences me to work as a toilet scrubber in a prison?'

'So when you make your list of what you want a higher power to be, maybe don't include "punishing bastard",' she says.

'I don't have any idea how this is stopping me from wanting to eat,' I say.

'Neither do I, to be honest. All I know is that it works for me, but any time I go back to thinking I can run the show, I get stuck back in that cycle of obsession and depression. It's not worth it.'

'But how do I actually *do* it? Turn my life over?'

'Just do the footwork. Do whatever seems to be the next right thing.'

I tell her I'll consider it. 'Good on you, sweetie,' she says, pulling a deck of cards out of the inside pocket of her denim jacket and grinning. 'Now, would you like an angel reading?'

•

Six months ago, if someone who was into cat analogies and angel readings told me to write a job description for an imaginary BFF and act as if they existed, I would have laughed in their face. Having said that, six months ago I was living on doughnuts one day, raw spinach and air the next, and visualising coasting my bike into traffic.

Job description for my Holy Goat
A. Works cosmically on my behalf 24/7. Even when I act like a moron. My Holy Goat doesn't hold grudges.
B. Pops better thoughts into my head than I am capable of on my own.
C. Wants me to have a career that doesn't involve cold-calling people.
D. Somehow, somehow, helps me eat normally and stops me from bingeing, starving and twenty-four-hour grazing.
E. Has a ~~GSOH~~ VGSOH ... because this whole thing is completely fucking ridiculous.

I ring Malin with my list. 'That's awesome, sweetie!' she says. 'I'm going to steal some of those for my higher power.' Cosmic plagiarism. Why not?

'Now what do I do?'

'Act as if those things are already happening. See what happens.' I will give this Holy Goat experiment forty days, like a spiritual *Rocky*.

In hindsight, maybe I should have put on my Holy Goat list 'wants to make me rich'. I've answered twenty job ads this month and haven't even had an email of rejection. But I don't know if my Holy Goat has much sway when it comes to the recruitment process.

What would Malin say? 'Do the footwork.' I send out a dozen yoga teaching resumes to gyms, workplaces and studios across the city, then I make a call I hoped I'd never make again. Now I have an interview at the call centre tomorrow.

•

My interview is in three hours. I start feeling hungry after breakfast and spy Gil's leftover pizza in the fridge. If I've learned one thing these past months it's that one bite leads to two days of feasting (and not turning up to things like job interviews).

Holy Goat, you're up. Stop me from wanting to pick up food.

Nope, still want it.

What would Malin— *'Do the footwork!'*

What's the footwork in this situation? *'Call someone. Write in your journal. Get on your knees and pray. It doesn't matter: the footwork is whatever you need to do to be able to feel the feelings you're trying to push down.'*

What feelings? I sit on the stairs next to the kitchen and try to relax my tummy. Oh! I feel like shit because I'm going back to the call centre, which I vowed never to do, and which absolutely no one my age is doing because they've all got careers, whereas I am just learning how to function! Interesting. What does that feel like? It feels like crap. What does crap feel like? Heaviness. Sadness. Loneliness.

Don't judge it. Just breathe.

And what's the next feeling? … Nothing. The hunger is gone. Time to get my interview clothes.

The call centre is on the main street of a gentrified suburb where wealthy retirees wear the latest hiking gear to walk teacup poodles to their local cafe. Outside the building, it takes me a full minute to contort my miserable mug into a 'hire me!' smile. I thought I'd never have to wear an office-appropriate blouse again. I used to be a contender! I can do so much more than survey people on how satisfied they are with their Yellow Pages delivery ('One to ten, ten being extremely satisfied, one being *as if you still use it?*').

Do the footwork. Act as if. I need work. I am doing the bloody footwork. Here I go.

2.32pm: How does anyone fluff a call centre interview? The two women interviewing me asked me to name an instance when I took initiative. I said, 'Rewriting the survey questions at my last call centre so I could get through them more quickly.' I thought this showed initiative *and* cost-effective efficiency. But they glanced at each other, frowned and wrote something on their notepads. Maybe that was the wrong kind of initiative?

2.34pm: What is happening, Holy Goat? Do you not want me to pay rent at the end of the month? Do you want me to live off alms from my free yoga classes? And if so … what are alms, and how do I cook them?

2.35pm: I'm at the tram stop when my phone rings. It's a friend-of-a-writer-friend. The uni she teaches at needs a new writing tutor. I start next semester. I can't believe it. Earning actual money from something I am actually trained in.

I get on the packed tram and see that the only seat is next to a woman in spiky black heels and a Vivienne Westwood leather jacket, the kind of woman who would never work in a call centre. She lifts up her sunglasses. It's Emily! I bound over.

'I think it might be a miracle,' I say after telling her about my do-the-footwork-call-centre-interview-screw-up-turned-better-job-offer. 'I've been acting as if a higher power exists and it's working. Or is it working because I'm getting off my arse?'

'Who gives a shit? If it works, it works. Trust, me,' she says, grinning like she knows something I don't. 'It'll change your life.'

·

Gil had been trying to get me to watch *Game of Thrones* with him for months, but it just looked like boobs and beheadings, so at first I said no. More recently, though, seeing an opportunity to get him literally onto the same psychic page as me, I told him I'd watch an episode if he read *The Road Less Travelled*, a classic text on spiritual growth. One chapter per episode.

But converting spiritual heathens proves to be a thankless task. After dinner we sprawl on the couch to fulfil his end of the bargain – him reading the book and me pretending to read a commentary on the Sutras, but really supervising him reading. So far it's been very disappointing. Instead of furrowing his brow in concentration and looking up from the book every so often to gaze into the middle distance and have spiritual epiphanies, every thirty seconds he lets out a huge sigh and mutters under his breath about 'patronising twaddle' or how 'everyone knows this stuff already'.

This confounds me. What feel to me like massive revelations, Gil just seems to take in his stride. Is it possible that he can't see the point of learning about evolving the self because he is already evolved? And more alarming, could it be possible that it's *me* who could learn from *him*?

Naaah, I don't think so.

Teacher training went late tonight. Graeme got on a roll talking about the Five Obstacles to Realisation, and I didn't get home till quarter to ten. I had planned on getting Gil to read more of *The Road Less Travelled* so we could discuss it and I could point out things he'd never considered before, but I'm so tired. So when Gil suggests *Game of Thrones*, I agree to one episode before we continue his reading. I mean, *he* continues his reading.

3am: The deal was Gil would read one chapter per episode, but somehow we've finished the season and thus *The Road Less Travelled* must remain un-travelled, at least until I get new leverage.

I'm yet to receive any direct communiqué from my Holy Goat, so instead I go for a walk in the park in the morning and mentally offload my problems to the trees. Why not? It's no more insane than kneeling before two planks of wood nailed together into a cross.

On another morning, I go to a class at the Live Free studio and am the only one who stays back for the optional meditation. As I sit, an intense loneliness that has been on the periphery for months suddenly overwhelms me, and I sit there, crying silently in the empty room like an idiot. After a while my breath calms and I start to feel hot. Then the weirdest thing; I suddenly have an image of myself in the studio, except I'm no longer alone. Sitting behind me is a row of Wild Things, the enormous beasts from the children's book, like an invisible, Wild-Thing cheer squad just for me. And that terrible loneliness lifts.

Is this really how my Holy Goat chooses to express itself? Invisible *Wild Things*?

My first class teaching at uni. Please don't let them be able to tell that I haven't had anything in print – or even internet print – for years. It's alright, they're just kids! Young adults. Totally fine. Should I wear jeans to be relatable? Or try to look professional? Jeans. Act natural. What do I do when I'm nervous in front of a new yoga class? I ask them to go into downward dog posture and focus on their breath. Can you do that in tutorials?

The room is on the third floor of an old sandstone building and freakishly hot. Outside the classroom, I say a silent prayer: *Holy Goat, please teach through me, please teach through me.*

It's their first class together, so there's no hubbub of chit-chat when I enter, just nervous silence. Their eyes bore into me. I set up my notes and pens and try to slow my breathing but get so light-headed I nearly pass out as I'm writing my contact details on the board. I turn around and there are still twenty young adults sitting at their desks, staring.

Act as if. Act as if you are a teacher. I look at my run sheet: *Introduce self.*

'I'm a writer and I've written for all these publications –' I meant to pass around some magazines but I'm literally pelting the front row with them – 'and I wrote a book and a movie and it got money and had a producer' – I leave out the bit where the money ran out and the project died – 'and I wrote for Australia's best-loved TV soap!'

See? I am a Real Writer. I deserve to be up here teaching you. *No one needs to know that all those projects fell apart, I got more or less fired, had a semi-nervous breakdown and now sit in a room with people talking about ways to cope with life that don't involve sugar and laxatives.*

Oh no ... now they're all looking at me with *sympathy* because my voice is shaking. *Please, Holy Goat, what is an acceptable version of downward dog?* Get them to talk to each other!

'Now, because one of the assignments is profile writing, as a way of introducing ourselves, I'd like you to interview the person next to you for ten minutes then spend another ten minutes writing it up as a profile, in the voice of your favourite publication. Then we'll read it out to the class.'

Lots of groans, but they dutifully start chatting. *Brilliant idea, Holy Goat! I got them to stop looking at me AND managed to tie it into their assignment. You rock!*

The rest of the class goes well, in that I stop sweating and they continue to think I'm their teacher until it's time to wrap up. Some smile as they walk out and I suddenly feel high as a kite. Teenagers are such arseholes when you're a teenager yourself, but these ones were really quite lovely. When they did speak, they seemed curious and interested and … not jaded. It's refreshing. At what point did I, and everyone I know, start thinking we had it all figured out? That we didn't need to wonder anymore?

Kate rings as I'm walking home to see how it went. 'I have no idea. But I felt less like throwing up as the class went on, and they had "thinking face" when they did exercises and I *think* they're coming back next week,' I say.

'Are there any little shits?' she asked.

'I don't think so. But they were surprisingly *quiet.*'

'That's first-years for you. They're all terrified of looking stupid in front of each other.'

They're terrified?

The following week they're still not speaking, except one student who raises his hand after I've described the next exercise and says, 'Um, didn't you get us to do this *last* week?'

Shit shit shit. Did I? Surely not. 'Yes,' I reply. 'And now I'm asking you to do it again because you are fundamentally different to who you were last week.'

Jesus wept. Is this what teaching is about? Tap dancing to get students to say something and passing off your own mistakes as learning opportunities? I must remember to be more Robin Williams in *Dead Poet's Society*, less Kim Jong-un.

•

Is life going well because my Holy Goat is real? After class I get three calls: one from a posh gym in the city asking me to teach Power Yoga, one from a yoga teacher I met at Susan's workshop asking if I can take over her class at a university college, and another from a woman who runs yoga classes for a law firm asking if I can teach 'Desikachar' style. Susan says Desikachar is not a fancy way of saying 'desk chair yoga', but a teacher who focuses on uniting breath with movement in a way that is safe for pretty much everyone, not just gym bunnies. I say yes to each and make a note to learn what those styles of yoga actually are.

The college class is a lesson in adaptability and 'learning from my students' (totally screwing up and putting it down to experience). The students drift in straight from the dining room, some holding plates and still munching. Assuming that, because they are youngish, they'll want a strong class, I include a handstand. I go around, physically supporting them one by one as they give it a go, then promptly drop one of the students on her head while I'm encouraging her to face her fears. (We haven't yet covered 'regaining teaching credibility' at teacher training, but there's time.) Eventually I realise that what they really want is rest. I've never met a more tired group of students than these teenagers: two fall asleep in Savasana, and though I'm tempted to leave them there, I have to wake them up because the Dungeons and Dragons group have booked the room straight after.

My first Power class is ninety-nine per cent awesome, one per cent aberration. The gym, at the business end of town, looks like something from *2001: A Space Odyssey*. Toned corporate-types slip out of the change room and attach themselves to complicated machines that look like they could make you a latte and filter your blood while they check your heart rate.

I'm running late, so Xavier, the 'wellness consultant manager' meets me at the door, clips a headset microphone onto me and pushes me, smiling, into a studio the size of a stadium with floor-to-ceiling mirrors. 'Namaste guys!' Xavier yells at the fifty people lying on the floor. 'Here's your new Power Yogi!'

Fifty faces look up at me expectantly. *Just do the next right thing.* Power classes are pretty athletic, so you assume people will have a certain degree of fitness and experience before they show up. I've planned an energetic class based around a handstand, which we will practise against the wall.

Halfway through the class I take a sip of water and the lid comes off my water bottle, soaking the front of my t-shirt. No big deal, I just ask the class to come into downward dog so I can quickly change my top while their heads are down. Then I keep them in downward dog a little bit longer, and I use a woman in the front row as a visual reference as I call instructions for the pose.

'Spread the fingers, push down with the hands and lift the hips,' I call to the class. I noticed the woman earlier – she's clearly an advanced student, but there's something else that impresses me about her. I just can't put my finger on it.

Though I'm looking at the woman, my focus is on my peripheral vision as I keep tabs on how the rest of the class respond to the cues, so it's only with half my attention that I notice the woman is not spreading her fingers.

'No, *spread* the fingers, *spread* them, or you'll lose stability,' I call out.

Suddenly the woman looks up at me. She looks confused and … annoyed? At that moment I remember what had so impressed me about her. She only has one hand.

Gil groans in agony when I get home and tell him the story. 'I can't go back,' I say. 'Maybe one of the goddesses could teach it?'

'You have to go back,' he says. 'And you should definitely write about it. It'll be therapeutic.'

I make a noise that sounds like a happy agreement, but my heart sinks. I haven't written anything beyond responding to job criteria for a long time. It's painful to be reminded of something I used to love but now can't do without suffering a panic attack. People say it all the time: 'Oh, you should write about that!' like it's so easy. But for me, writing, showing up at the desk has become an exercise in self-torture, showing up to all the ways I will never measure up.

•

Later that night I'm writing up the lesson plan for next week's writing class. It's on the subject of 'pitching articles'. Once again, I feel like an absolute fraud. I haven't written a word in months, much less pitched anything.

One of my talking points for the class is on maintaining morale, and why racking up rejections is a sign of progress because it means you're trying. Of course I don't believe that for a second – rejection hurts every single time, and the more you rack up, the more dispirited you are, until you eventually think you're so crap everyone laughs when your name comes up attached to something, and the powers that be are all living it up in a grand Deciding Room somewhere saying, 'Oh, bless her heart, is she still giving it a go?'

But fucking Malin. Her voice is like a mosquito buzzing round my head in the middle of the night when I'm trying to sleep. *Next! Right! Thing! Justdoit!*

Write an article, I tell myself – just one. It's just an article, it's not meant to be your life's work. It'll probably get rejected anyway, so fucking go to town and enjoy it.

I write quickly, then follow the pitching formula in my lesson plan step-by-step, and send it off to a magazine. *Now let go of the results, sweetie.*

It's the battles no one else sees that are the most significant. I go downstairs, feeling like I've woken a sleeping beast and slain the shit out of it.

•

This morning I go to a yoga class, and afterwards I stay to meditate in the empty room. As usual the first thing I feel in meditation is a crushing sensation of failure, but I suspect those feelings are present most of the time, and it's only in meditation that I slow down enough to feel them. (And I wonder why everyone rushes out of the room when it's time to meditate. Who *wouldn't* want to feel all their underlying crap?)

But this morning I'm so tired of battling that stuff that I just give up and sit in it.

Hit me with it, Holy Goat. Give me your worst.

It's like being shot.

There's a moment in the Bhagavad Gita where the warrior Arjuna is listening to a pep talk from his charioteer Krishna (who has just revealed that he's really God in disguise).

'Okay, Krishna,' says Arjuna. 'If you're really hot shit like you say you are, if you really are God, then prove it.'

And Krishna smiles and says (I'm paraphrasing), 'You poor little thing. If I showed you my true face it would blow your tiny mind. You want the truth? *You can't handle the truth.*'

And Arjuna says, 'Yes I can; go on then.'

Suddenly the skies open in an incredible psychedelic light show, then Krishna flies through the air, turning himself inside out and back again until Arjuna is so freaked out by the splendour that he begs Krishna to stop.

'See?' says Krishna, 'You've already peed yourself, and that was just a fraction of all my coolness. I'm God, now get over it.'

All of a sudden my heart feels like it's filling up so fast it's going to explode out of my chest. Energy zaps out of every corner of my body and beyond the borders of my skin. I'm so scared I might explode that I think, 'that's enough now', because it feels like I'm just a tiny container for this brilliant light, and the light is so big it's struggling to be contained into such a small vessel. And a voice in my head says, *This is all that you are and only a fraction. You can't even handle how much power you truly have.*

And then my own thoughts: 'You were looking for this ... in *food?*'

•

When I get home I open my email and see a message from the editor of a magazine about my pitch for a story on being a newbie yoga teacher. He not only accepted it, he asked for more. I don't believe it at first, and I have to read the email a few times. Outside, the chefs in the restaurant are banging pots and swearing in Italian, and life goes on.

You think life is in the big moments, where you stand up and get a certificate or a round of applause or marry someone or win a race. But it's making every mistake there is to make teaching your first yoga class and getting over yourself enough to enjoy it. It's walking out of a low-paying tutorial liking the students and liking yourself. It's sitting on the stairs and feeling the feelings and showing up to the next thing. It's getting the email you never thought you'd get again, saying that someone wants you to do the thing you love doing. Just another thousand words, please. And maybe some ideas for the spring edition.

The doorbell rings and it's our neighbour, an events caterer, dropping off a massive box of muffins left over from a breakfast job she's just finished. I thank her, and still in a daze, put the box on the desk and re-read the email. I feel a rush of elation (it is literally the first thing I've had published in five years – I am officially not a fraud), followed by nausea. They want more articles. I'm going to have to deliver.

When I look down, the box of muffins is just a box of crumbs. Two months' abstinence, gone. But that isn't the worst thing: I didn't even notice it at first, but for the past few weeks I've had a sense of being accompanied – of being held by something – and now I'm alone again with my black heart. I can already see what will happen. The shame that lasts for days. Then eating to numb the shame.

Just do the next right thing. I call Malin. Instead of the lecture I'm expecting about being in denial and abstinence not being something you can test out and play with, she is kind. She asks how my 'spiritual' connection is. 'I am too dark and cynical for celestial help,' I say.

'It's not your higher power judging you that keeps you separate, it's *you* judging you,' says Malin. 'You're not locked out, sweetie. It's guilt that's keeping you away from your higher power. Let yourself out of that jail right now. It's not what God wants for you.'

God. The G-word.

'But when you've done something wrong, shouldn't you …'

'*Be punished*? You atheists are so superstitious. God doesn't work like that,' she says. 'Anytime you drift out, just row back to shore. Skip the drama.'

I suddenly have no fucks left to give if my Holy Goat/higher power or whatever other name Arjuna's charioteer might go by is real or not. I no longer care if I look ridiculous, I no longer care to argue, because the results of my forty-day experiment are clear: whether it's real or not, things go better when I look for the good in things and 'act as if' there is some benevolent being operating in my life. All I have to do is 'the next right thing' and take my hands off the rest. If that makes me weak and in need of a spiritual blankey, so be it.

What I do know is that trying to dissect faith – find definitive evidence for or against – wrings all that is mysterious and wonderful out of life. And where's the fun in that?

Eight weeks after Dad's transplant we meet for lunch in a French cafe he likes in the city. His skin is a normal colour and there's a tiny bit of flesh and muscle underneath. It's like seeing a happy ghost, someone I thought I'd never see again.

We have French onion soup and steak tartare. It's nice to

remember that 'sane eating' means being able to enjoy food as well as cutting the stuff that triggers you. Dad is in fine form, cracking jokes and actually talking excitedly about things that have nothing to do with illness or viral loads or ... fizzy lemon.

I tentatively asked him about the hallucinations. Specifically, Jesus. He pauses for a long time. 'I know that I don't know,' he says finally. 'And that's okay.'

A week later he's back to ridiculing Christians, Jews, Muslims and Knights of the Jedi Order. But his lack of cynicism was nice while it lasted.

•

Some Sundays I get up at sunrise and jog through the park before teacher training.

It's the end of autumn. I jog down avenues of English oaks and Elm trees, their paths a glowing carpet of golden leaves. I still don't hear my Holy Goat, but I'm open to its possible existence. 'Act as if' said Malin, and so chat to my Holy Goat and wait for a reply. I never seem to hear anything back, but in the silence that follows, when all I hear are the leaves rustling with the wind, whatever worries I have seem to have lifted.

I get to my favourite part of the park. It's a straight path up a small rise, at the top of which sits a beautiful stone fountain adorned with Greek Gods and cherubs. This morning as I jog up towards the fountain, the sunlight is so clear, individual rays literally illuminate each drop of water. I know I'm exactly where I'm supposed to be, and I can practically hear the cherubs serenading me. Surely a sign, finally, that my Holy Goat really Does Exist, and Expresses Itself *in All Things*.

I'm so blinded by the celestial sunlight through the water that I don't notice a man smiling at me from the bushes behind the fountain until I'm metres away. My eyes track down and see that his tracksuit pants are around his ankles and he is holding his penis.

I freeze. Then I'm enraged. *What the fuck, Holy Goat? Do you want me to get this serenity thing or not?*

I look directly at the man. Late forties. Blonde hair. Thin. Human. And what a pathetic specimen if he needs to get his thrills by trying to scare women. Suddenly I hear Jorge's voice – *'If you only remember one thing about today, let it be that Tantra is the ability to see divinity in all things'* – and I remember the final point in my Holy Goat's job description: Very Good Sense of Humour. And then I laugh. A look of confusion crosses the flasher's face before he quickly pulls up his tracksuit and runs towards the carpark.

Watching him scurry back to his car, I mentally practise Tantra on that poor little fountain man, though perhaps not the kind he might have wanted.

10

Shadow Yoga

The winter semester break is almost here. As I walk to yoga at six every morning it's so dark it feels like the middle of the night. Fortunately, the Live Free studio is humid and womb-like, so it's easy to crawl onto a mat and wake up slowly. I leave once dawn has broken, and the early morning dew makes my nose run and my sweat freeze.

Later I walk home past student houses, window sills lined with half-empty beer bottles and overflowing ashtrays, feeling insanely healthy in my post-yoga glow. Every morning I pass the owner of the beauty salon on the corner of my street as she sucks down a ciggie in her white smock, her oxygen-starved skin suffocating under layers of bronzer. I want to place my sweaty palm gently on her arm and say, 'You know, darling, you'd look *so* much fresher if you took that $242 you spend on Crème de la Mer and spent it on a six-month yoga pass?' And though she would not thank me, I would know that I had led the horse to water and the rest was up to her.

Yogic smugness. No one ever admits to it, but it's either a blessing or a defect to be overcome, depending on where you are on the navel-gazing journey.

I wrote another article for the yoga magazine and have started pitching for another online news publication. I don't know how this happened – once upon a time that sort of thing would have had me quivering at my desk, but I just kept close to my Holy Goat and followed Malin's formula of *Just do the next right thing*, and then the news site said yes to the pitches and I've been taking one step at a time from there.

I've sent my old editor the one or two short stories I managed to choke out when I finished the TV show. Had I stopped to think about it I would have realised it was an insane thing to do, given how flimsy they are, but I was on a high and felt invincible.

•

Before the evening's philosophy class begins, Jorge gathers us in a circle. For the first time since I've known him, he looks flat.

He tells us that he's been 'reassessing where he stands' in his teaching and wants to 'maintain integrity with us' by keeping us up to date.

I'm confused – is he quitting teaching? During the break, one of the goddesses spills the beans. The founder of Jorge's yoga lineage was recently busted cultivating a sexual relationship with selected students he called his 'coven', under the guise of tantric guidance.

Unfortunately, his name is inextricably intertwined with that form of yoga, and so the many people around the world who, like Jorge, have invested faith, time and money in training and certification in that lineage are having to weigh up whether they want to continue or start again in a whole new style. But it's not just the money and time that's been lost. What I see on Jorge's face, that look of total confusion and disillusionment, is probably just a fraction of what some of the women involved with the teacher might feel.

One of the stories I'm researching for the yoga magazine is about sexual abuse in the yoga community. I wish I could say I was shocked by how many well-known swamis have preached celibacy in one breath and commanded their students to screw them in the next. Funnily enough, while the majority of people practising are women, the majority of teachers who found their own lineage are men (and when women put their names to a new style it usually takes many more years to build up a community of students). And yet they're less likely (actually I haven't read of a single case) to grope, rape or otherwise harass their students. I think that's what I like about Susan's approach: she points out when the yoga emperors have no clothes. Because just like that other bastion of abuse and cover-ups, the Catholic Church, yoga cultivates its own brand of mystique that discourages close questioning or challenging authority.

Whenever I go on about this stuff to Malin she inevitably trots out some tired cliché like 'What's happening in your own backyard?' followed by 'How's that inventory going?' 'Nowhere' is the answer. Since getting more work for the yoga magazine and teaching, the fun process of documenting all my resentments, plus all the shitty things I've done, has been surprisingly low on my list of priorities. But I still can't quite justify dropping it altogether. The people who are doing well in meetings often talk about its effectiveness – specifically its humility-inducing qualities – and the people who come to meetings and moan about the same thing week after week don't seem to be working the steps at all.

Malin suggests setting a date to go over the inventory together as a motivation to finish it. Personally I don't see the point of reading it out to her, but then, it wasn't by following my own logic that I racked up two months of abstinence.

•

My old editor, Andie, calls. She's read some of the stories I sent! But her voice is not jubilant?

'Some of them are great but, let's face it, they're a bit all over the shop, aren't they?' (All over the shop? – they are *delightfully eclectic!*) 'We're not sure this is for us, but we want to get you in for a chat.'

Okay, so it's not rejection, but it's not *yes please, keep going*. What's up, Holy Goat? What is your plan? The publisher's office is on the top floor of an old banker's building in the city, and when I arrive Andie ushers me into a meeting room with a view of the river. While she fetches the publicist, I stand at the window and gaze down upon the city. *One day I will* ~~make you my bitch~~ *serve you.*

'The problem is that no one knows who you are,' Andie begins. I like Andie's directness, I just don't like it when it's directed at me.

'I had a look online,' says Emma the two-year-old publicist, 'and technically you don't exist. You do know about Twitter, don't you? And Instagram?'

'Instagram!' I scoff. 'You mean, the platform for organic blueberry-eating narcissists?' Emma and Andie look at each other. Good start: reject their ideas and display an unwillingness to compromise!

'Yes, well, we need them to jump on *your* bandwagon,' says Andie. 'Look, this is a lovely little book, but the only time anyone publishes books of short stories by authors when nobody knows who they are is when they have *exquisite prose*.' She lets that hang for a moment. I suddenly realised how lucky I am that Andie had even brought me in for a meeting.

'You need to become *part of the conversation* so people are actually interested in what you have to say.'

'But what do people talk about?' I asked.

Andie gets Twitter up on her phone. 'Ah! Here's Sam's account.'

Sam is a pretty-boy author and darling of the left who lends his cuteness and puns to every current affairs program on TV, radio, podcast and print. I loathe him. Andie scrolls through his tweets, chuckling.

'See, here he's making a joke about what the Nationals leader said, and then all these well-known people retweet it, and it's like eavesdropping on a conversation.' Between people wittier, smarter and better connected than you.

On the way home I ring Kate. 'You're not on Twitter, are you?'

'Oh god, no. Wild West of the internet.'

I email Andie. *Kate's not on Twitter.*

Kate is a best-selling author, beloved by all. She doesn't need to be on twitter. You need to get your hands grubby and self-promote.

•

Operation Build Identity. I'm on an email list for an internet marketing guru called Marie Forleo, so I nick my friend's login details and unlock her secrets of branding. I ask my mother to take photos of me for a website and social media.

'Oh, you poor thing,' she says when I tell her I have to brand myself or sink into oblivion. 'There's something sort of shameful about promoting yourself, isn't there?'

I sit under the clothesline next to a writerly-looking brick wall. 'Don't worry, darling, we'll crop out the pegs,' mum assures me as I repeatedly throw my head back and laugh candidly. Internet guru Marie says that when building a brand it's important to know your 'brand personality'. Is 'Hot Doris Lessing' an acceptable brand personality?

Later I think about what Mum said. It *does* feel shameful to market yourself. To say, 'Here I am, look at me. I am something. I am someone.'

I agonise for hours over the first tweet, then check every few hours to see if I have any followers. Eventually a Russian sex lady follows me, and Andie. I think Andie did what they call a 'pity-follow'. But that Russian sex lady has no personal connection, so she must really like me!

•

Career-wise I may be trying to build an identity, but at the moment fight club and yoga are all about shedding it. For instance, one of the things that you're meant to do with your inventory is weed out all your character flaws and ask your Holy Goat to remove them. Purify. In yoga there are two approaches to dealing with bad qualities: number one, from my observation, is the 'spiritual bypass'. Anything that remotely triggers envy, rage, unholy lust or pride, you simply banish from your life under the guise of self-care. But I like the Bhagavad Gita's approach, where you get in there and slaughter them.

There's a famous section where Arjuna, the great warrior prince looks over the battlefield. His clans are at war with one another, and on the eve of combat, he confesses to his charioteer Krishna that he can't wage war against an army made up of members of his own family.

'How can I fight these people?' he says to charioteer Krishna. 'They're my family!'

'It's not about Arjuna killing his relatives,' Graeme says when we unpack it in teacher training. 'It's an analogy for being willing to let go of our negative traits, which are based on a limited sense of self. The fight is not between family members but between the higher and lower parts of himself. But it feels like a death, because it is like a death for the ego. We crave the familiar, even if it causes pain.'

I'm confused. Who *wouldn't* want to get rid of all their crap parts?

'It's not that easy,' says Graeme. 'First you have to be willing to see your own flaws. The Swiss psychologist Carl Jung explains this really well in his concept of the "Shadow". Jung taught that we all have aspects to our personalities that we don't like and so keep hidden, even from ourselves. But if we deny them, they have the power to run riot, so we project them onto others. The idea is that whoever we judge is actually mirroring something we don't like in ourselves.'

'But if you don't have judgements, then how do you know who you are and where you fit in?' I ask.

Legal Aid Grace Kelly smirks at me across the room. Just when you think you're becoming spiritually evolved, God shoves someone like Legal Aid Grace Kelly in your face with all her smugness and yoga perfection. Program says that harbouring resentment leads to eating your feelings, so I've been praying to my Holy Goat about Legal Aid Grace Kelly, but I'm not getting any answers. I've tried everything to dissolve my loathing of that woman. I've tried seeing her in white light. I've tried training my eye to sweep a few inches above her head when she's in the room, figuring that if I don't let her into my line of sight, one day the universe will comply and open up a sinkhole beneath her.

'Judgement has its place in learning and growth,' says Graeme. 'But eventually you need to come back to a place of "knowing innocence". Besides, the judgements we make are really what we see in ourselves, projecting the shadow parts we don't like onto other people so we can condemn them.'

Yes! I saw that exact scenario on *Wife Swap: Utah* last night! I tell the goddesses excitedly: 'Mormon Mum hated Slutty Mum's daughter because Mormon Mum secretly wanted to go back and whore it up in her high-school years.' I'm quite pleased about finding one of the yoga Sutras in *Wife Swap*.

Across the room, Legal Aid Grace Kelly whispers something to one of the vegans, who titters. *Smirk smirk smirk.* My face grows hot with embarrassment.

'I'm sorry,' says Legal Aid Grace Kelly, twisting her mouth to keep from laughing. 'It's just that you always seem to have such an extensive knowledge of commercial television.'

Oh! It's a classic 'I'm more spiritual than you' yoga burn. For the rest of the class I stew on how much I loathe her. Open my heart to that pious piece of Aesop-scented gristle? I don't think so.

During the break I ring Malin. She asks me to list all the reasons I hate Legal Aid Grace Kelly. 'Where do I start?' I crow, marching through the city, frightening Sunday shoppers. 'Prissy. Uptight. *Smug.* She acts like she's so much purer than the rest of us. Says snide things about others behind their backs,' I continue. 'Wears quirky, boho hair ornaments that look like they were designed by Swedish hipsters in an artisan colony.'

'Wow,' says Malin. 'I don't remember the Swedish hipster hair thing on your inventory, but the rest of it sounds pretty familiar.'

What is Malin saying?

•

Legal Aid Grace Kelly is not alone in her particular brand of toxic perfectionism. Anytime I have to interview a yoga teacher for a freelance story, a good fifty per cent of them will follow up every half-decent quote with 'but you can't print that', and then give me some lofty spiritual pronouncement so boring and sanitised it essentially says nothing. One of the interviewees insists I send her quotes back for editing, and then strips everything away except 'I have more than twenty years' experience in teaching, and my students see immediate results. Yoga is profoundly beneficial for both mind – and body!' I particularly like the dash. It's as if she's about to say something interesting – then doesn't!

My writing students also seem to be suffering from print-fright. So far their opinion pieces have all been written in this passive, boringly formal style, seemingly designed to put you off reading. I don't get it. They're supposed to be the brightest of the bright, but they seem to be writing opinions they believe they're *supposed* to have, rather than the opinions they *actually* have.

I've booked an empty office for consultations before my students hand in their final folios, and have noticed a distinct pattern in the conversations I'm having.

Girl student: I have this idea for my feature article, but I'm pretty sure it sucks.
(*They tell me their pretty good idea, which has clearly been agonised over.*)
Me: Excellent! Here's how you could make it work.
(*Spends ten minutes making suggestions and pumping up their confidence with reference to past classroom successes.*)

Girl student: Thanks …! *(Fiddles with neat document-carrying vessel.)* I'm pretty sure it won't go anywhere, but I'll try anyway. *(You get the feeling they won't get around to actually sending it anywhere.)* Thanks anyway for a great semester!

As opposed to …

Male student: So here's my idea. *(Presents half-baked idea with utmost confidence.)* I'm aiming to send it here, here and here. What do I need to do to make sure it gets published?
Me: Fix this point here, make sure you include that counterargument and send it to X, Y and Z.
Male student: Done! I know we only get one consultation with you, so I'll just email it to you to proofread.
Me: Nope! *(I'll mark it but I'm not their copyeditor.)*
Male student: Worth a shot. *(Grabs handful of dog-eared papers and sweaty backpack off table.)* Greatclassbytheway, thanksbye!

And you kind of know that even if they don't send it off, when they do figure out what they want, they'll go for it like a bloody rhinoceros.

> *Girls! We run the world, Girls!*
> *We run this mutha …*
> (or we will once we have been vetted by a panel of experts
> Fully Qualified to Give Approval, who have publically stated our ideas
> are officially beyond reproach. And then …)
> *Girls! We run the world!*

The students' next assignments are meant to be personal essays. I can't face reading sixty pieces on the topic of the evocative sights and smells of their dead grandmother's house, so I give them a pep talk about following their curiosity and showing up and revealing themselves.

'The point of your writing is not to *sound impressive*,' I say. 'The point is to make people want to *read what you have to say*. When you try so hard to 'get it right', your writing ends up being bloodless. *Nice*, but bloodless.'

They look at each other nervously.

'It's very different to academic writing,' one student says.

'Yes,' I say. 'People are supposed to enjoy reading it.'

During the consultations, one student was practically in tears about redrafting her piece because she literally could not figure out what her opinion was supposed to be.

'It's not "supposed" to be anything – it's supposed to be what you actually think, as long as you've got the arguments and evidence to support it,' I say, but she looks at me like I'm speaking another language. Of course, under careful questioning she found she *did* have an opinion, and seeing her piece it together was like watching that YouTube video of the chimpanzees who see the sky for the first time after spending their entire lives inside a research facility.

Wooo! Term break in two days!

·

I've finally hit on the perfect formula for both branding and getting more freelancing work: write an article calling people out in an amusing way, then … that's it. Just call people out in an amusing way. It's fun, it's easy and you never have to look far for a subject.

Admittedly it's a brand personality that gets a good workout among all the other freelancers, but it's a popular technique for a reason.

·

Getting my hands grubby with self-promotion requires a lot of purifying, so for the semester break a couple of the goddesses and I have booked in for a short stay at an ashram just outside of Melbourne. It turns out to be the very same ashram that Goddess Jo-Jo raved about at the teacher training information night, the one where she and her fellow goddesses 'liberated themselves from their outer layers, bathed in the beautiful Luna energy and rubbed oils into each other's bodies'. It just so happened that this annual Wild Woman Goddess Weekend was going to coincide with our stay.

'You sure know how to have fun,' says Gil.

Yes, getting woken at five every morning might not be everyone's idea of fun, but the rewards are an inner sense of cleanliness and purity, something my non-yogi boyfriend and his cousin can only dream about.

•

Annabelle and I drive to the ashram a day early. Being English, Annabelle packs as if we're going on a three-day survival tour of the outback. She has a three-litre water canteen, compass, heat packs and enough beef jerky to supply a vegetarian ashram population with iron for a month.

We pull into the carpark in darkness. Stepping out of the car into the icy country silence, I take a long, slow inhale of the eucalyptus. Heaven. Far from the city lights and pollution, the sky is crowded with stars.

We're met at the gate by a shaven-headed man in orange robes. He introduces himself as Swami something-or-other, though the label poking out the back of his orange polar fleece says 'Greg'. Swami Greg motions us to take off our shoes and leads us to the deserted dining hall, where some leftover vegetarian food has been kindly set aside for our late arrival. Large portraits of two men, the smiling head of the ashram's lineage and his Australian offsider, beam down over the dining hall. They look strangely familiar, but I can't remember where from.

'After the evening program, the ashram maintains silence until dawn,' whispers Swami Greg, and leaves.

Annabelle and I eat our lentils in silence. After teaching all week, it's nice to stop talking. I think of Gil and Cousin Neddy, whooping it up to *FIFA World Cup*. He was right. Yogis sure know how to take a holiday.

•

We're woken in the middle of the night by someone ringing a cowbell inches from our window. I peer through the curtain and see a bald twenty-year-old woman in orange robes wandering outside the dorms and thrashing her bell like a saffron town crier. In the darkness behind her, zombie-like creatures shuffle in the direction of a field. I check the ashram schedule with a cigarette lighter: *5.30am – Morning fire ceremony*. It seems like something that can be slept through.

At 6.30am I creep down to the yoga hall and try to blend in with the others shuffling in from the fire ceremony. The hall has floor-to-ceiling windows overlooking the ashram lake, and as a hundred of us watch the sun rise over the water, I'm grateful for the 'silence till after breakfast' rule. It's so nice to be with people without having to talk.

One of the rules of the ashram is that we are not allowed to wear form-fitting clothing of any kind (even yoga leggings) in case we arouse lust. Spicy food is also banned, and apparently so is walking at anything more than a semi-comatose shuffle. From the inoffensiveness of the spices wafting from the kitchen to the gentleness of the practitioners in their wide-legged tracksuits, who don't so much walk as gently glide, the whole place feels like one big tranquiliser dart. Everyone wears either white, yellow or orange – the different colours represent how 'realised' you are. (I do wonder what the purpose of realisation is if you have to wear special clothes to announce it … maybe you get to use the express queue at meal times?)

The yoga practice is notable in that it involves movements so gentle it feels like sleep in motion. Perhaps anything more vigorous would incite the flames of lust we keep hearing about? But the slow pace of the practice forces me to focus, and by the relaxation at the end I start to notice every thought and sensation like a silent witness. One of the things I notice is a kind of underlying 'bracing' type of tension. It feels like it's been there for a while. When the teacher asks us to inquire about any strong physical sensations that arise, I 'ask my body' what's up with the bracing and am suddenly flooded with fear. I haven't been using food to cope for months, but I'm full of fear that it's just around the corner, waiting to be picked up again. There's an expression in program that 'the disease is always in the corner doing push-ups', and I feel absolutely powerless.

'Have you noticed their eyes?' Annabelle whispers on the way out.

'Yes!' I say. Everyone either has the blissed out expression of the heavily medicated, or they look hard and angry.

After breakfast, a platoon of orange-robed women hands out brooms for the morning karma yoga. It's odd that so many of the people who wear robes seem like disapproving schoolmistresses. Whenever I cross their path I have the distinct feeling I'm getting the once-over. Are my garments suitably sack-like?

Something about this relentless focus on 'purity' makes me feel like the ashram itself has something to hide.

•

The next morning I'm woken again by the cowbell, but this time it's ringing inside my head. I shimmy out of my sleeping bag and peer through the curtain, straight into the eyes of the saffron town crier, who rattles her bell inches from my face and seems to be smirking.

I snap the icicles off my shoes and take my place in the zombie conga line, which leads to an enormous clear plastic tent in the middle of a cold, wet field. Holy Goat, this better be deepening our connection something chronic.

I shuffle into the purifying tent along with dozens of my fellow yoga-bots. Inside it's freezing and damp, and the fire at the centre provides all the warmth of a sodden candle. Two women with downcast eyes shuffle aside so I can squeeze between them on the ground. Dew quickly soaks through the straw mats and chills my bottom to numbness. Why must the journey to purity be so unpleasant?

Someone passes me a booklet of chants. After each line we mime throwing something from our heart into the fire. It's meant to symbolise chucking all the crap out of yourself (I think), but I feel curiously unmoved. Forty-five minutes of chanting in an icy puddle later, all I can think about is defrosting my arse-cheeks. And then the chanting resumes.

'Didn't we just do this one?' I whisper to the woman beside me.

'Oh, yes,' she says, eyes shining. 'But we sing it 108 times – 108 is a very auspicious number!'

Why. *Why* is it such an auspicious number? I suspect the answer is 'tradition'. Which means 'don't question it.' I'm all for purity – that's what I came here for. But it feels like someone has shrouded the ashram and its occupants in a heavy blanket, designed to smother any trace of spontaneity, energy or ... *spirit*. And telling people something is an 'ancient tradition' seems like just another way to control them.

I look around the tent at the earnest, cold, dedicated chanters. What have we ever done that needs purifying? (Except maybe have the odd thought crime about murdering Legal Aid Grace Kelly in her sleep.) Why are we the ones getting up before dawn to purify ourselves? What about the people buying disposable fashion that destroys our environment and enslaves Asian garment workers? What about the people flogging pink gendered bullshit to little girls and teaching little boys to be aggressive dictators if they want to get ahead? What about the politicians ripping public funding out of public health and education so they can give tax breaks to billionaire donors who spend their holidays eating unsustainably sourced salmon and banging trafficked women on oil-spilling yachts?

What about THOSE arseholes?

For distraction, I turn my attention to the booklet of chants. There's another photo of the spiritual head of the ashram. The way people worship him like he's a god makes me uncomfortable. I'm all for slaying the ego, but it feels more like people are surrendering one ego to service a larger one. Are we sitting here in the pre-dawn ice because this man told us to?

Before we left, I'd sent off a column to my editor. In the afternoon I stealthily scout around for internet reception to check if it's getting many hits. And holy crap! It's been shared dozens of times already and every time I hit refresh, more people are sharing it, commenting and tweeting. But that's not all – people are also sending me personal messages telling me to go to hell and die (in that order). Being Someone seems like a recipe for poor mental health.

You fucking lefty cunt, wrote a gentleman fan. *I'm not going to stoop to your level, but I hope someone drowns you in a soy latte till you die.*

The cowbell rings for a meditation session, but I ignore it and open another message:

I have reading you're articles and your the worst attitude writer I have ever read. Seriously I am just saying because someone needs to tell you.

It starts to rain and people hurry inside but I'm glued to the spot, hitting 'refresh'. Jesus Christ. Am I the recipient of these readers' collective shadow?

'Alice! Look at your legs!' Annabelle calls from the door of the meditation hall. I look down to find my legs covered in bull ants. I was so absorbed in the comments, good, bad and ugly, I didn't even notice them stinging me.

One of the conditions of coming to the ashram is that you do 'karma yoga', which is 'service through action', like working in the garden or kitchen. It's also an excellent way to offload the shit jobs that nobody wants to do, like cleaning toilets. Funnily enough, while women are zealously cautioned against wearing any kind of fitted clothing, the lust police are strangely blasé about the men taking their shirts off in the veggie garden.

Since all the jobs have been assigned by the time Annabelle and I report for duty, we head to the lake to enjoy the serenity.

A woman in orange robes steps into our path. 'Where do you think you're going?' she says. I tell her there were no jobs left so we're going to go down to the water.

'So what if there are no jobs left? Karma yoga is about *humility*,' she says, handing us brooms. 'Sweep this path till the bell rings.'

I looked at the stone path. It's clean. I look at the sun glistening on the lake's surface. 'But there's nothing left to sweep,' I reason. 'Surely it would be okay for us to enjoy the serenity of the natural world?'

'That's not the point,' she says. 'The point is *humility*.'

Really? The point seems to be about rigid control, but we dutifully make a show of sweeping, then once she's out of sight, Annabelle and I stash our brooms behind a rock. *My* kind of spiritual connection doesn't need to announce itself with robes or ugly haircuts. My Holy Goat and I are tight.

9.35am: I did not come here to let my hiking boots languish in a dorm that reeks of lentil farts. The ashram is in the middle of a beautiful forest, so far from civilisation that you can walk for days and not see anyone. I intend to commune with it.

9.50am: The forest is completely silent – we're so far in we can't even hear the cars on the road. So relaxing to finally get away from schedules and directions. I forgot to bring water, but we won't be gone long.

11.45am: There's nothing like getting up at the crack of dawn and walking for hours to whet the appetite. 'Shall we head back?' says Annabelle.

11.54am: Lost! We are lost!

12.45pm: We have four hours of daylight before we'll need to find food, shelter and a discarded animal pelt for warmth. I have been extremely calm so as not to alarm Annabelle. She doesn't realise that the Australian bush is a harsh and unforgiving place.

To keep her from panicking I tell her stories from my childhood.

'Isn't that the plot of *Stand By Me*?' she says. (Possibly – I am delirious from lack of food.)

12.48pm: Annabelle pulls out her enormous water canteen and I glug it down. (As I am at least five inches taller, I need more water.)

2.15pm: 'Surely they do a head-count?' I say.

'Don't you remember what Swami Greg said when we got here?' Annabelle replies. 'This forest is notorious for bushwalkers getting lost. He showed us that book at reception where people sign out when they go for walks and sign back in.'

'As if anyone actually does that.'

We can't panic. As the only person present with a hotline to a Holy Goat, I must assume command.

I close my eyes and pray. *Holy Goat, please show me the way out of this forest.* When I open my eyes I see a gap in the vegetation, which looks like a side path leading off the main track. *Universe, is this a sign?* A bird flies across the path. Definitely a sign.

'My internal compass says it's this way!'

3.16pm: The further we walk, the more convinced I am we're going in the right direction.

'Are you sure? It's been over an hour now,' says Annabelle.

Annabelle keeps making noises about retracing our steps, and it's getting on my nerves. I have to tune her out so I can listen to any guidance my Holy Goat night be trying to get through. *God, please show me what to do. And make Annabelle shut up so I can hear you better.*

3.36pm: Low blood sugar. I might be having visions.

4.07pm: Executive decision: 'Annabelle, we need to start looking for a tree hollow to shelter in for the night. We need to boot a wombat out of its hidey hole, nestle together to keep warm, and by dawn there'll be a search team of swamis out to rescue us.'

Annabelle protests, a sure sign of panic.

'Stay calm!' I bellow.

'*How. About. We retrace. Our. Steps?*' she says. 'As I have been saying for hours.'

'Genius idea!' (Though she has NOT been saying it for hours.)

4.28pm: The road! The road! I cling to Annabelle and wail, 'We were minutes from freezing to death under a strip of bark!' I can't help but be pissed off at my Holy Goat. I'm doing all the right things, and he can't give me a decent direction?

5pm: We burst into the dorm, having survived our Spirit Quest. The other goddesses have finally arrived and are lounging around on the beds, including Jo-Jo who booked herself into her second Wild Woman retreat, which will be on this weekend.

I hug them with an affection I didn't know I had.

∗

In the middle of the night, I wake up sweating from a nightmare. I dreamed about the black dog again, the one I used to dream about before I started yoga teaching.

It came back, and again it was trying to break out of the house to be near me. It was scruffier than I remembered, with grey, worn-out whiskers and patches of fur missing. Again it trailed around after me, nipping me occasionally, but it meant no harm – the dog was unskilled and messy, but all it wanted was my acknowledgement, to be allowed to be near me.

But this time it was accompanied by a white dog: a beautiful white husky. Unlike the black dog, it was fast, smart, glossy and highly trained. And deadly in its precision. I heard it snarl, and then it came for me in a flash of white. And I knew then that it could destroy me.

In the morning I take my porridge to a sunny spot away from the dining room and piece together my thoughts. It's not hard to figure out what the dream is about. The ashram's piety gives me the shits, but I've been chasing purity just as hard – albeit in a different way. I never knew purity, or the pursuit of it, could be so toxic.

Are we in the yoga community trying so hard to transcend our flaws that we don't actually accept them?

In the afternoon we have an hour of free time. My inventory is sitting in my bag, incomplete, and I'm finally so sick of procrastinating that I actually finish writing it.

Now that I can actually see the flaws on paper, I suddenly get what Arjuna felt on the eve of battle. If I let go of all these shit bits – the anger, the judgement, the pride – then who am I?

'It's not about Arjuna killing his relatives,' Graeme said. 'It's an analogy for being willing to let go of our limited sense of self. But it feels like a death, because it *is* like a death for the ego. We crave the familiar, even if it causes pain.'

For me, letting go of those parts that kept me going for so many years, feels exactly like a kind of death.

●

Full moon. I sneak my phone down to the lake again while everyone is chanting, and call Malin.

'I'm worried that working program is making me some personality-free robot like the people in the ashram.'

'You think those things are what makes you who you are?' Malin asks. 'It's not about purity. It's about recognising that you developed those traits as a means of survival, but they're no longer serving you. It's about being honest about what those things do *for* you, and what they now do *to* you. And only when the pain it causes outweighs any good are you able to let them go.'

I think of all the ways I try to build myself up, 'be someone' to mask feelings of inadequacy.

'It feels like it's not enough to just be "good". I have to be "special". *Exceptional,*' I say. 'So when my piece got accepted by the magazine, part of me said, "See? You're special!" And I just want more of that feeling.'

'What does it give you?'

'I guess security. If you're special enough you can blind people, so they can't see the bad stuff. But what it does *to* me is that it keeps me separated from people. Lonely.' I pause as something new occurs to me. 'It's weird how the further on you go, the less and less program has to do with food.'

'Food brings people to program, but it's really just a symptom of not having the skills to deal with life on its own terms. Even over and undereating served you well for a long time. It's only when it stopped serving you that you became willing to do something about it. Not everyone finds that willingness.'

Malin gives me a prayer to say when I'm ready. 'Asking your higher power to remove those traits – for you it's judgement, perfectionism, specialness – that's symbolic. It's about being willing not to hide behind all that bullshit you use to build up your ego. That's the stuff that keeps you separate. That's the stuff that keeps you isolated,' she says.

After we finish I call Gil, and in the background I hear soccer and various men, Gil's cousins, whooping.

'Ask her if they've done the oiled-up massage yet,' someone says to muffled giggling. I get off the phone quickly and turn away from the lake to head back to the chanting.

As I'm walking back up to the dorm I hear the distant rumble of drumming. High on the hill overlooking the ashram is the light of a distant bonfire. It's Jo-Jo and her wild goddesses beating the drum of sisterhood. I think of Gil and Cousin Neddy smoking spliffs and playing *FIFA World Cup* back home, and just for a moment I regret selling Jo-Jo and her sacred goddess rituals out for entertainment value.

●

Our last day. The saffron town crier has gone back to her job as a financial planner in the city (we bonded last night over vegetarian slops) and been replaced with a weedy teenage boy who just doesn't inspire the same fear. But today I leap out of bed for the fire ceremony: I have a job to do.

After chanting each mantra, the people surrounding me mime reaching into their hearts and throwing something into the fire. This time I join them, silently saying the prayer Malin gave me. If 'having personality' means standing on a tree stump obsessing over how many strangers are tweeting about you while ants bite your legs, maybe I can stand to lose a bit. When I open my eyes I see we're all still a bunch of messy, clueless people, just like every other person on the planet. And that doesn't seem like such a terrible thing to be. So that's it. I've been trying to show off, to prove how smart and wonderful I am, when all I need to do is own up to being a human being, as clueless as everyone else.

On our final night, dozens of us gather in the hall to chant Kirtan with some visiting musicians. I close my eyes and let the vibrations from the voices sway through my body. And for a little while, the separation between me and the others disappears. The rules of the ashram may be stifling, but is it possible they also create these tiny, perfect pockets of peace?

●

I'm back home, but something has shifted. There are still days when everything feels like a struggle, but a lot of the mental crap I didn't even know I was carrying around seems to be falling away of its own accord.

Something else has changed, but it's happened more

incrementally. Since committing to yoga and program, that weight of loneliness doesn't feel so heavy anymore. Like the mask I didn't know how to take off is slipping.

I mention it to Joel when I go to a meeting a few nights after the ashram. Joel, who I once judged so harshly. 'One of the biggest surprises for me in program was that when I stopped covering up, my relationships improved,' he says. 'The only people who drifted away were people I'm probably better off without. It's like that authenticity attracted similar people, and repelled people who were living with their own masks on.'

That made me laugh. Joel's vulnerability *had* repelled me when I first came to program, because I felt like if people saw who *I* really was they'd reject me. And I tried to pass this shame on to other people by judging them. Sometimes I think that the most 'healing' thing I ever did was tell the truth in that first meeting. When I went there to get tips on controlling food, I didn't realise that coming out of hiding and letting yourself be truly seen is the most purifying act of all.

I've been trying to get in touch with Emily for weeks but she hasn't been answering her phone. The last time I saw her, she spoke about courage. How she admired my courage in showing up to that first meeting and being honest. I hadn't ever thought of myself that way before. At the time I thought of what Malin says: 'It doesn't matter what other people think of you. The only thing that matters is what *you* think of you.' Somewhere in the last few months since I stepped into this godforsaken *I don't know* space I've started to feel proud of myself.

And more than any karma yoga, it's actually incredibly humbling to be able to listen to other people in meetings, normal people – students, tradies, actors, even a detective – admit they haven't got it together. You can have the shittiest day and turn up in the foulest 'I hate the world' mood, and some stranger tells a story that absolutely cracks you open. It turns out that middle-class white girl problems are pretty universal, and the things that separate us aren't so great after all. And somehow God lies in this connection. At the end of every meeting we go out into the night and I see well-dressed and not-so-well-dressed people get into their cars, and I think, 'If I saw you down the street I would never guess this was going on for you.'

●

A few nights later I'm researching the story on sexual abuse in the yoga community for the magazine and I finally remember where I'd seen the gurus who founded the ashram. As part of a nationwide investigation into institutional child sex abuse, former students of a yoga community spoke about being offered to the community's 'spiritual leaders' for sex. It was the ashram.

Former victims, some just teenagers at the time, spoke of forced abortions, and being passed around different teachers. One spoke of being raped with a double-barrelled shotgun and being forced to drink the founder's urine as a form of contraception, all while other followers were ceremoniously tossing their impurities into a fire. One of his victims was only a young girl. She was told that the higher up the person who was abusing you, the greater your spiritual advancement.

Senior members of the community were complicit in the abuse. One of the ashram's founders had a 'spiritual wife', who was in charge of bringing him girls to abuse. Everyone in the community would see these girls being led to the head of the swamis' rooms, and yet said nothing. I think of the sack-like clothes we were told to wear, so as not to incite 'lust'. What a joke.

The abusive swamis are long since gone (one died of the effects of alcohol abuse while leading an alcohol-free ashram), but many who I believe tacitly condoned the abuse by their silence were still there during my visit, including the woman who was running the ashram. Under questioning she said that the young girls at the ashram could be 'very flirtatious'. The hypocrisy is hard to stomach: forcing people to cover up while the spiritual head, and his underlings, were quietly procuring women for sex.

I try to reconcile that knowledge with my own experience at the ashram, which was at times blissful, at times shrouded in a confusing sense of oppression.

One of the Yoga Sutras pops into my mind – Sutra 1.49: *The inner state of knowing must come from within; not from someone else's experience.* Did all those people who knew about the abuse say nothing because they thought the abusers were their conduits to something greater? Is that what happens when we make another human being our Holy Goat?

For the article I'm writing on sexual abuse in the wider yoga community, I interview a woman who was abused under the guise of spiritual advancement by the leader of another prominent Melbourne ashram (in a different lineage). Something she says stays with me: 'I will never trust anyone who claims to be closer to God than I am.'

•

In spring, Malin and I meet at a cafe to go through my inventory. It fills three notebooks. Malin is dressed down for the occasion; fake fur and model make-up, but the heels are only 'high' as opposed to 'teetering'. We sit on one of the couches up the back, and I clutch my notebooks.

'I'm a bit nervous about reading this to you,' I admit.

'Don't be,' she coos, fluttering her spidery lashes at the barista. She waits till he's gone then turns to me, lowering her voice.

'Okay, sweetie, I'm going to tell you a joke that someone told me when it was time to do *my* inventory,' she says. 'A guy goes to read his inventory to a priest, and he's shaking with fear. "I've done some terrible things, Father," he says. "I had sex with a chicken!" And the priest pauses for a moment and looks sternly at the man. "Tell me the truth, son. Did yours die too?"'

Malin slaps her thigh and chuckles. 'So go ahead, sweetie,' she says, dabbing a mascara-threatening tear. 'Give me your worst.'

In the end, it takes two sessions to get through my inventory. We finish it off over dinner at an open-air Italian restaurant. It's a warm spring evening. Some kind of meeting has just concluded next door to the restaurant, and the attendees are all spilling in for coffee. Malin knows them all, of course, and if it isn't the doe-eyed Italian waiter interrupting my deepest darkest secrets by coming up to '*Bella Bella Bella!*' at Malin, it's a steady stream of dudes from the meeting.

'I'm so sorry,' Malin whispers after an ageing photographer pulled up a chair for a friendly chat that turned into ten minutes of trying to get Malin's number. No sooner has Malin fobbed him off than one of her old friends 'Damo' settles in to reminisce about merry drug binges he shared with Malin in days gone by.

'Damo!' Malin says nodding at me. 'I'd love to chat but she's doing her inventory.'

'Oooh, sorry! Good luck!' He wanders off to join the other table. Another man from the meeting walks in, clocks Malin and heads over.

'Stay away, Sammy! She's doing her inventory!' yells Damo, subtle as a truck. 'Good for you, darlin'!' says the new guy.

'It works if you work it!' calls Damo. So much for bloody anonymity.

'We can go somewhere else if you like,' Malin whispers. Hell no! Watching the hopeful romantic dance playing out in front of me is much more fun than reading my inventory!

Later, as I wait at a pee-soaked tram stop under a bridge in the seedy end of town, the warm evening breeze brushes over my bare arms and legs and I feel indestructible.

It's the first uni class of the new term and still no one is talking. I look out of the fourth-floor window. There's a cloudless spring sky, with students sprawled out on the South Lawn below. It reminds me of an afternoon three months earlier, when I looked through the window at a plane soaring through the sky and asked Dad to name everything he saw to bring him back to the here and now, because he thought he was dead.

Now I'm in a room of eighteen-year-olds for whom the worst thing in the world would be to get laughed at by their peers.

Before the break they handed in their personal essays. Reading a bunch of them in one go was mesmerising. I can't believe these shy people who barely say anything in class have such passion locked inside them! And they're all *completely mad*. Their writing is so funny and painful and vulnerable, and every one of their pieces is about *the same things*: belonging, loss, desire, hope. And yet when it comes time to workshop them anonymously, they clam up, terrified that their classmates will know the work was theirs.

Life is so goddamned short.

I try to think of the most ridiculous, dumbest interpretation of the readings and offer it up to the class. Laughter. Someone tentatively corrects me. Another person jumps in with their interpretation, then someone else proposes a different theory and connects it to one of the supplementary readings. And finally I sit back and enjoy watching the first real class discussion since I began teaching.

11

Dharma-Rama

Shortly after we returned from the ashram, Annabelle went AWOL citing a work crisis. It turns out the 'work crisis' was her calling her new boss a 'toxic motherfucker' during a counselling session, and she was counselled right out of a job. She took a payout, flew to Koh Samui, qualified to be a yoga teacher in a ten-day training course and, according to Facebook, now teaches at a five-star Thai wellness resort catering to wealthy executives and Russian oligarchs. Her Instagram feed is full of sunset yoga sessions, cocktails in coconuts and pictures of Annabelle in harem pants teaching in a beachside studio with the caption, *Love what you do and you'll never work another day in your life!* Even knowing that everything on Instagram is bullshit, I think she's genuinely happy – at least more so than when she was crying into her designer handbag in the fourth-floor ladies' bathroom.

Tonight Graeme devotes a whole session to the philosophy of dharma, as outlined in the Bhagavad Gita, which says we all have a purpose – a 'dharma' – and our job is to figure out what that is and do it without fuss.

Clearly, yoga and cocktails in the tropics make up Annabelle's dharma. I, on the other hand, would still very much like to know what mine is supposed to be. I'm currently teaching six yoga classes a week, writing like a mad person, and I'm still just barely making rent. Once I hit 'enter' on the final marks for the students I will halve my income. The thing is, I actually love tutoring at the uni, feel privileged to do it and adore each and every one of my writing students, even the shit ones, because they show up with such sincerity. When I'm teaching or writing, I feel like all is right with the world. But neither of them pay well, there's zero job security and I keep thinking I'm supposed to be doing something more impressive.

Malin says 'turn it over to your higher power' so often it has become meaningless. If my higher power has any big ideas s/he should try speaking up about it for once instead of leaving me to look for mystical clues in fountain drops.

In Graeme's Bhagavad Gita analogy (or as Jo-Jo calls it, 'rapping the Gita'), when Arjuna is freaking out on the eve of battle because he's had enough killing and pillaging, he whines to his charioteer, Krishna (really God) that he really, really wants to call it a day.

'Call it a day, motherfucker? Call it a *day*?' says Krishna. 'You're a warrior, so warry! (And maybe pillage!) You're not supposed to have *opinions* about it, you're just meant to get out there and do it!'

'Follow your dharma' is like 'follow your dream' except that it's not necessarily the thing you *want* to be doing, it's the thing you're *meant* to be doing. Which can be inconvenient; since the course began, most of the goddesses, like Annabelle, have either changed jobs or become extremely unhappy in the jobs they have. (Except Jo-Jo, who has 'always been living my dharma, baby, I'm just changing the *frame*'.)

As for me ... does the world need one more yoga teacher telling them how to stretch their pectoral muscles and giving them a feel-good 'look inside' aphorism while they're doing it? (And yet, I've been helped immeasurably by the right teacher at the right time.) Does the world need one more short-story author or pithy internet writer cracking wise and calling out? Probably not. (And yet reading what others have to say in these forums always makes me feel less alone.)

Graeme says our dharmas might not make sense from the outside. 'But if you're ever near someone who is acting in their dharma, it's magnetic,' he says. He tells us about a man he met who was shining people's shoes on Oxford Street in Sydney. 'He was so present, so precise and happy – who's to say shoe shining wasn't *his* dharma?' All well and good for Graeme to say – his dharma, in addition to teaching – was having an uncanny knack for playing the stock market.

'The Gita says it clearly,' Graeme continues. 'On action alone be thy interest, never on its fruit. It's also there in the Sutras. Sutra 1.12: *Abhyasa Vairagya*. "Work without attachment to the results." Here Patanjali is telling us to turn up every day to our yoga practice, but stop looking in the mirror to see if our poses are getting better-looking. Never do the job just for the money. Do the job for the sake of doing it well.'

Said as only someone who invested early in Google can.

•

To help us find our dharma, and as an early graduation present, Jorge is taking the whole class on a Your Life Purpose weekend retreat at a Buddhist centre in the mountains, which is 'infused with the transformational vibrations of all who have meditated before us'. We carpool up on Friday evening, and after being assigned an individual monk's cell for the weekend, follow a trail of yellow rose petals from our cells into the meditation hall, which had been decked out in spiritual doodads. I have to hand it to Jorge: he sure knows how to create a sense of occasion.

During the weekend, we will also be 'discovering our bliss, aligning with our Source and tapping into the wisdom of the group to reveal our Unique Soul Mantra'. (I sometimes feel a bit silly going away to do these sorts of workshops. Like, will it solve the crisis in North Korea? But then I forget about them and come back to me.) I'm really hoping my dharma isn't 'make minimum wage until your body packs it in, you can no longer teach and your fingers will no longer type.'

First thing Saturday morning we Uncover Our Bliss.

'There are four stages to living in your bliss,' says Jorge. 'First of all, ask yourself what lights you up? Something that makes the hours fly by, and that *gives* you energy, rather than taking it away?' I don't think 'watching Netflix with Gil' is what he means.

'To truly live in our bliss, we must first embrace our weakness. That thing we're afraid people will find out, the one that makes us different? It's also our greatest strength,' says Jorge as we take notes. 'Everything you've ever experienced, especially the hardships, have given you the unique skills and abilities to be able to do something in a way that no one else can. Look at your life experience to this point. What skills have you learned?'

To demonstrate, Jorge tells us that his first career was as an optometrist. (Jorge, resplendent in his star-spangled fisherman's pants, surrounded by rose petals, was an *optometrist*?) 'And what that gave me was the ability to look into people's eyes – *really* look – which has been a wonderful blessing in my work as a transpersonal healer.' He's right. Jorge really does have the ability to look *through* you in a way that dissolves your defences but doesn't feel creepy.

'The final question; of all those things you've listed, what gives you meaning? What is really worth pursuing? And here's a clue: it's not "when I get the money I'll follow my bliss". It's the *inverse* of that. When we know our soul's path and we *serve* with that in mind, then abundance comes to us in ways that we cannot even imagine.'

It's hard to argue about bliss with a man whose zest for life could power a lightbulb factory, but still, I have questions. What if we think we've found our bliss, but the abundance is not yet forthcoming?

Yoga teaching is enough to cover basic living expenses if I teach a dozen classes a week and never get sick or take a holiday. And though it's been a dream to earn a living wage (or even half of one) from writing, somehow in the writing world, flattery has become a substitute for payment. Current 'job offers' include:

We LOVE your writing – how would you like a weekly column? If it gets more than 300,000 clicks we'll give you $15 per story! Original content only.

We've been following your work and think you'd be a GREAT match for our readers … we follow the Huffington Post *business model…*

'What's the *Huffington Post* business model?' I ask Kate.

'The *Huffington Post* pay nothing but they've got heaps of readers (or they used to). People who say they use the *Huffington Post* model pay you nothing, and then hope that you won't notice they only have ten readers.'

I put the conundrum to Jorge.

'What if following your dharma is risky? And you don't know where it might lead or if it's worth pursuing?'

'Faith and action,' says Jorge. 'We rarely get to see the whole path, but if we're really honest we can always see that next step. Following your dharma is about trusting that the path will reveal itself when we're ready.

'One of the tricks of Resistance is "if I never try it, I can never fail". The point of dharma is that you've got to take your ego out of it. You've been tapped to do a job. So just "be the vessel" and let spirit, the Divine, work through you. Because when you shift your motivation from "what's in it for me" to "how can I serve", everything starts to open up,' he says. 'I'm not kidding – there's a whirlpool of energy around you when you change your motivation to one of service – you can't *not* succeed.'

It reminds me of teaching my first yoga and writing classes. When I stop thinking, 'Convince them you're a good teacher and don't fuck up,' and switch to, 'How can I teach this in a way that will be a) fun and b) leave them a bit better off than when I walked in?' the students (and I) have way more fun. Which I'm pretty sure equates to learning more.

In the afternoon we put the answers to all these questions together, and consolidate them into a succinct phrase beginning with 'I am the one who ...' It's incredibly cheesy, but as the goddesses read out their mantras, I'm surprised at how apt they are.

Back at our cells we find that Jorge has stuck a quote by Joseph Conrad under all of our doors: *Follow your bliss and the universe will open doors where there were only walls.* I wonder if that works in North Korea?

We are to reconvene after dinner because Jorge brought down a 'very special treat' for us to enjoy together.

>Things I hope our special treat is:
>- The new season of *Game of Thrones*
>- Jorge telling us what our dharmas are so we don't have to figure them out ourselves
>- Chardonnay and sleeping pills
>
>Things I hope our special treat is not:
>- Charades
>- A Heart-Centred Group Activity
>- Healing (in any capacity)

Jorge's very special treat is a movie (Good!) called *You Can Heal Your Life* (Sounds bad!). The gist of the plot is that a lady is unhappy because she has negative self-talk that becomes a self-fulfilling prophecy. So then she switches to positive affirmations and has positive experiences. So far, so rocket science. But they put something in these motivational movies that work on you like ecstasy. I find myself nodding along. After all, we are biologically programmed to look for the negative in order to survive, so countering that negative bias is something we actually need to be taught. But we've relegated it to the frizzy-haired-cat-lady section of the bookshop.

At the film's conclusion Marta is nonplussed. 'Well that's great for everyone else, but I am *so crap* at affirmations and I can never seem to get them right!'

'*You are programming yourself for failure!*' Jorge roars, and bans Marta from saying 'I can never' and 'I always mess this up'. Marta burst into tears.

'I'm not going to run out of the room like I always do!' Marta sniffs. 'I'm going to sit here in my heart space and feel!' And the goddesses dutifully form a heart circle around her.

Before we go to bed, Jorge announces that he's leading a tour through India at the end of the year, right after our graduation.

'*And* we'll be getting a very special treat! A trip to Amma's ashram!'

For years I've heard stories about Amma, the 'hugging saint'. Amma's powers were supposedly discovered when, as a young girl growing up in a small Indian fishing village, she had a knack for healing sick cows by whispering in their ear. People travel from all over the world then queue up all night to have Amma hug them. Dubbed 'the great mother', Amma, a large cuddly woman in her sixties, has hugged tens of millions of people worldwide. It's not just any hug: it's meant to be some kind of *transmission*. A hug from her is said to heal people from great pain, induce spiritual awakenings and just generally impart a sense of otherworldly, mind-blowing love.

It sounds like goddess sorcery of the highest order.

·

For our final morning's Closing Circle, we express the lifelong learnings we have gleaned over the weekend, and swear not to tell anyone our Unique Soul Mantras which are never to leave the sacred circle. Jorge gives us a quick reminder to watch out for 're-entry syndrome' (you come home on a spiritual high, only to be confronted with dirty dishes and asbestos).

When I get home I manage to keep my 'I am the one who ...' mantra to myself for about half an hour before I blurt it out to Gil. As I could have guessed, he falls about laughing.

'Oh excuse me,' I say, as he wipes tears from his eyes, 'is your Unique Soul Mantra, *I am the one who ridicules my beloved's heartspace?* or is it, *I am the one who sprinkles corn chips on the couch?* Oh, I know! It's, *I am the one who should go to Syria to see what real bombs do.*' (It's a low blow, but my heartspace needs strong defence.)

Gil says that 'on reflection' my Unique Soul Mantra is very accurate, and he won't tease me. Instead he'll get it printed on a coffee mug in case I forget.

In the morning I get a group email from one of the goddesses. *Is anyone else's partner acting like a* complete cock-head? Re-entry syndrome is real.

·

I return home to the final university teaching week full of pumped-up Robin Williams *Dead Poets' Society*-send-em-out-to-be-awesome enthusiasm. It might be a Robin Williams too far to make them do the kind of affirmations Jorge taught us, but I can at least get them to pitch their articles to actual publications instead of letting them languish in my marking folder.

One student clamps her lips shut and shakes her head. 'I'm not pitching,' she says. 'I'm not ready.'

'Why not?' I say. 'Your pieces are great. What have you got to lose?'

She glares at me as if I'm an utter moron. 'What do you mean, "What have I got to lose?" Like, what if they say *no*?'

She looks genuinely angry, and I'm surprised to see that the other young women are also frowning at me, waiting for an answer.

'Well ... you tell me,' I try Jorge's 'I know the answer but Imma make you say it' trick. 'What *would* happen if they said no?'

'I'd lose my confidence and never send anything out again!' she yells. Jesus wept, is *that* it? I give a 'you can do it!' talk but what I really want to say is, 'Who are you, to never have to face rejection?'

But as I'm walking home I remember how I curled up into a ball with my num-nums for a couple of years after my own long run of rejections, and the person I want to yell at most is myself back then.

•

Every morning I say my affirmations in the mirror. Jorge said I was blocking myself with a deep sense of unworthiness so 'I love you, I really love you,' is meant to be my opener. I giggle through the first few because the whole thing is so ridiculous, but after a while you get numb to the silliness of it and it seems to work.

The only thing more embarrassing than mirror affirmations is getting busted doing them, which Gil did this morning. It's actually more embarrassing than if he'd busted me making sweet love to the shower head (not that that's possible since ours is non-detachable – I'm just saying, I've heard people do it and it's supposed to be fun).

'Gross! That stuff creeps me out,' he says. 'It's just emotional masturbation. It's like a co-dependent relationship with yourself. Ugh.'

So far, so predictable. The next morning when I'm in the shower he comes in with the free takeaway coffee the bakery woman always gives him when he buys bread. (Gil, like Jorge, gets free stuff chucked at him wherever he goes, and is in fact miffed when it *doesn't* happen. *I* don't get free coffee. Or anything. Gil says it's because 'you look like you don't like people'.) There's silence for a moment, and when I peer through the shower curtain he's holding his free coffee musing at his reflection in the mirror.

'I'm a handsome man,' he says, nodding thoughtfully. 'These colours suit me. I look like Ragna from *Vikings*.'

'Ha!' I say sticking my head out. 'See? You're doing an affirmation!'

Gil blinks at me. 'That's not an affirmation. It's just a fact.'

The amount of work it would take me to reach Gil's base level of self-entitlement beggars belief.

•

Gil may think affirmations are bullshit, but they've been working a treat for me and the other goddesses. Since Jorge's retreat, Jo-Jo has manifested a job teaching underprivileged children in India, Legal Aid Grace Kelly manifested another fuel-efficient Volvo and I have manifested two high-paying weekly yoga classes at a beachside health club, plus a corporate yoga class.

The walk from the tram stop to the health club (like a gym, but more expensive and you get free apples) is like walking through a gated community without the gates. Or the people. I pass multi-million-dollar waterfront properties that seem entirely uninhabited. Occasionally a pack of MAMILs (middle-aged men in lycra) whizz past on $20,000 bikes or a 'well-preserved' woman power walks by with a small fluffy critter. Other than that the streets are deserted.

The gym is chilly, dark and expensive. Dance music pumps through the speakers, which seems at odds with both the time (9am Sunday) and the beach view. Jorge says that teachers need to create a sealed cocoon that makes people feel safe. I'd like to see if even he could transform the icy sweat-on-polished-concrete room into a womb-like yoga hub in the thirty seconds I have after Pump class finishes. As the student trickle in, I decide against manically trying to 'create community' in the brief moments before we begin, as most are busy Blue-Steeling their reflections in the floor-to-ceiling mirrors.

I put on some music and introduce the theme of the class. On the other side of the room, one of the students is texting.

Holy Goat, how am I supposed to teach connection to a higher source when their higher source is WiFi? Worse, how am I going to teach these people to embrace *messiness*?

Just get them into their bodies.

I get them moving and the class starts to engage. Maybe the

problem is me? Maybe I'm intimidated by the monied surrounds and projecting soullessness onto the students?

In the middle of the room a woman crunches her lower back every time we come into cobra pose. My own back almost goes into spasm just watching her. As the class continues a sequence, I position myself beside her and quietly suggest she modify the pose to protect her back. She makes something that sounds like a hiss. Surely not? I look at her, confused.

'I *said, could you go away please?*' she repeats slowly. 'You're putting me off.'

I look at her. Did I hear her correctly? She turns to me with a face like a Year Ten girl about to rip out her nemesis' hair.

'Of course!' I stutter and scuttle away, stunned. I want to run out of the room, but both the shittest and greatest thing about teaching is that you just have to keep going.

After class, some of the other students offer me a tiny smile. (Did they hear? Is it a pity smile?). It feels like a millilitre of Arctic ice melts.

I walk back to the tram stop along the deserted beach and call Susan.

'How do *you* approach classes like that?' I ask.

'I don't,' she says. 'I only teach people who are literally begging me for a spot in my class.'

'Oh, that's so helpful, thank you,' I reply and she laughs. Susan is semi-retired and says that as soon as her students start to shit her too much she's giving it up. For some reason this makes her students adore her even more. 'It's like teaching the corporate yoga class,' I continue. 'The place seems designed to strip away any trace of what makes us human. Then I come in telling them to embrace messiness and feel like I'm asking them to do a fart in a lift. How do you teach surrender when the whole atmosphere is about control?'

'You don't,' says Susan. 'You new yoga teachers are notorious for trying to fix everyone, but they don't need fixing and you're not

God. Bring their attention to their bodies, their breath. Believe it or not, your students have their own inner wisdom, and if you can create space for them to access it, that's all you need to do. It's not about you,' she says.

I thought I was being financially responsible in going specifically for higher-paying classes. But if both my dharmas are unreliable fiends, then they may as well be fun.

•

Something's snapped. Somehow in having my expectations dashed over and over, writing has become fun again. Since my old editor, Andie, said I could keep sending stories through, I've been beavering away at the short story collection. I've got a self-imposed deadline of Christmas, and have put myself on a strict writing regime: two hours in the morning before teaching yoga at lunchtime, then the rest of the afternoon in the Biochem library at the University. I'm on a nodding relationship with the other regulars – a couple of international students stranded over summer, and a guy who honks loudly while he watches Eddie Murphy movies on his laptop. Whenever I need to pee I make eye contact with one of the international students and they nod. We're like the Cosa Nostra of the Biochem library: we look out for each other, and newcomers must be tested for a week before we can trust them with 'pee-watch'.

Whenever I try to work at home, my strict writing regime proves to be an excellent way to get the house sparkly clean, answer long-forgotten emails and excavate body hair. It also seems to unearth a familiar feeling: the unrelenting desire to eat.

Eventually I ring Malin about it, and she gets straight to the point. 'What are you really hungry for?'

'Reassurance,' I say without missing a beat. 'I want someone to come and say "you're good at this, it's worth the pain and frustration and no money".' Malin laughs and tells me to send them her way.

'But I've seen your paintings and they're great,' I say.

'Well, most of the time I think they're crap!' she says. 'Listen, I think we all have a gift and it's not our job to figure out if we're "good enough". Our job is to surrender and do it. Because the tighter I hold onto the hope that my work will be successful, the more attached I am to the outcome, the more I start to hate painting.'

'But what about making a living? Is this my dharma to always be on edge, financially? I thought it was "do what you love and money will follow"?'

Malin laughs. 'Who the hell said that?! I don't have all the answers, sweetie. All I know is that every time I've been tempted to give up painting, something's always given me a sign to keep going. Once I was literally about to call the estate agent and tell them I had to break my lease when an old collector friend called to ask if I had anything for her. Besides, you love teaching and writing. And since you've been doing it, haven't you found a way to pay your rent? Haven't you always been taken care of, even if it was at the last minute?'

I love/hate it when Malin's right.

Does the world need more whimsical short stories from middle-class English lit dropouts? Is it my place to ask? I'm going to paraphrase Krishna in the Bhagavad Gita: 'Stop asking questions, shut the hell up and get the job done.' Or as Graeme's favourite Sutra says, *Abhyasa Vairagya*, 'Work without attachment to the results.'

My Holy Goat still has not revealed himself or herself in a flash of blinding *This is your dharma, Jedi!* But before every class and every writing session I say a little prayer that Jorge taught us about 'being the vessel' and keeping my ego the hell out of it, and everything seems to go okay. Malin says this is proof that my higher power exists – I suspect it's proof of the power of self-delusion. But if it works, who cares?

Today, for example, I was meant to teach a yoga class in the city straight after donating blood. I parked my bike in front of the building feeling so faint I had no idea how I was going to get through it, and halfway through the class I completely forgot where I was and what I was doing.

Please just teach through me. Let me get through the class without fainting or babbling, I thought. We sailed through the rest of the class effortlessly, and at the end one of the regulars came up for a chat.

'What did you do?' she says. 'That was amazing!'

'Really?' I say, too vague to conjure some lie about when preparation meets inspiration. 'I was totally out of it.'

'Well, whatever you did, keep it up cos it's working for you.'

So now all I have to do is drain half a litre of blood before every class.

*

Maintaining connection to my secret best friend, my Holy Goat, is a full-time job. I wake up and my first thought is 'hello cruel world', then I purify that thought by making a mental gratitude list. Then I list all the things I'm powerless over (food, people, Gil coming to yoga with me and becoming a better and more compatible person), and hand the whole thing over to my Holy Goat as I ask for direction for the day. What that looks like is me thinking, *What should I focus on today?* while putting the kettle on, and then trying to let my mind go blank.

(To be honest, my Holy Goat is quite pedestrian in its guidance. Usually a thought will pop into my head while I'm having a shower, something earth-shattering like, 'Just do one thing at a time' or 'Slow down and listen to people'. I bet Oprah gets way better stuff from her Holy Goat. I bet she gets high-level business advice like 'Oprah – syndicate!' But sometimes, not often, an entire scene or conversation for a story, or else an entire outline for an article will pop into my head and I'll scramble to write it down.)

Then throughout the day I try to notice when I have thought crimes like jealousy or resentment or selfishness, forgive myself for being a bitch, and then look for ways I might have contributed. (Usually, in my opinion, by being too loving and trusting a person in a world of selfish cunts. Malin says that's not the point of the exercise.) At the end of the day I just hand the whole thing over to my Holy Goat.

The cost of all this is 1: Time, and 2: Furtiveness. People like Jorge may feel comfortable kneeling before a homemade transportable altar, but I still cower in stairwells before classes to whisper a quick prayer out of earshot of anyone who might think me a crackpot.

The rewards: no desire whatsoever to binge, starve, purge or otherwise mess around with food. Fewer fights with people, even just in my head. I don't know how it works. I don't know why it works. I just know that it does.

Something weird is happening. I'll take all morning to get a bit of writing momentum, then something will shift and all of the words will come in a great rush, but it feels so overwhelming I just want to make it stop. I used to numb those feelings with food, and the cravings are as strong as they were when I first came into program.

'Classic upper-limit problem,' says Malin the next time we meet for coffee. 'The closer I get to the next level with something, the more I self-sabotage. Last week at work, a collector bought three paintings. I went home and all I wanted to do was binge for two days.'

'Great. So what do I do?'

Malin shrugs. 'Someone suggested visualisation.'

'Did it work?'

'I dunno, sweetie. Too scared to try it.'

On my way home I listen to an interview with a rabbi/

psychotherapist. He says that there are two Hebrew words for fear: one is the 'lizard brain' fear about survival in a harsh and cruel world, and the other one is the fear of expansion.

'It happens when your ego senses that you're on the verge of letting it go,' he says. 'It's the fear of expansion, being close to God, of filling up a larger space than you feel safe being in.'

One of my favourite writers, Haruki Murakami, says that in all writers is a kind of poison that you can only get out through writing. But you have to keep yourself scrupulously healthy, because if you don't, the poison will destroy you.

At least once a day I burst into tears in the Biochem library toilets. Trying to match the words on the page with the finished work I have in my head is absolutely crushing. I've been crap at plenty of things before, but being crap at something you care about is different.

Taking writing seriously again is forcing me to pull out every yoga and fight club trick I know to get through the terror. When I want to give up, or overeat I hide in the toilets and make program calls. I meditate at my desk with my eyes open so people won't think I'm asleep. I tap into 'nature's pharmacy' and do pranayama breath practices in the stairwell, huffing and puffing to get an adrenalin boost. I do mini-yoga practices in the chemical engineering section of the library because no one ever goes there.

All in all, it's a glamorous way to spend the summer.

•

Somehow, by yoga-storming my way through, I've finished the collection. I have no idea if it's good or bad, what matters is it's *done*. I print out my proposal, ride my bike to my old publisher's office in the city and, ignoring Kate's gentle caution ('the slush pile is high and self-replenishing'), I knock on the door and hand the proposal envelope to the receptionist.

'Does Andie know it's coming?' she says, pinching the corner of the envelope like it's an old tampon.

'Yes,' I lie. 'She said to give it to her straight away.'

Heading back down in the lift I feel a wave of shame (*it's not good enough, everyone is laughing at you for even trying*), but the thing about practising yoga and fight club like a second job is that they show up for you when you need them most. This time it's in the form of a mental pep talk from Krishna in the Bhagavad Gita. *You feel ill because of your attachment to the outcome*, I think. *Let go of the desire. Let go of the outcome. Do your fucking job.*

And my job, at this moment, is to ride my bike two blocks north and teach a yoga class no one else wanted to teach – and for good reason. On paper, the job sucks. The city gym where I teach has a stall at a university open day down the road, and my boss asked me to teach a yoga class *in the middle of the university food court* to encourage people to sign up for gym memberships. It's basically teaching an internal, mind-body-centring practice while a bunch of teenagers try to cram in lunch between information sessions. So much for Jorge's safe cocoon.

Just show up. Show up with your full self and do it like you mean it. That's your job.

I park my bike and locate the stall, but there is literally nowhere to teach. Every inch of the cafeteria is either covered with stalls spruiking maths tutors and protein drinks for study, or students with ginormous backpacks slowly shuffling from stall to pizza stand to stall.

The gym's membership manager, who is co-hosting the stall, looks at me glumly. Not a soul is stopping to talk to him. Instead, there's a huge crowd playing a free version of Gil's car racing game at a nearby games stall. Figures. 'What a wash-out,' the manager says. 'You can go home if you like. Don't worry, you'll still get paid.'

Fuck that. *Abhyasa Vairagya*, mo-fo – work without attachment to the results. If I have to spruik 'come ye, come ye', I will. Feeling like a complete nong in my yoga outfit, I stand in the middle of the room and yodel, 'Yoga class, over here, starting in ten minutes. No experience necessary. *Come and get some innnnnerrrr peeeeeeeeeace!*'

And fuck me if a handful of tentative-looking people don't start loitering with shy intent! None look like they've ever done yoga and I love them instantly. Three are wearing jeans, one a miniskirt, and a couple are clutching sandwiches, but hell, we can improvise. I shoo some Dungeons and Dragons players from a sticky corner of the student lounge, ignore the hoards passing through, and within minutes we're on all fours cat–cowing, then noticing our soft tummy inhales. And goddammit if we don't practice some yoga!

At the end of the class they all lie in a row with their legs up on the cigarette-burnt couches, totally oblivious to the hoards shuffling past them, and I'm overcome with an odd feeling. Is it ... *nurturing?* Somewhere, in that crowded lounge, they have found a little gap, a moment of pause, and I helped them do it.

Riding home on my bike, I realise that for the first time in a very long time I've done something purely to be of service, and it's made me happier than anything else I've done recently – including handing my book to the publisher.

•

I'm ever impressed by my brain's ability to ignore what it doesn't want to see – in this case, Christmas. It's been almost a year since I lay in bed wishing I was dead, and somehow the city has transformed into a Christmas wonderland while I've remained blissfully ignorant.

I've arranged to meet Kate after a reading of her new book at a city bookshop. When I arrive she's signing a stack of books, but something is different. Instead of the usual envy, I actually feel a *warm glow in my tummy*. I even re-merchandise the rest of her books so they're more prominently displayed (booksellers love that), and discretely re-shelve authors I deem competition under 'gut health'.

The bookshop is in the 'Paris End' of the city, so-called because it has both a Hermes store *and* laneways that smell like pee. After the signing, Kate and I have coffee at an outdoor cafe, and as we bask in the early summer sunshine I silently congratulate myself on finally being able to have a conversation that doesn't revolve around resentment or chakras.

Kate, too, has changed. Though outwardly railing against the dearth of decent black 'non-mumsy' maternity wear, a softness seems to have settled over her. She presses my hand firmly to her tummy. It's a physical reminder that my dear friend is about to cross the sea to a foreign land while I stay on the shore and ask what the weather's like. She's already moved with her boyfriend to a house in the suburbs, and it's all I can do not to ask her if she's been roaming IKEA lately.

After coffee, we planned to pillage Target of gender-neutral yellow baby singlets, and I wait for Kate to go to the toilet for the 600th time before we go.

I'm idly people-watching when my eyes lock onto the figure of a young woman, who seems to whisper along the footpath like a ghost. Despite the hat, she is bundled up in *Vogue*-casual woollens, but even they can't hide the skeletal shoulders and arms underneath. Her features are incredibly familiar, but I can't place her. I try to hide my stare as she approaches.

Then I realise: Emily. She looks dreadful. Gaunt. Wasted. It's her, but so much less of her – I realise just how many weeks it's been since I last saw her, since she replied to my calls or texts. She's about to pass, less than two feet away. I want to run up, hug her, exclaim and cross-examine, but I would have to explain to Kate. Then she glances up, and for a second I glimpse her face. It's a shock. She's so closed in on herself that I let her pass, unhindered.

'Right! Are we ready?' Kate calls brightly from the doorway. I wave and nod, but as I watch Emily disappear down the street, my heart leaps in yearning and regret. How could I let her pass? 'Let's go,' I say.

Later, amongst the tiny terry-towelling jumpsuits and plastic cups of Target's baby section, I can't let go of Emily's emaciated face.

She looked sick – and not just physically. I want to tell her I saw her and am worried, but what would I say? 'You look too thin'? Any comments about weight could be misconstrued, rebelled against or taken as encouragement to keep going. Maybe I could be casual, 'Hi, I saw you, you look great, how's it going?' But who the fuck am I kidding? And if I can't tell her I'm worried, who can?

I finally piece together a text: *Hi Emily, how are you? I just saw you on the street but was with a friend so didn't say hi. I'm worried because you looked quite frail. Are you okay?* Frail. It's not fat or skinny. It's also not the truth: *skeletal*. My phone beeps almost immediately. *Ha ha, yeah, up shit creek at the moment, but got a new job. Will give you a ring. Great to hear from you.*

I didn't realise how much I'd missed her.

12

The Inner Light That Knows No Sorrow

I've made an excuse to get out of Christmas this year, but I still end up driving by my aunt's house on the way home from Gil's hill-tribe family's extravaganza. I sit in the car, on the street across from the house, and through the window I can see everyone just sitting down to dinner, no doubt passing around something delicious and exotic on beautiful plates. I feel a yearning to go in. They're my family, and that's where I belong. But something stops me. It's the feeling that I'll have to pick up my mask at the door. If you must wear a mask, do you really belong? I start the car and drive home, then luxuriate on the couch. Messy, mask-free and content.

·

Some Sunday nights I go south of the river to meet Malin for coffee in the posh end of town before fight club for people with weird families. In addition to being therapeutic, it's also absolutely fascinating: the stories and characters are better than any predictable crap you might see on Netflix.

I think Malin and I are becoming friends. She's even shown me a photo of her without make-up and spidery lashes (much more beautiful), which I think symbolises crossing an inner-circle threshold.

Malin recently got a job in a department store selling designer clothing to wealthy ladies, and even though I'm glad she no longer has the financial worry of how to support her painting, I'm sad that all the quirks that make Malin Malin – the vintage lace, the six-inch platforms, the embroidered cat jacket – have been sanitised away. Still, it does make me look differently at all the same-same fancy folk I see working in those places … who knows what devilish penchants and unseemly habits they're really hiding?

Today, for the first time in ages, I have only good things to talk to her about. Every now and again the food thoughts creep back in, but they're no longer the thundering commandments they used to be, and I can't remember the last time I acted on them. But the fact is they are still there, and food *is* my default way of dealing with anything vaguely uncomfortable, so I keep going back to meetings and *feeling the feelings* and calling people. When I do, it's like a broom comes through and sweeps away all the crap.

'I'm teaching all the time, even though I'm not earning much, and I've got a really good feeling about the short stories,' I say. 'Plus, I've been abstinent for months, *and* I've been following your advice and trying to be more of service.'

'Did I say that?'

'Yes. People call *me* needing help.' (The one person I want to call – Andie – is not calling. I finally cracked and sent her an email last week to check if they'd decided. She says they were having a meeting in two weeks.)

Malin laughs. 'Are you sure there's not some part of you getting off on being needed?'

'Of course! I just feel good and want to share it.'

'That's great,' she says, brushing her talons through her enormous mane. 'It sounds like you've got it all going on.'

Do I detect a *note*? 'I wouldn't say everything's perfect,' I say defensively, 'but I'm definitely better than I was.'

Malin laughs. 'Relax, sweetie-pie, I'm glad everything's going well. I just know from my own experience that I start getting into trouble when I think it's 'me' doing it. I'm not hearing much God in there.'

•

While I'm on my way to a lunchtime class, my old yoga student Jade texts to say how much I'd meant to her as a teacher. I'm surprised, given how things ended. I text back something vague and positive. My phone pings straight away. *I'm actually texting from hospital.* She writes. *Depression.*

I'm taken aback, but my class is about to begin so I send a 'hang in there' text. My phone rings as soon as I turn it back on after class. 'I hope it's okay that I'm calling you,' she says. 'I just felt a real connection to you … would you like to visit me?'

Well, it's not like you can say *no*.

The clinic is a tram ride away and is disappointingly nondescript. When I arrive, jade seems happy to see me. We go straight into the courtyard so she can smoke as she tells me about the treatment, and how because of 'the things that were done to me' in her past, shocks were necessary. Something about the highly charged environment makes me slow down and enjoy the sun filtering through the trees in the small courtyard. A few other patients are also smoking nearby.

'They're bitches,' Jade whispers, face entirely placid.

She resumes her story and something in her energy changes. As she begins talking more specifically about her past and the people in her life – family, ex-schoolmates and colleagues – a bitterness creeps into her voice and something in me recoils. I'm all for blaming others, but for the first time, in Jade, I see how that bitterness and anger can literally keep you imprisoned.

I maintain my expression, but inside my head is screaming *get out of here.*

Beneath her words I hear fury, blame and victimhood, and it's uncomfortably familiar. I realise it's just an amplified version of what

I've been carrying around all year. The illusion that we're two old friends shooting the breeze gets chipped away.

As I'm going, Jade gives me a huge hug. 'I feel like I can really talk to you,' she says again. She texts me the next day to say I cheered her up. *Would you like to come and visit me again?*

'I'm not sure what to do,' I say to Malin the next time we meet up. 'If someone's asking for help, I should do it, right? Isn't that what program says: to keep it – serenity – you've got to give it away?'

'I'd tread very carefully if I were you,' she says slowly. 'Experience is non-transferrable. People have their own higher power, and it's not you.' It's the second time she's said this to me.

'When I speak to Jade it's like trying to fill a vase with a hole in the bottom. It just felt good ... like I'm finally in a position to help someone,' I say. 'But the victim stuff made me really uncomfortable.'

Malin is silent for a moment. 'Have you thought of looking at your own lack of forgiveness?' I give her a look and she laughs.

'Ugh, fine, yes I do see your point,' I say. 'But to be honest, things have been going better since I put my family in the too-hard basket.'

'Ahh,' she smiles into her piss-weak coffee then looks at me pointedly. I did, once, take out the inventory I'd written, and the list of people I needed to make amends to. There are people on that list who I've stolen from, lied to, bitched about, kind of semi-manipulated, sure, but they weren't entirely blameless themselves.

'See, most of these people actually did something to *me first*, and I'm just doing whatever I did *in reaction* to them,' I explain. 'And I know you think I'm talking out of my arse, but I just don't think I need to make amends to anyone.'

One amend is to an old friend I've not spoken to in years (or, technically, she hasn't spoken to me. Potato–potarto.) It takes me twenty minutes to explain to Malin why *I'm* not the one who caused that fight.

'But the fact is that it's weighing on you, and you do have a part to play,' she explains.

'It's not about excusing their behaviour, it's about apologising for *your* part so you can let it go and move on. You want to know why you never get a sense of your higher power? It's there, but resentment will block that connection every time.

'I only became willing when carrying that resentment got so painful and tedious I just couldn't do it anymore,' she goes on. 'But you can only make amends once you've forgiven someone. I started by praying for the people on my list, praying that they could have everything I wanted for myself, even if I hated them while I was doing it.'

'Surely that's counter-productive?' I say.

Malin shrugs. 'I don't know how it works, I just did it every day, and eventually I started hating them less and even started seeing things from their perspective. We're all just doing the best we can to get our needs met, even if we fuck it all up sometimes. Forgive, make amends for your part. *Even if* –' she continues, as I open my mouth to butt in '– from the outside it looks like they had it coming. I'd rather be happy than "right". I just had to let that shit go.'

As we leave the café and say our goodbyes on the street, Malin looks thoughtful.

'You know, when I first came to program I really needed to isolate myself to get a foot in my recovery. And it's much easier to be spiritual when the people who trigger you aren't around. But we're not meant to do this in isolation. Unconditional love, forgiveness … *that's* a real spiritual practice.'

I tell her I'll think about it.

∗

I start with the easy ones: money. I calculate that over the months I worked at the TV show I stole several hundred dollars' worth of chocolate and stationery. Malin suggests I make a time to see the

Office Manager, go in, confess my sins and pay back the money. Ha! As if. I know it would make a great story to share in meetings (almost without exception, when people try to return money to old managers, workplaces or shopkeepers, the amendees are profoundly touched by the person's humility and generally say 'don't worry about it') but there's just no way in hell.

Instead I borrow a book from Kate on 'enlightened giving' by the ethicist Peter Singer and research which charities spend the most on the wretched and the least on air-conditioning their head office. I choose the Fred Hollows foundation, a charity that restores sight to people with eye disease in developing countries, as a worthy recipient for my guilt cash. My receipt says my donation had restored sight to more than a dozen people, and whether that's true or not (no one ever says, 'Thank you, your donation covered postage for our annual mail-out!'), a warm glow sweeps through me. Remorse never felt so good!

(Two days later someone from the charity rings to see if I want to become a regular donor. When I tell them it was one-off guilt money they laugh nervously as if I may have killed someone and get off the phone quickly. Silly-billies. Killing someone would be at least $500.)

Next on my list is the Marie Forleo digital marketing program whose login details I 'borrowed' from my friend when I set up my website and social media. But there was no way I could buy it myself, or pay back the price tag. But the program *was* useful, and I know they donate a portion of profits to charity. I email their customer service person offering to pay instalments, and she very graciously suggests I just give what I can afford to charity instead. I hit up Fred Hollows again and now another dozen cataracts are being cured out there, now in Marie Forleo's name.

Icky, though, is the prospect of actual face-to-face amends to real people in my life. Fortunately my crimes have been pretty pedestrian, except for a couple of personal offences that an outsider might see as heinous, but that I knew were totally justified. Ish.

Finally I can't stand it anymore and ask my ex-friend if she'll meet me for coffee. When I arrive at the cafe I can tell she's wary. It's been three years since we last spoke, and there's a lot of awkward small talk until finally I broach it: 'A few years ago I said some things that in hindsight were probably a bit harsh.'

She looks at me cautiously.

I continue. 'They probably weren't nice to hear, and I should have handled the situation better. And I just wanted to tell you that I'm sorry.'

I sit on my hands and zip it. Listening to what the other person has to say without defending or justifying your actions is part of the amend, and I'm determined not to defend myself from the litany of accusations I'm sure are coming.

I'm wrong.

'Thank you for saying that,' she says after a long pause, and for the first time I do feel truly sorry. We part cordially and promise to get back in touch, though I know we won't. But yet again something is sweeping through me that I've never felt before. Is this what serenity feels like? To give up the fight; to stop defending? To forgive? I think of Jade and wish that feeling, one day, for her.

·

I accidentally let Marta die today. We've got two days of First Aid and Occupational Health and Safety training, and we're taking it in turns being accident victims. I was meant to be resuscitating Marta, but instead I was thinking about what I'll wear at my book launch, and wondering why it's taking Andie so long to let me know. Is it possible that I'm not the publisher's top priority?

·

In our last philosophy classes before graduation, Graeme asks us to distil what yoga philosophy means to us into a short paragraph and read it out to the class. The goddesses couldn't distil a shopping list into a short paragraph. For some incongruous reason everyone's personal yoga philosophy references birds spreading their wings (or, in Marta's case, 'spreading their wingspans'), so it takes several hours and many tortured analogies to get even halfway around the circle.

I can't bear to think about not seeing these women twice a week anymore.

We end on a gentle reminder from Graeme not to let our heads disappear up our own arses in the name of yoga.

'The cornerstone of yoga philosophy is Svadhyaya: self-study. But Svadhyaya can lead you into becoming what I call "a connoisseur of your own neurosis",' he says. 'Know thyself, but when you overly identify with your story, it becomes a barrier. The Dalai Lama says that a spiritual practice is pointless if it doesn't make you any kinder. Remember that.'

I think of all the angry-faced people in the ashram, and remember Gil imitating me meditating. Legs crossed and hands in a peace mudra while hissing orders at him with my eyes closed – determined to shut the world and all its fuckwits out until I get serenity, now! I'm all for kindness in theory. But the Dalai Lama doesn't have a partner who shits him sometimes.

'The solution,' says Graeme, 'is there in Sutra 1.36: "Cultivate the inner light that knows no sorrow." And, guys, that light is in everyone – not just your yogi friends.'

During the break, Graeme compares notes with some of the goddesses on their Yoga Journey. He sits next to me.

'I've noticed a change in you too,' he says. 'When you started ...' Graeme lowers his brow like a mad gorilla. 'But your whole face has changed. You laugh occasionally.'

•

On my way home that night I get a call from a familiar number. It's Emily.

'Yeeeeaahhhh, I got your messages,' she says. 'Sorry I've been AWOL. I went to rehab in September, but … I had to get out of there. They didn't want me to leave, buuutt …' She laughs – *what can you do?*

'Oh, that's okay,' I say, breathlessly eager to keep her on the line. She sounds like the same relaxed, lackadaisical Emily I know, and I'm having a hard time connecting her voice with the pale waif I saw on the street a few days ago.

'I mean, you're back at meetings though, right?' The irony of our role-reversal is not lost on me.

'Yeah, nearly … I went to my first one last week. It was good, but full on.'

I can empathise. The times when I've most needed a meeting are also the times when I've most wanted to run out the door.

Emily tells me she's back at work in an ad agency, but she had to break up with her boyfriend. I'm surprised – it sounded like it was working.

'He was really supportive, but it was like, "If I let you see what's really going on …"' She laughs again. 'It all just got too hard.'

I don't challenge her. But I make her promise to call again.

•

Emily rings while I'm charging through Chinatown to teach a class in a tiny massage studio. 'Oh my god, I'm so tired! I'm covering a bunch of other people's yoga classes over summer. It feels good to be in demand but it's exhausting.'

'Ahhh, you love it,' she says.

'I love *whingeing* about it,' I reply and ask how she's doing.

'Oh, yeeeaahhh, you know …' Sick. She's sick.

'Oh, me too!' I babble, trying to make her feel better. 'The food thoughts have been creeping in since I've been so bloody manic. Not a lot, you know, just here and there …'

Emily doesn't say anything and I cringe – *I'm doing it again.* It's okay to stop pretending I don't know she's depressed. I look at my watch. Class in five minutes.

Fuck it. I perch on a milk crate in the alley under the studio and take a breath. Be present. 'So, tell me what's been going on?'

•

I've been working through my amends, but I'm clueless about how to approach the final one: family. How do you make amends for resentment? Malin told me this is a living amend, where instead of having an 'I'm sorry' conversation, you enact a fundamental change to your everyday behaviour. Forgiveness. I always thought forgiveness was such a wishy-washy word, as soft, fuzzy and potent as fairy floss.

Gil and I go to my parents' place for my dad's birthday. These days seeing him is like walking into that movie *Cocoon*. (A group of octogenarians are given a new lease on life when they swim in a pool occupied by alien pods. Why not?) It's as if the past few years never happened.

Before dinner my mother sits down with a stack of cards on her lap. She tells me that my grandfather's painting of her had recently sold at auction. I ask, but she says she doesn't know who they sold the picture to because they keep that stuff private. It would be an investment for somebody, I guess.

'Jesus!' says Dad, and I get that familiar rush I feel whenever one of my grandfather's pictures is sold for some huge sum, as if in some way it's a reflection of my own worth. But the second feeling is worse. It's this knot of resentment that sits in your stomach, like poison. It feels like you've been winded, because of who he was to his family. And here is a picture of his daughter, making another rich banker richer.

But when I look at my mother, her eyes are shining. 'I wrote to Sotheby's and asked if they had any catalogues with the picture left over, and they sent these.'

She picks up the cards on her lap. 'I framed one for you.'

My mother has carefully cut her own portrait out of the leftover auction house catalogues and pasted them onto cardboard frames she's made for Liz and me. She hands me a picture, and something about the grace and acceptance embedded in this simple act humbles me.

When Liz and her boyfriend arrive, Dad is in his element, showing off and making jokes no one gets but him. At one point he threatens to take Liz's boyfriend and Gil into the front room and beat them with wire coathangers, then cackles like the whole thing could become a fond memory. *I* know it's a reference to Joan Crawford's character in *Mommie Dearest*, but do they?

After dinner, Mum brings a birthday cake to the table, candles aflame. There are a few false starts as no one quite knows who should kick off the singing, but we get through. It feels like a significant moment – like one of us should say something to mark not just his birthday, but his still being with us.

I ask Dad what things he can do now that he's missed doing. 'Dance,' he says, without skipping a beat, his mouth full of cake and strawberries.

'Go on then,' I say. He looks at me, eyes twinkling. *Dare me.* 'We're waiting,' I say. Mum's clearing the plates while Liz and her boyfriend are discussing pot plants, and Gil is trying to pretend to follow what they're saying. Dad rises from the table and puts on a CD. Everyone is still talking, and I sense he would like some kind of introduction.

'Behold, the birthday boy,' I say as the first strains of Bonnie Tyler's *Total Eclipse of the Heart* start to play. Gil and Liz's boyfriend look at each other, confused. Liz is already halfway under the table in mortification.

'*Turnaround,*'

Dad stands with his back facing us then slowly turns his upper body while his feet stay planted. As Bonnie sings about loneliness, he drags spirit fingers across his eyes ...

'*Turnaround,*'

Dad jump-turns, full-circle this time.

'*Every now and then I get a little bit tired*
Of listening to the sound of my tears'

Liz's boyfriend starts clapping slowly and nodding at us. We all join in, except Mum, who is standing frozen next to the fridge, a stack of plates in her hand, her expression unreadable.

The song starts to build and a look of anguish covers Dad's face as he sways his hips and reaches to us, his public. The drums kick in,

'*And I need you now tonight*
And I need you more than ever'

Dad reaches for the stars, pulls them down to his chest, and he's off! As Dad's movements become more frenetic, the music swells and his eyes roll back in his head.

The chorus is in full swing and Dad's hand are in the air. '*I don't know what to do and I'm always in the dark*'

Point to the sky! Point to the corners! YOU get a car and YOU get a car and YOU get a car and YOU get a car!

'*We're living in a powder keg and giving off sparks!*'

'Woooo!' yells Liz's boyfriend.

'*Forever's gonna start tonight!*' Bonnie cries.

Dad throws himself on the floor and kicks his legs in the air.

'It's the dying fly!' yells Gil.

The song continues for seven minutes. Just as we think Dad's flagging, he revs up again. As the final notes fade away, he performs a move I've not seen on any dancefloor but feel impelled to name 'the reverse butterfly': wrapping his 'wings' around himself and curling up into a little cocoon on the cork tiles of the dining-room floor, the dying flutters of his wings finally curling around him as he becomes still. Or as still as someone can be when they're gasping for air after a seven-minute performance illustrating what they've missed most about life.

The next day, Mum calls while I'm having breakfast.

'Well,' she begins, and I wait patiently. 'Well,' she says again and I count my breaths. 'That was a lovely evening, wasn't it? And ... quite a performance. So unexpected.' I agree and, sensing there's something else, wait it out.

'You know ... I was speaking to my friend Annie,' she continues (Annie works as a counsellor), 'and she said a lot of women take years to realise their partners are cross-dressers.'

I snort tea out of my nose. 'Mum ... do you think Dad's a cross-dresser?'

'No, of course not!' she says. 'Don't be ridiculous.'

'I think maybe he was just being a bit, you know, enthusiastic?'

'Oh, yes, I know!' she pauses. 'I'm just saying ... a lot of women don't realise.'

•

When I get home, I look through some old things in my room. I find dozens of cards my grandmother has painstakingly drawn for me, and I think of her raising four young children while her husband painted, her own art career always coming second. I find a book my mum put together full of all my artwork and stories after she'd seen me cop a little verbal smackdown from a family member. I think it was her way of saying, 'Here you are: not nothing.'

I think of something Kate said, about how they had to bring a counsellor to talk to everyone in her rehab centre after they read the book on how much our families mess us up. The counsellor said that you have to realise that everyone was just doing the best they could. My family weren't vile torturers, just your average emotion-denying WASPs. Is that really so terrible?

Malin says that the first person most of us need to make amends to is ourselves. 'Treating yourself well means not denying your needs, but only taking them to people who can meet them,' she says, before giving the old program slogan about not going to the butcher's shop for milk.

There are worse things in life than choosing to discuss different strains of lettuce as a way to bond with people you might otherwise squabble with. There are worse things than finding ways to make the simple routines of everyday life – cooking, cutlery, how we dress – beautiful. Maybe I've been so caught up in the way I think people *should* show love that I've missed the ways that they do. And maybe I've been so focused on making myself a hero to the people who aren't close, that I've stopped showing up to the people in front of me.

•

I speak to Emily every few days, which is oddly reassuring. Whenever she calls I go and sit in the backyard in the sun. I've only recently discovered how nice it is when you talk to someone who doesn't try to change your experience or 'fix' you, and I'm trying to do that now for her.

One day she rings while I'm having lunch at the little outdoor table in the yard, but this time she isn't in a good place. As she speaks, Ginger rubs against my legs, weaves in and out of the potted ferns then rolls luxuriously in a patch of sunlight under the washing line. What could be wrong on a day like today?

'I'm bingeing every day, I just can't stop,' she says. 'I can't feel contact with my higher power. I keep praying for it but I can't feel it.'

I know what it's like to be in that pit of despair and how hard it can be to hear anything outside your own rambling thoughts.

'I think the one thing I always get stuck in when I'm depressed is mistakenly believing that that's who I really am,' I say. 'That all the times when I'm happy are just illusions. It's not true. Depression is just information, it's telling you something … it's just shit when you don't know what that is.'

What I don't say, because I know she won't believe me, is how much I admire her strength in just showing up and being honest. And I know she'll be okay, even if she doesn't, and I'm kind of looking forward to saying, 'I told you so' when she comes out the other side.

As I listen, a gentle breeze rustles through the fronds of the fern. I want to tell Emily about what Graeme says, about what the Yoga Sutras call 'The inner light that knows no sorrow.' But I hate having theory quoted at me when I'm in a shit place, so I'm not going to do it to her. What would I want to hear in her position? Hope. I would want understanding and hope.

'To be honest, I've never really heard my higher power, but I find meetings help me feel it through other people,' I say, hoping I don't sound too pious.

'Yeah,' she says flatly. 'I've gone to a couple.'

'And is it helping?' I ask.

'No!' She laughs. 'But I'll keep going.'

Just stay in touch.

An image comes to mind of a net, of all things. I want to place a safety net under Emily, just for a little while. I know she'll be alright, but I also know that it's scary when you don't know that yourself. I could call other members, but one of the rules of fight club is that you don't talk about the other people in fight club. I find myself 'strongly hinting'/begging Emily to see a psychologist. So much for 'holding space' and not trying to fix her. After she hangs up, I think of that day I saw her on the tram, when I told her I would give the higher power thing a go. 'It'll change your life,' she said, glowing like she knew something I didn't.

Later, as I walk to the tram stop to get to a teaching job, I focus on each step of my feet on the footpath. The sun is out, and the trees beside the tram stop have started to produce tiny green buds.

I think of the place I was in, for years. And how I systematically crawled out of it – was hauled out by the loving hands of people who didn't know me. People who let me speak and listened, and let me listen in return. The people who saw me go up and down, and up again, and knew I'd be okay, so I believed it too. 'That's what we do in program,' Emily had said, during that first phone call, when I was so freaked out that someone could see me.

And now it's me who knows Emily will be okay – even if she doesn't.

•

I've started teaching private yoga classes one morning a week. I walk home just as the city starts clanging to life, sometimes stopping at the market on the way home or meeting Gil on his way to work for coffee. Teaching forces me to slow down, drop whatever's going on in my head and get present to what's going on in the class. The effects linger for hours afterwards.

Today as I walk home through the honking traffic of the city, I try to hold on to that sense of witnessing life without judgment for as long as possible.

I get to a busy intersection near the market and as the light turns green and I start walking, I'm hit with a profound sense of gratitude – though to who or what I don't know.

For the past few months I've felt like something has been falling away, and now I know what it is. That feeling of wearing a mask, or covering up. Of not being quite good enough. I know I'm not good enough – I live in a hovel, my clothes aren't right, my jobs (all of them) are what others might call hobbies, and Gil and I frequently neglect to declare our love for one another on Valentine's Day. My biggest achievements this year are showing up to rooms I never would have chosen to be in, and listening to people I once would have ridiculed. And one day at a time the desire to binge or diet and purge is being taken away. I'm excited by the work I'm doing because it challenges me and brings me into contact with people who I actually like. And most days I feel a current running underneath everything that feels close to peace.

I'm still not hearing my Holy Goat, I still don't know how to 'build a relationship' as everyone at fight club says. But if he/she is there, and if they have a hand in any of this, maybe that's enough.

•

I finally get an email from Andie: *Sorry it's taken so long! We're having a meeting on Friday to discuss.* That's good! It's not a no, it's more like '*I* love it, just give me a week to convince everyone else.' I put the bottle of champagne Gil won at his mother's church trivia night in the fridge. It's not top-*top* champagne, but I plan on drinking so much of it I won't know the difference.

'They'll probably have the meeting around late-morning, after coffee, and then Andie will call at lunchtime,' I tell Emily breathlessly on the phone. (Isn't hearing about me-me-me the best thing to get her out of her own troubles?) 'I actually feel quietly confident. This is my dharma.'

Friday comes. Then Friday afternoon. I guess they've just popped out to lunch. Everything has its time, a time to sow a time to reap, a time to grow (a time to weep?).

3pm: 'Maybe they're having an afternoon meeting?' says Emily, sounding anything but convincing. I will act surprised. Modesty, that's the way to go. I will tell others how surrendering to *Abhyasa Vairagya* – work, without attachment to results – was key to my creative success.

5pm: *No call???*

•

On Monday night I'm running late to get to an after-work Power Yoga class in the city gym. I'm just clipping on my bike helmet and the hideous reflective vest Gil bought me when I have the compulsive urge to check my email.

There's something from Andie.

… it's just a little too hit and miss … While not everyone gets your

snarky tone, usually I don't mind it, but in this case ... it's a no.

The critical voice is immediate and unforgiving. *What were you thinking? Don't you get it yet? Nobody wants your work. Your voice is wrong. You are wrong. 'Snarky tone.' You knew those early stories were dripping with cynicism – why? Are you an actual bitch, or just pretending to be one?*

My class begins in ten minutes, but the shame's like a grenade I need to diffuse. I quickly dial Emily's number, hoping she'll somehow put it in perspective in the next thirty seconds so I can clear my head and teach, but all I get is her answering machine.

Shit, I need a class theme. Usually I just teach whatever's been going on for me, dubbed in Sanskrit. Shit, they're all in there now, lying down. Okay, showing up ... showing up ... Shit! Okay, 'Showing up to the shit bits of your life.' There's gotta be a Sutra for that? Oh crap, *Abhyasa bloody vairagya* is the only one I remember off the top of my head.

If you're real, Holy Goat, please don't let me infect the class with my rage, humiliation and disappointment. Bugger, arse, bum! Please just put a screen around any shit I have to give off and only let the good stuff out and in. Amen. Sonofabitch.

Then I remember something Susan said once when I complained about the days I didn't feel like teaching. *When you teach, it's not just for them. Let the yoga work on you too.*

Teaching is so immediate that I forget my own worries for most of the hour. At the end of the class, the late afternoon sun bounces off the city skyscrapers and through the windows of the gym. Everyone looks so peaceful, and I'm struck by the fact that these thirty-two strangers have all come together at the end of a frenetic work day and, just for ten minutes, they can share in a moment of peace. *That's what it's all about, isn't it?* I think. *We all bloody suffer and we're all here together in this room, giving it a crack.*

As the students lie with their eyes closed in Savasana, I make up a heart chakra meditation. 'Imagine a golden orb at the centre of your chest, feel the warmth,' I begin. Around the room brows furrow in concentration. I look down at the city street below, office workers pouring out of skyscrapers and rushing to tram stops, shoppers jostling on escalators with shopping bags. 'Now see if you can visualise a thin, golden thread climbing from the orb up through the crown of your head … eventually connecting to all the other threads, sending love to those who need it.'

A slow smile spreads over the face of a woman in the top-left corner of the room and slowly ripples out to all the other students. I wish they could see what I see, some thirty people lying silent and still as a wave of peace rolls through the room. I look back down to the street: the sun is finally poking through the clouds, bathing the city buildings in a golden light.

Once again, yoga saves me temporarily from insanity, but the peace only lasts until I get home. Then I'm hungry. Like *hungry*. I try calling Emily again, but this time the phone rings out.

I wake up in the middle of the night, my muscles rigid, my singlet drenched in sweat. I dreamed Emily and I were speeding along in some kind of getaway vehicle, but the car was too small and too light – it barely skimmed the surface of the road.

After driving for hours we desperately needed to rest and pulled over in a field beside an abandoned shed. Inside it was dark and dirty with nothing but a dusty old mattress and a coil of rope on the wall. I was so tired I crawled onto the mattress and fell immediately into a deep sleep within the dream. I awoke to Emily gently shaking me, whispering that she'd seen a snake. I looked up and realised it had been hanging on the wall, coiled up like a rope, watching us the whole time we were asleep. But now we were awake and it was coming for us both.

As it slithered down the wall, my eyes trailed its length – it was the kind of snake that could swallow lambs whole for breakfast. In the gloom of the shack, its yellow eyes gleamed. It sensed our body heat, like Predator, and was attracted to it. It was coming for our very aliveness. It wasn't evil – it was just following its nature.

I looked at Emily. Her eyes had locked with the snake's and she couldn't move. I grabbed her hand and told her it was time for us to go, get back into our getaway vehicle and go home. But she was mesmerised.

I shouted and dragged her to the car, but it wouldn't start, and when I got out I saw that our car was stuck in quicksand. I looked around, but Emily had disappeared.

•

On Thursday I go to the lunchtime meeting. But I'm still angry about my manuscript getting rejected, and so I sit there and stew, barely able to focus on what anyone else is saying. How is this happening? I do yoga. I have *surrendered*. I fucking PRAY for god's sake – not that I ever hear anything back. Why is the universe not giving me what I want?

At the end of the meeting it's Malin's turn to share, but she seems distant and confused.

'I'm sorry, I'm not travelling well,' she says looking at her hands. She tells us that someone who used to come to the meeting took her own life on Monday. But it couldn't be Monday. I spoke to Emily on Monday.

Didn't I?

I hear a noise in my throat, and one of the long-timers crosses the room to hold my hand.

So that's why the phone rang out.

•

Emily's funeral is held at Gil's family church, opposite the uni where I teach. I recognise the priest. He's meant to be one of the 'good' priests, but still, the Emily I knew was such a funny, wry person

– it feels completely wrong to say goodbye in such a formal place. I see Malin on the other side of the church, but I can't be bothered battling through the crowd, so I stay where I am.

The priest swings incense around and murmurs a few nonsensical prayers I imagine he says at every funeral. It sounds so distant, completely disconnected from anything I imagine God to be: just ritual and empty words.

Emily was looking for you, and you were nowhere. Will you be nowhere for me too?

Here. I have always been here. I will never ever leave.

Emily's sister and parents take turns speaking. Seeing her family smiling and telling stories, it's so clear that the person I knew was just a tiny fraction of who she was. A very intimate part, but not the whole. It is a fully rounded person who is now gone, not an illness, or a recovery buddy. Music plays and they run photos of Emily on a projector. It makes me smile to see what a dork that teenage Vogue-girl had been, chubby cheeks, cigarettes and a 90s-grunge wardrobe I would have envied.

The priest says something lofty, and I remember someone somewhere telling me that suicide was a sin. I have a horrible image of Emily being turned away. But the priest describes a celestial scene where she's being loved and welcomed, and even though I don't believe in heaven or hell, it comforts me. I hope it's true.

After the funeral I put on my runners and some head-banging music and go to the university gym. I feel alive, *weirdly* alive, so I crank the music and run and run until the sweat pours and the swearing stops.

The next day I don't move from the couch. The goddesses are all at training – we're meant to pick our dates for our final exam classes today. Gil is playing a game on the computer, and it's nice to be in the same room and not talk.

I always thought it was ridiculous when people in meetings called it a 'deadly disease'. I forgot, or didn't connect it to how I wanted to ride into traffic a year ago.

It's strange when you realise how much you love someone just because they're human. The struggles? Whatever. Everybody struggles. You want to brush aside their concerns and tell them you're not listening because their fears are silly and will be gone soon. And that's what I did say to her, right?

Your mind does funny things, of course, when someone you care about kills themselves. It would be arrogant to think I could have stopped it, but if I *could*, what would have been the right thing to say? I would have said whatever it took to reach through the phone and hold on to her. I would have said, 'It's just being caught in a rip, and if you just let go – don't struggle – the current will bring you back in.' Did I say something like that? To just hold on? Maybe I forgot to. I would have held on to her any way I could, but I don't think Emily would have liked being held. She would have just laughed that wry laugh.

Through the window that looks into the backyard, I see the sunlight on the ferns and the birds fossicking around the lemon tree. From the restaurant across the laneway come the crashing sounds of pots and cutlery as the chef berates his sous chef in Italian. Gil comes and wraps his arms around me on the couch for a while before going back to his game. *This is normal. This is sadness. You don't need to change it. It's just there.*

I sat opposite her on the tram. She told me that once you get a connection to something greater than yourself your life changes. And then she lost it. She told me she'd been praying so hard to find it, but it was gone.

A few days later I call Malin. She's quiet when I tell her what Emily had been saying before her death. How she'd been praying to her higher power for help, but got nothing.

'What's the point of having faith in something if it abandons you when you need it most? What is the point of praying to God or a higher power or Universal Consciousness if it's nothing more than superstition? What's the point if it isn't there when you have nothing else?'

Malin asks me how Emily was in the weeks leading up to her death, and whether she was in relapse.

'Yes,' I reply. 'Every day.'

I hear Malin exhale. 'I don't have all the answers, sweetie,' she says softly. 'I don't think it's God who abandons us. But it's hard to connect when we're turning away.'

It's simple, really. I know absolutely nothing. I have no answers. I thought I'd figured out how to live, but all I'd done was overlay a complicated sequence of words and prayers and routines over my life to keep the chaos at bay. An elaborate, awesome-in-its-effort game of self-delusion. Hooray for the attempt. But no matter how much work you do, how much yoga, meetings, meditation, analysis, sometimes you get knocked down to your knees and you just have to make it through the day without doing anything to screw yourself up even more.

But life can be beautiful and fragile, and we must love and love and love and cherish the people in it, even the shit ones, and never take any of them for granted. It's nothing more complicated than that.

The first weeks of the year are a blur. When I teach yoga and uni classes, something clicks into gear. I step into the room and everything flows without too much effort. But as soon as the last student leaves, a dullness sets in, and once I get home it's harder and harder to get off the couch.

I haven't felt like writing anything ... what's the point? It makes me laugh out loud when I think of all the weekends I eagerly set off for the library with my laptop, like I'm someone, doing something worthwhile.

A real yoga teacher would know how not to feel this way. There must be something, a Sutra or something, a practice that would make me not feel this way. But I couldn't be bothered doing it, even if I knew what it was.

·

All I remember of my final exam class for yoga teacher training is one of the assessors commenting that I prowled the class like a tiger in a cage. And Mum came along as one of the students to support me, which meant more to me than I thought it would.

Graduation is at Susan and Graeme's place in the mountains. Gil comes along, and we gather on the top of their hill for the ceremony. Jorge reads us all a poem and hands us a certificate, while Susan and Graeme's Golden Retriever licks our hand in congratulations. Each teacher gives us a small present – incense, a poem. Susan's gifts are 'healing rocks', which look suspiciously like the gravel from her driveway. 'I ran out of time to go shopping,' she whispers as she gives me mine. 'But I saved the biggest piece for you.'

The goddesses and I perform a dance depicting our yogic journey, involving much fluttering of hands and whooshing of arms to demonstrate highs and lows. Later we make a date for a group practice session at Jo-Jo's place in a couple of months.

As we drive home, Gil looks thoughtful. 'It was really something, wasn't it?' he says.

'You mean the graduation?'

'No, all of it. I thought it was just some cult you disappeared to every Sunday and Thursday, but when I saw you all today … I dunno. You guys really seem to have had something special.'

'We did,' I say.

I'm glad he thinks so, because at the graduation I told Jorge to sign me up for his 'Delights of the Yoga Motherland' tour of India.

13

Hugging Saint

Pale ladies with UK ancestry are not built for the South Indian tropics. My damp, once-white shirt sticks to the pleather seats, and though the windows on the minibus are open, the jungle on the way to Amma's ashram is still.

They say India is a place of contradictions, and so far on Jorge's tour we have saluted the sun at dawn in the Sivananda ashram and had our crotches illicitly grabbed by local men in Varkala. We've honoured Hanuman, the monkey god, during a dawn practice at the monkey temple in Hampi, then watched the adult children of Russian oligarchs haggle over rupees with impoverished shopkeepers in Goa. Jorge himself is lovesick after splitting with his partner days before we left Melbourne, and has been expressing his sorrow through song, keeping everyone awake crooning mournful love songs on the overnight train journeys.

But all the while I've just been waiting for Amma's magical hug. All year I've had to listen to people rave about all the great stuff they get from their higher power, but I still haven't heard a peep. And while I've always dismissed those who say they 'found themselves in India' as wankers, if there are spiritual transmissions to be had, I *need* to get me one of those magical hugs. It's possible that hug could be an energetic transfer of whatever certainty other people get from 'God' – a quiet confidence I can draw upon whenever life gives me lemons.

There are eleven other goddesses on the bus, plus Gil.

'If a charlatan sorceress ends up snatching your soul, someone needs to get your empty shell onto a plane back home,' he said when he told me he'd bought a ticket. Gil's only condition: he's not going to submit himself to 'The Witch' for a hug. ('Sure!' I said, but my plan is to push Gil into Amma's arms at the last minute. It's a small act of deception to get us onto the same plane, spiritually speaking.)

The goddesses have adopted Gil and his rigid hamstrings as a kind of tour mascot, and he has accepted this role in surprisingly good grace, rising early to stiffly salute the sun, his bass *Om* anchoring the goddesses' off-key soprano, and even politely asking for seconds of the ashram fare, even though it lacked Gil's favourite ingredients of pig, cow and Henny Penny. As the goddesses waved their arms at the sky for Jorge's New Moon Goal-Setting yoga ritual, Gil awkwardly flapped his arms along with them. As we Planted Seeds for the Auspicious Year Ahead, Gil dutifully set some life goals (which were a big surprise to me) and read them out to the group. I thought for sure Jorge's obligatory 'stare into the eyes of a stranger' first-day group bonding ritual would tip Gil over the edge, like it once did me, but he just furrowed his brow in concentration and did his best to 'welcome another's soul with his heart', which I must admit, softened mine. (Though he drew the line at New Year's Eve primal screaming.)

On Jorge's instruction, we've all dressed in white to meet Amma, except Gil who is defiant in blue. Minutes before we arrive at the ashram, Jorge stands at the head of the bus and gives us a pep talk.

'Now ladies-and-Gil, when you're waiting to see Amma, try to hold a question or prayer in your mind. It will gather power as your turn approaches. And remember, it can take up to a week for Amma's blessing to manifest, so keep an open mind.'

Throughout the trip, Gil has maintained his good-natured ridicule of 'The Witch'. But as the jungle thins out and we get closer to Amma's ashram, he grows silent.

'Are you alright?' I ask. He turns to me, pale and eyes wide. Sweet Jesus, he's nervous.

'Just promise me one thing,' he says. 'If I start jumping around like Hanuman the monkey god, please just put me down humanely and tell my mother it was a bus accident.'

Woooo – he's going for a divine and mystical hug!

•

Amma's ashram rises out of the jungle like an oasis. It's more of a small city; hundreds of people from all over the world dressed in white, bustle about serving food, sweeping paths, chasing children and hosing pathways. There are dozens of food stalls, bathroom attendants (the 'bathrooms' are more like closets with a bucket in them, but so what?), and even a ticketing system for the hugs. The hierarchical vibe of the ashram I visited in Australia is missing, and I overhear the bathroom attendant tell someone she used to work as a psychiatrist in New York. Everyone has those soft-soft eyes of the truly surrendered. (Or insane.)

'Group photo!' Jorge yells before we all dive into the nearest food stall. A bell rings while we're waiting for samosas and chai and a hush falls over the complex. Around us everyone from canteen workers to bathroom cleaners down tools and bow their heads. There is a palpable feeling that we're about to be in the presence of a living deity.

On tiptoe, I peer over a row of tourists. Striding along is Amma: short, round and beaming as she is escorted to the great hall by a troop of armed female guards.

The hall is already packed with Indian families on rows of chairs. The proceedings onstage are magnified by two enormous screens with the chants written up in English and Hindi. 'We bow down to she whose limbs are perfectly blessed ... To the mother goddess whose every utterance is honey, we bow down...' and so on. Onstage, there are already a hundred people coiled around in a tight queue. We've been told that Amma routinely hugs people without a break for up to eight hours. Sorceress or not, I am in awe of her stamina.

Jorge has already bought us all tickets for the express queue, and as we enter the great hall, an attendant from Oregon points to our group. 'One! Two! Three! Four! You go up!' Gil is ahead of me in the group, and Jorge and I are still standing below the stage, waiting to be called up.

I've been avoiding Jorge on the trip. He has a sixth sense for spiritual rawness, and his speciality is 'making you *go there*' when you least want to. So I'm not surprised when, as what's left of our troupe take seats to await our turn on stage, Jorge plops down beside me.

'And you?' he says kindly. 'What are you hoping for from Amma?'

'Ooh, I don't know,' I say my eyes wandering to avoid his piercing, former-optometrist gaze. But it's hard to maintain a facade when someone looks at you with such compassion.

'I just want someone to believe in me, I guess,' I say, my voice cracking. Around us hundreds of people are chatting and laughing, patiently awaiting their turn. They'll wait all night if they have to.

I look at Jorge, willing him to do his magic forest sprite thing, say that one perfect thing that will take the pain away, but he doesn't. He just looks at me.

'When are *you* going to believe in you?' he says and shakes his head sadly. And then the Oregon acolyte is calling us up.

Once we're on stage there is little room to move, and the air is sticky and stifling. Rows of chairs coil tightly around the stage. Over the next two hours we slowly nudge closer to where Amma is sitting, one chair at a time. Herding us through are white-clad assistants, all blissed-out just to be serving Amma. I'm told to roll my calf-length pants down, but otherwise they're unobtrusive.

A few rows ahead of us, six assistants surround Amma, pushing people in towards her. They whisper in Amma's ear and hand her prasad (offerings) to give her huggees, taking their devotional offerings in return. I look closely at those who've had their hugs for signs of transformation. Once they're pulled gently from Amma, they either weep or look so dazed that an assistant has to lead them to their seat on the floor behind the Great Mother. There, they can sit in meditation as long as they like, integrating the experience as they bask in her presence. I've been looking at them for signs of Hanuman-style derangement, but they're all just smiling weirdly and sitting quietly.

As our turn approaches, instruction sheets are passed down the line. 'Wipe your face before your hug. Don't rest your weight on Amma. Instead, put your hands on the chair on either side of her. Repeat your personal mantra as you wait, to keep your mind pure.' I focus on my prayer. *Holy Goat, please let me know if you're there.*

Finally, only five people remain ahead in the queue. As my turn approaches my heart slows to a dull thud. The gentle buzz of chatter dims and all I hear is my own breath and that voice in my head, slow and clear.

What could she possibly give you that you don't already have?

What? No, no, no! I need her to give me something – a bolt of realisation – to finally hear the voice of my Holy Goat and know it exists.

I fight the feeling that I'm here under false pretences. Haven't I done my part? I've done the practices, stripped back all that isn't 'me' – so now what's left? Whose hand can I hold? I want to be restored, given back to myself. I want that sense they talk about in one of Jorge's chants; that nothing is missing. I want validation. I want to know I'm not on my own anymore. Please don't let it just be me.

You already have everything. You have someone you love, who loves you. You're doing work you love. You have family. You know how to look after yourself. You have me. You have sanity. You have love.

I've gone from not caring if I rode into traffic to living a life that is meaningful to me, even if it doesn't look like much on paper to anybody else. I'm in recovery for an eating disorder, I've made internal peace with my family, am doing work I enjoy, and short of Gil turning into a monkey god, am with someone I love. If I can't see those things, then no other person, no guru, no 'mystical hug', will ever be enough.

I remember something Malin said after Emily died: 'It's us who turn away.'

I just thought I'd feel different. That one day something would come along to take all the fear and uncertainty away.

If I take that away, you won't be human.

I'm a few feet away from Amma. A female assistant asks me, 'What language?' and if it's my first time. She gives me a yellow sticker to put on my blouse. Finally I am kneeling at her feet.

'English, English,' the attendant whispers to the Great Mother. Strong, wiry assistants take control, grabbing my hands and placing them firmly on Amma's chair so I can support my weight without leaning on her. Someone pushes my head down, into her chest.

It's like falling into a large, warm pillow. She seems to hold me for a long time, and I don't know what to do. I stiffen. I'm trying not to lean my weight into her, but she pulls me deeper into the hug with insistence. I collapse into her arms involuntarily like a dead weight, and the wiry hands of her assistants are the only things holding me up.

She rocks me, whispering in my ear, 'My darling, my darling.' And then the assistants pull me back and Amma smiles into my eyes and that's it.

I stay on the stage until the last few in our group have their turn. I feel completely spent. I feel like crying. Nothing happened.

I held my question, my disappointment, my sadness, and nothing happened. I queued for hours and nothing happened. I look at the other members of my group. They all have that 'so much bliss, so much love' look in their eyes. What's up with that? My hug was faulty! *Nothing happened.*

Our group is to spend the next couple of days cruising the backwaters of Kerala on houseboats. On the bus ride there I can barely speak with disappointment. At night Jorge gathers us all on one of the houseboats to share local cane cider and recount our experiences with Amma. Oceanic feelings. Love. Support. One woman's six-month-long toothache disappeared after the hug. Another person wrote a poem about the experience. One woman couldn't speak: she could only sit there with tears shining in her eyes. But mostly they just smiled that funny smile. Even lovesick Jorge has been all but restored to his formerly bouncy self.

Motherfuckers.

'Alice, would you share with us your experience?' Jorge asks.

'Actually, bugger all,' I say. 'I could pretend something happened, but I feel a bit gypped, to be honest.' The goddesses look alarmed, some look embarrassed for me. Good! Smug bastards. But Jorge just grins.

'Remember, in addition to being the holy mother, Amma is like Kali, the destroyer of illusions. Just notice what comes up for you over the next few days and see.'

Finally it's Gil's turn. Before we left, I would have given anything – *ANYTHING* – for Gil to finally catch up with me and have a spiritual experience.

'Well – *ahem*!' Gil clears his throat and suddenly comes over all bashful. Oh please, no. Not him too. Then using the language of video games, he describes a deeply spiritual experience.

I go to bed early and watch the banks of the Kerala estuaries drift by the bedroom window. I feel completely empty, as if Amma's hug flushed out a hope I didn't know I had. Gil lies beside me and wraps me in a hug.

'I'm sorry. If I could take what happened to me and give it to you, I would,' Gil says. 'You know, when Jorge told us to pray for something while we were in line, my prayer was for you. I prayed to Amma that if she had any blessings to please give them to you.'

This just made me feel worse. I asked him if he was at least converted to the yogic path, and he just shrugged.

'Naah, not really. I mean it feels good and I'll do it while we're here, but, meh – not for me.' Figures.

The next day, while the others nap and chat as our boats cruise languidly up the river, I sit on the bough and stare at the water, brooding. Why didn't anything happen? Am I not worthy of a blessing?

I'm here. I'm always here.

There is a little voice that talks to me which has been quiet for a very long time. And it only shows up when I'm either very, very quiet, or very, very desperate … I heard it on that Christmas night when I wanted to die, and again in a yoga class when I knew I'd lost control over bingeing and restricting. It's my voice, but it feels different, like it's telling me something I've always known, but have somehow forgotten.

I'd only ever heard it once before, when I was sixteen years old, standing on a train platform in France with my suitcase. In the distance I saw the mother and daughter who liked to weigh me, speeding off in their car, and I knew I'd never see them again. I sat on my suitcase, not having a single soul on that side of the world I could call, and felt silence. From that silence the voice arose. *I guess you'll just have to rely on me now.*

It's us who turn away.

No one, no guru, can teach you something you don't already know. All they can do is trigger awareness of the knowledge that is already there, lying dormant. But we can't see it unless we clear the fog and look. We can't hear unless we get quiet and listen. That voice is so easy to dismiss. I didn't have to come to India. I don't have to chant, wear beads, pour salty water up my nose. It's just there when you listen, and then the more you listen, the more you hear it. And maybe my Holy Goat has been with me all along – it was me who was turning away.

•

A few days later we're on an overnight train hurtling towards Mysore. Every fifteen minutes Gil accompanies me to the horrific train toilet so I can vomit. The 'bathroom' is a small cupboard with a hole in the ground. Head down, I can see the tracks whizzing past as I hurl my guts out. With one hand, Gil holds me steady so I don't fall into the hole; the other presses against the toilet wall to stop us both from slipping and falling into the pee of hundreds, sloshing around our ankles.

Another wave of nausea. I squat down and watch the tracks hurtle by until the nausea passes. Life is messy and just when you've got it sorted and found a modicum of serenity, something else comes along and you're railing against the chaos. And when you realise that, as Malin would say, you've drifted away from shore again, you can either curse and cry or ride into boat traffic or you can pick up the bloody oars *one – more – damn – time* and start rowing. And I'm so glad I did. Because everything and everyone good in my life, I encounter on that long, gruelling trip back to shore.

'Again?' Gil asks. I shake my head and he passes me a Wet One. We go back to our train bunks, pull the curtains and I try to sleep while Gil keeps vigil, certain we'll be mugged by bandits if we close our eyes.

Around 3am, somewhere between Mysore and Hampi, I hear someone crooning outside my bunk. Most likely a lovesick native, curious about my flaxen hair.

'*In a place that won't let us feeeeeeeeel*
In a life where nothing seems reeeeeal'

A lovesick native who knows all the words to *Miss Saigon* and has perfect pitch.

'I have found you— I have found yooooouuuuuuuu'

Uh-oh. I know who that is. Last time we took a train he sang *Les Miserables* from Goa to Mysore.

In the bunk above I hear Gil groaning softly and I smile. Gil proposed a few days ago, but holding my hair back while I vomit onto the train tracks whooshing by below is definitely the most romantic thing he's ever done, second only to travelling across the world to hug a sorceress and be serenaded by a lovesick forest sprite. Sometime in the future my 'hive of Aspy WASPS' will join in holy in-law matrimony with his enabling Catholic hill-tribe, and who knows what mysteries our collective Holy Goats have in store?

'... *It's telling me to hold you tight and dance like* –'

I pull open the curtain and Jorge beams, throwing his arms open for the finale

' – *it's the LAST NIGHT OF THE WOOOOOOOORRRLD!*'

The Indian family across the aisle break into rapturous applause. Jorge bows, and I throw up.

Acknowledgments

All but one of the events in this book took place over a two year period, and are adapted from diaries I kept at that time. Most names have been changed, and in some instances two people have become one. I've also condensed some events and changed the order, slightly, of others. Not knowing I was to turn them into a book, my diaries mostly consisted of petty grievances, feelings as strong and changeable as the weather, and rude impressions of people. So my first acknowledgement is to the people depicted within these pages, and also an apology, really, for being such a twat.

A big thankyou to Jo Butler for being *Bad Yogi*'s first champion, and also the wonderfully stylish Jeanne Ryckmans at Cameron's. Ruby Ashby-Orr was the most astute, diplomatic, flattering-without-outright-lying, and most of all skilful editor I could have hoped for. Thank you Ruby. I'd also like to thank Grace Breen, Martin Hughes and the lovely team at Affirm Press. And thankyou Josh Durham for the terrific cover.

I'd like to thank my family, in particular Mum and Dad for supporting the book (and who really wants a writer in the family?) and Liz for your steadfastness and care. Thank you also to Freda and Charlotte, and a special thanks to Mum and Lucille for taking care of Charlie while I wrote.

I am most grateful to my teachers – too many to name here, but for this book I'd particularly like to thank Heather Blashki, Andrew Mournehis, Leigh Blashki and Pamela Speldewinde.

To my yoga goddesses, well. Your radiance is just too damn bright to be confined to the pages of a dusty book, so instead I'll say that getting in Patanjali's rowboat with you during those intense two years was one of the joys of my life.

Kathy Winton and Kate Holden, thankyou, thankyou, thankyou.

Marnie Pantano, by what divine intervention did you come my way? Thanks for putting up with me, still. Sancia Robinson, Rachel Thomson, Claire, Maggie Scott and Winnie Salamon – thankyou for nudging me forward. And thankyou Anne Jeffs for your unflappability and faith in me.

Charlie and Finn, it turns out your Granny was right (don't tell her). Having you melted me in all the right ways and I hope I can make you proud.

And finally to Gil. What can I say? You've shown up for me in ways I never knew I needed. Thankyou, my darling.